Learning me your Language
PERSPECTIVES ON THE TEACHING OF ENGLISH

Edited by
MICHAEL JONES
and
ALASTAIR WEST

with an introductory article by
HAROLD ROSEN

You taught me language, and my profit on't
Is, that I know how to curse. The red plague rid you
For learning me your language.

                Caliban in *The Tempest*, Act I, scene II

STANLEY THORNES (PUBLISHERS) Ltd.

Published by Stanley Thornes (Publishers) Limited,
Old Station Drive, Leckhampton, Cheltenham GL53 0DN

© Mary Glasgow Publications Limited 1988

All rights reserved. No part of this publication may be reproduced or transmitted in any form or by any means, electronic or mechanical, including photocopy, recording, or any information storage and retrieval system, without permission in writing from the publisher or under licence from the Copyright Licensing Agency Limited. Further details of such licences (for reprographic reproduction) may be obtained from the Copyright Licensing Agency Limited, of 7 Ridgmount Street, London WC1E 7AE.

Typeset in Great Britain by concept, Crayford

Printed in Great Britain by St Edmundsbury Press Limited, Bury St Edmunds, Suffolk

Acknowledgements

The publishers are grateful to the following for permission to reproduce copyright material:

A. L. Hendricks for his poem 'John-Crow' on page 161; Tony Harrison for the extracts from his poems 'Wordlists' and 'The Queen's English' (in *Selected Poems*, Penguin, 1984) on page 135; Methuen & Co. for the source for the illustration on page 210 from *Fundamentals of Psychology* by C. J. Adcock (1959).

Every effort has been made to contact copyright-holders of other material reprinted in this book.

Contents

Preface *Alastair West and Michael Jones*	iv
Struck by a particular gap *Harold Rosen*	1
Perspectives for Kingman *Harold Gardiner*	15
*A model of the English language *Leslie Stratta and John Dixon*	21
*Studying communications or studying language? *Douglas Barnes*	32
A primary perspective *Fred Finney*	41
Quaint moonmarks *Dennis Carter*	51
Language is a special need *Bridie Raban and Michael Strutt*	58
Some lessons from language monitoring *Dennis Brook*	68
Language or English? *Carole Edwards, Jenny Moorhouse and Susan Widlake*	77
Language and gender *Ros Moger*	96
Language in the secondary school *Dave Gilbert*	100
*Definitions of English *Shropshire National Association for the Teaching of English*	108
A bird and the charabanc *Andrew Stibbs*	116
Objectives for language learning *Pam Czerniewska*	123
Variety, more than the spice of language *George Keith*	133
On Advanced Level English Language *John Shuttleworth*	148
Language on the English curriculum *John Keen*	154
Teachers learning *through* language *Pat D'Arcy*	163
Ministering to their needs? *Peter Traves*	171
A reader's guide to the Kingman Report *Alastair West*	185
A view of language *Dick Hancock*	201
Language and understanding *Martyn Lloyd*	208
*Evidence submitted to the Kingman Committee *by the National Confederation of Parent-Teacher Associations*	212
*Evidence submitted to the Kingman Committee *by the National Association of Advisers in English*	218
*Evidence submitted to the Kingman Committee *by the National Association for the Teaching of English*	223
Index	247

*Denotes articles submitted to the Kingman Committee

Preface

The immediate origins of this book can be traced back to some conversations at the International Oracy Convention held at the University of East Anglia in April 1987. For many of the teachers, teacher trainers and advisers who attended it, that convention provided the first opportunity to share with colleagues their hopes, anxieties and speculations about the Kingman Committee's inquiry into the teaching of English language whose membership and terms of reference had been announced a few weeks earlier. Those contributions to the Oracy Convention which threw light upon the Committee's working assumptions did nothing to allay that feeling of apprehension. Nor has the unease been dispelled by later events. Indeed, intervening months have shown the Kingman Inquiry to be but one element amongst many in a wholesale restructuring of the education system in which we work – financial delegation, open enrolment, and the national curriculum proposals, including testing at 7, 11 and 14.

The more general context for the book is the continuing professional discussion about the teaching of English prompted by various recent official publications and initiatives. Between 1981 and 1984 the Assessment of Performance Unit, whose establishment was one of the recommendations of the Bullock Report, published a series of reports on language performance in schools. In 1984 HMI produced the first of the Curriculum Matters series, *English from 5 to 16,* a copy of which was sent to every school. It included elements such as age-related objectives which caused considerable concern within the profession. Its very format, which set out objectives before principles, invited misrepresentation. The press duly obliged and complex issues were distorted through simplification, as a later and subtler HMI paper acknowledged:

> the document was widely reported in the daily press in articles which were lively, variously informed, partial, superficial and mischievous in their representation of its contents . . . The headlines in particular were unhelpful; they concentrated on the issue of 'knowledge about language' which they reduced to grammar, and dubbed the recommendations as a call for the restoration of practices which were clearly and specifically criticised in the document itself.
>
> *English from 5 to 16: The Responses* (1986)

The publication of the *Responses* paper in 1986 did something to restore the faith which so many English teachers had previously had in HMI, but it did not receive the headline treatment accorded to its predecessor. The damage that had been done in confirming ill-informed prejudice was never put right. What the Responses recommendations did instead was to launch the idea of 'a national inquiry into knowledge about language, to focus opinion and guide policy formation about what should be taught about our language and what needs to be known by teachers and pupils'. In a lecture at Pangbourne College on November 7th 1986, Education Secretary Kenneth Baker announced his intention to set up 'a high level independent committee to recommend what pupils in our schools should know about the English language'. On January 16th 1987 it was announced that Sir John Kingman, Vice Chancellor of Bristol University, would chair the inquiry and a week later the full membership of the committee and their terms of reference were published.

However welcome the inquiry might be as an opportunity to refine and redefine where we now are in our thinking about language and learning, much of the publicity surrounding its announcement dismayed the teaching profession. A disturbingly high proportion of its members had little direct experience of teaching English in maintained schools. The National Association for the Teaching of English was excluded. And the only English adviser invited (for whose inclusion those who know him are profoundly grateful) was there only in a personal capacity and not as a representative of the National Association of Advisers in English.

As we write this preface we are aware that the educational landscape has changed considerably since the book's inception. But we hope now, as we did at the outset, that the book will serve two functions. We see it as playing some part in helping to shape events at a time of rapid change, and to shape them in a manner that reflects the widespread professional consensus exhibited in the book. Our second hope is that this collection will contribute to a longer-standing debate about language and learning in our schools, and that it will offer some perspectives of lasting value to those involved in bringing language to life.

Our decision to produce a book which would be published at much the same time as the Kingman Report itself was scheduled to appear has imposed very tight deadlines and we are grateful to Mary Glasgow Publications for taking on a project with such a timescale. Our main debt is to Harold Rosen for agreeing to write an introductory article, and to the many contributors whose commitment and sense of the importance of the issues at stake have led them to produce articles at such short notice. Different perspectives and personalities are reflected in the range of views that people hold as to what stance should be adopted towards the Kingman Inquiry. However, what matters more than unanimity over the temporarily important issue of the setting up of an inquiry is that there should be – as there is – a great deal of common ground over the permanently important issue of how we can respond to and respect children as language users.

Royalties from the sale of this book will be donated to the National Association for the Teaching of English and the National Association of Advisers in English.

The terms of reference of the Kingman Committee

The Kingman Committee's terms of reference are to recommend:

1 a model of the English language, whether spoken or written, which could:
   a) serve as the basis of how teachers are trained
   b) inform professional discussion of all aspects of English teaching.

2 the principles which should guide teachers on how far and in what ways the model should be explicit to pupils, to make them conscious of how language is used in a range of contexts.

3 what, in general terms, pupils need to know about how the English language works and in consequence what they should have been taught, and be expected to understand, on the workings of the language, at age 7, 11 and 16.

STRUCK BY A PARTICULAR GAP

HAROLD ROSEN

Harold Rosen is Emeritus Professor of the University of London in the Department of English and Media Studies at the Institute of Education. His teaching, writing and research have been concerned with the teaching of English and, more generally, language in education.

> I am working towards national agreement on the aims and objectives of English teaching in schools in order to improve standards, but I have been struck by a particular gap. Pupils need to know about the workings of the English language if they are to use it effectively.
>
> Kenneth Baker (DES press release, 16.1.87)

Let us disregard the cynical laughter back there triggered by the idea that Kenneth Baker is interested in working towards national agreement. We must not be diverted by unpleasant memories of how teachers woke up one morning to discover that Mr Baker had been struck by the particular idea of taking away teachers' negotiating rights. We should by now be so inured to attacks upon teachers and schools in the public system that we should have become impervious to shock or surprise. We have come to expect the worst. Indeed we may have cajoled ourselves into believing that we had seen the worst. The Secretary of State has shown us that the unthinkable is being thought and said and may soon be done. Yet when the Kingman Committee was set up and we learned of its terms of reference and its bizarre composition, we still found reserves of incredulity and dismay. There will be more to come unless we find ways in print, in talk and in the classroom to resist, counter and challenge. This book is one such effort.

The terms of reference and official pronouncements about the committee revealed a significant change from the discourse of *English from 5 to 16: The Responses* (DES, 1986).

> The responses to *English from 5 to 16* . . . make clear that a prerequisite to a national policy statement about the teaching of English is agreement about what all our children should be taught about the English language and how it works.

(The assumption is made) that it is possible for the profession to agree broad categories of language experience which should be offered to pupils . . .

Agreement, agreement? More of that later and of *English from 5 to 16*. Meanwhile we should all take note that the Kingman Committee did not come into being as a result of an irresistible popular demand. It did not emerge from a ferment of discussion, it was not a response to a profession crying out for a definitive and authoritative statement from a collection of clandestinely nominated individuals and its topic was not selected for priority after a thorough canvass.

Let us take a look at the committee itself. It is not, of course, my intention to deal in personalities. My guess is that it would be a pleasure to sit down with most of the members of the committee and discuss the teaching of English, the English language and language more generally. But wearing their Kingman hats they must accept that they have been caught up in a political process. Mr Kenneth Baker tells us 'there is disquiet'. But we do not see committees of inquiry set up every time a Secretary of State notices there is disquiet. Politicians are in business to create disquiet where none exists, to amplify disquiet when it suits their political purposes and to ignore disquiet, however vociferous, when it is critical of their policies. Committees of inquiry are the continuation of politics by other means. However, time was when it was necessary that such committees should establish their credibility by some semblance of a comprehensive representation of differing standpoints including those known to be opposed to the very thinking which led to their formation. Compare Kingman to Bullock and Swann. The government is not noted for its readiness to consult with those who do not toe the line. Professor Randolph Quirk who those in the know confidently predicted would head the committee went into print to declare his views. He dropped out of the running in spite of his acknowledged eminence in linguistic scholarship and his interest in language education. We can leave aside the virtues of those who finally survived what must have been a fascinating screening process. Who were the delicately tuned folk at the DES who were able to declare of some contenders, 'Lo! with a spot I damn him thus'? The result was a committee which left people agape with incredulity. The collective credentials of the members revealed shocking and obvious omissions. Had you asked those who played an active part in the field of English teaching they would have come up with a list of those who were *not* asked. The list of members constitutes a calculated insult to the English teaching fraternity. There are reasons to believe that there are members of Her Majesty's Inspectorate who were unhappy with the final outcome, but they are suspect anyway, coming under hostile scrutiny for their stubborn refusal to act as the ideological arm of the party in power. In sum, we are entitled to ask whether the committee contains a single member who can lay claim to having made a major contribution to the theory and practice of English teaching in the last quarter of a century. You will, however, find in this volume contributors who would easily satisfy that criterion and there are others not represented here. The committee does not contain anyone who can speak with the authority of recent experience and recognised achievement in the teaching of English in the comprehensive school, especially in inner cities. Ethnic minorities are not represented by those who have direct experience of multicultural education and linguistic diversity and are known for their creative contribution. It must have taken very adroit fixing to have by-passed so many obvious candidates. Why should English teachers respect the findings of such a rigged committee and embrace with enthusiasm its exhortations? It may be said in reply that the committee, as is customary, has called for written evidence from anyone who cares to respond. There are three examples of such responses in this book from organisations which were under an obligation to express the collective opinion of their members. We do not know what notice will be taken of their contributions, though I think it likely they will be treated seriously.

We can deduce that there was a certain sensitivity and (who knows?) bad conscience being felt in certain quarters. After all, criticisms and hostility were being expressed very early on and we should take some encouragement from the fact that it evoked a conciliatory gesture. It justifies the publication of this book. Out of the blue, in addition to the general invitation for the submission of written evidence, certain selected individuals were written to in these terms:

> The Committee recently issued a general invitation for written evidence from anyone with views on the teaching of English in schools. I am writing to you now, in recognition of the distinguished contribution you have made to English teaching, to invite you to submit written evidence, relevant to the terms of reference.

I do not know who else received this flattering invitation but I certainly did. I went through some prolonged and somewhat absurd agonizing about how to respond. It was not, to be sure, a matter of doubt about what I wanted to say but quite simply whether the very act of writing to a committee whose authority I did not recognise, would be a kind of betrayal. It was about this time that the plan for this book emerged from the energetic and competent activities of Michael Jones and Alastair West. That settled it. All doubts banished, I wrote the following reply.

Dear Peter Gannon

Thank you for your invitation to me to submit my views to the Kingman Committee. I am afraid I cannot accept it in spite of my great interest in the matters it is discussing. The committee was set up in a political context by a government with clear political and educational intentions in mind. That would not have mattered if the constitution of the committee itself had not made it abundantly clear that the intention was to keep off the committee anyone who had made a major contribution to the teaching of English and, more generally, language education over the last quarter of a century or more. The list of members reads like a calculated insult and a planned attempt to exclude the vigorous and sustained presentation of certain points of view. It hardly meets the case at this very late stage in the day to invite submissions from those who have made, as you write, 'an outstanding contribution'. Warm invitations of this kind confer no power whatsoever on those invited and their contribution can be completely ignored. You must surely be aware that you are inviting an obvious question. If these people have made such an outstanding contribution, why is it that not one of them is on the committee? Who struck them off the original lists and why? Or, if they were not on the original lists, there is an even more damning question to be asked.

Lest this letter be misinterpreted, I must make it clear that this is not a personal grievance. I am making a qualitative judgement about the committee.

I imagine your letter is a kind of 'amende honorable' in the face of many criticisms similar to my own which must have reached you. It will not serve. I have no knowledge of how any submission by me might be treated but I do have some unhappy past experience of the use of selective citation of my work. I do not want to risk being singled out in that way, however slight the risk. I much prefer to present my views, unfiltered, in a public forum and eventually in print.

I am sorry if this letter seems to you churlish and uncooperative. It is in fact a very moderated expression of the dismay I felt when I first read of the committee and its terms of reference. Since that time I have had the opportunity to learn that many colleagues of all kinds share that dismay.

I should be grateful if you would put this letter before your committee to keep the records straight.

Yours sincerely

Let me return to the context of the Kingman Committee's appearance. In the broadest terms I see it as one small tactical manoeuvre in the general strategy of bringing the teaching profession to heel, intimidating dissentient voices and closing down the options. To carry out its policy the government needs compliance, however sullen and grudging, by way of centralised control. There are two arms to this strategy: the first is brutal diktat, like the abolition of teachers' negotiating rights or the 'opting out' policy for schools; the second is the much more difficult business of trying to control what goes on in classrooms. Enter the Kingman Committee. The preparatory work had been done by *English from 5 to 16* which sent up the signals with its notorious list of objectives. People reading this could not believe their eyes. They could not believe that in the 1980s it could be seriously proposed that children should be taught a handful of grammatical terms. Coming from any other source it would have been drowned in hoots of derision. I say nothing of the other objectives, which attracted their share of critical onslaught. But we had been warned. It does not matter whether what is being promoted is an obsolete and discredited practice or an up-to-the-minute 'model' of sentence structure from the linguistic manuals. The intention remains to stir up the feeling amongst the susceptible that English teachers have sold out and left their pupils in the mire of ignorance about how language works. Not like those golden days when school leavers could happily discuss your noun clauses in apposition or spot an example of prolepsis. For grammar and definitions speak, in this context, with the voice of authority, remote and invisible. Mysterious and impenetrable forces have worked out how it should be with words.

This is not to say that direct and conscious attention to language should not figure in the language curriculum in schools in various ways, always bearing in mind that it should take the form of active exploration and critical investigation. You would be hard put to it to discover from Mr Baker's 'disquiet' at the 'particular gap' which has come to his attention, that teachers, in collaboration with linguists, have for years been working on just this question: there have been conferences and publications. The National Congress for Languages in Education, for example, has brought together the very diverse activities in schools and colleges in *Language Awareness* (Donmall, 1985). I find no hint there of a search for a model of the English Language.

English from 5 to 16: The Responses is a document which would make interesting study for an advanced course in language awareness. Presumably it is on the Kingman Commitee's reading list. Despite some of its extraordinary contortions in its effort both to accommodate criticisms and justify the original *English from 5 to 16*, it showed beyond doubt the importance of sustained and informed challenge to official initiatives. The objectives were rewritten in the light of the critical comments and some criticisms were frankly accepted:

> ... for most readers the objectives were misaligned and ... accord might be possible with substantially realigned objectives cast in broader terms.
>
> (p.18, para. 45)

Lovely words, 'misaligned' and 'realigned'! There was more realignment than this, on the subject of the 'age-related nature of the objectives' for instance. The force of many criticisms was acknowledged and accordingly

> . . . expectations might be redrawn in more general terms to accommodate the great diversity of children's abilities and rates of progress, as emphasised by respondents while still providing teachers with indicators as to progression.
>
> (pp. 8/9, para. 22)

Now compare that to the Kingman Committee's terms of reference:

> To recommend what, in general terms, pupils need to know about how the English language works and in consequence what they should have been taught, and be expected to understand, on the workings of the language, at age 7, 11 and 16.

Apart from the vacuous reappearance of 'in general terms', the conciliatory tone of the *Responses* is abandoned. For if the great diversity of children – not simply difference of ability – is to be accommodated and catered for creatively, what can be usefully said about what they can be expected to understand at specific ages apart from a few recommendations so vague as to be useless? More ominous by far is that, since the government has declared its intention of testing children at 7, 11 and 14 (diversity or no diversity), the Kingman Committee may be preparing, unwittingly perhaps, a blueprint for a set of gruesome tests.

The longest paragraph of *Responses* (p.19, para. 45) is devoted to knowledge about language. Not a word is said about this in the objectives. Perhaps the Inspectorate knew what was afoot better than the rest of us. We should have read that paragraph with every ounce of our hermeneutic skill. We would certainly have concluded that there was no need for a few more conciliatory objectives since something much more portentous was on its way. Read this passage in the light of what happened subsequently:

> It may be that a concentrated and thorough public discussion of the issues is needed; *perhaps even a national inquiry* (my italics) is required to focus opinion and guide policy formation about what needs to be known by teachers and pupils.
>
> (p.19 para. 45)

All credit to the Inspectors for suggesting that what is needed is 'concentrated and thorough public discussion'. Now we do know a thing or two about how to conduct thorough public discussion. We know about the usefulness of a preliminary document, about kinds of conferences which promote full interchange, about the availability of teachers' centres, professional associations, in-service programmes, staffroom meetings and so on. No vetted audiences, no closed doors, no monologues, no calculated leaks, winks and nods. We do not lack the basic expertise in how to give a democratic airing to controversial questions in order 'to guide policy formation'. There are euphemisms and evasions here. What exactly is a national inquiry? And what's national about it? Look at the Kingman Committee and ask yourself in what sense it can be called national and ask further how it has earned the right to pronounce and guide policy. Many of its members could be seen as raw apprentices who will be relying on various forms of documentation to learn hastily the rudiments of the subject – (knowledge about language) – sometimes from those who have been effectively barred from participating in the debate. To submit evidence or offer a written outline of a standpoint is worlds away from the active role of participant in the day-to-day give and take of ideas and the active process of collectively shaping a final outcome. Expert witnesses have been effectively marginalised. They can be ignored or selectively quoted and at the same time be used to give legitimacy to a venture known to be shaky at the outset.

All the signs are that there is muddle and mystery about what the Kingman Committee will actually be talking about. The actual terms of reference are clear and concise. The focus is exactly that set out in the *Responses*, i.e. what should be taught about language. The task, sharply circumscribed even through the intention of setting out 'a model of the English language', will inevitably take the committee into some very deep and perilous waters. However, a press release from the DES on 18th February 1987 at a stroke seemed to broaden the inquiry to include absolutely everything which teachers of English would consider their province:

> Sir John Kingman said today the Committee's terms of reference gave broad indications of the issues to which evidence should relate, but it would be useful to receive comment on the following specific matters:
>
> ● the needs of society in present day England as they relate to individuals' ability to communicate in speech and in writing;
> ● the needs of individuals, as they relate to skills of literacy and communication generally, in a rapidly changing world;
> ● the training – both initial and in-service – of this country's teachers in relation to those needs;
> ● English language teaching in primary, middle years and secondary phases of schooling.
>
> Sir John said the Committee would consider the evidence and might, at a later date, decide to invite oral evidence on the basis of the written material submitted.

It seems as though Sir John Kingman is proposing, in the short time available to him, to go over the ground covered by the Bullock Report, to which he makes no reference whatsoever. Is this a covert rejection of the Bullock Report? No one has enlightened us. It is difficult to take at its face value the intention to explore the specific matters listed by Sir John. One can only surmise that in its early days the committee members were fidgeting uneasily at the thought of having to isolate 'knowledge about language' from the practice of English teaching in general. Good for them, if that is indeed so. I hope it does not slow them down too much; theirs will be a very hurried excursion across the terrain. Sir John has also told us that there will be visits to schools and colleges. They will be asking a question or two, I have no doubt. They might ask, but I doubt whether they will, what English teachers regard as the most burning issues in English teaching today. They would come away with a long list, but in the substratum would be an abiding concern with the relationship of language to the culture of the students and the culture of the school, though only a minority would put it in those terms. I am confident that of all the issues and problems confronting teachers, knowledge about language, as construed in the terms of reference, would not come very high on the list, thought it would certainly be there. How did it achieve top priority?

Language as everyone keeps telling us these days cannot be understood without relating use to context. And that must be true of learning about language too. It is a fatuous exercise to lay down a syllabus for all children irrespective of who they are, the state of affairs in a given school, the rest of the curriculum and the culture(s) in the community from which the children come. The classrooms I know well in which many of the pupils are bilingual and often bi-literate offer a different range of possibilities from those which are completely monolingual. Any convincing language awareness programme must grow out of the linguistic resources available in the classroom, which are never meagre but always different. All the illusions of a national curriculum haunt the aspiration of laying down in advance what all pupils need to know about language. That is why all the work already done on language awareness is notable for the diversity of courses it has already generated.

The record is impressive and this is no place to record the wealth of materials already available. I have already referred to the volume brought out by the National Congress for Languages in Education (Donmall, 1985). It contains three appendices: a classified bibliography, a map of language awareness activities and a list of schools carrying out language awareness work. So much for Mr Baker's gap-spotting. What the documentation reveals is that courses have started with different goals, under different auspices and are aimed at different groups of pupils. The list of schools is classified into broad categories.

1   A course for 11- to 13-year-olds, to create awareness of and interest in 'language' as a preparation for foreign language learning.
2   A language awareness or linguistics element in Humanities or English for 11- to 13-year-olds.
3   A course in language development of children as part of a child care, preparation for parenthood and social studies course in fourth or fifth years.
4   Introduction to linguistics in the sixth form (possibly as part of General Studies).

No doubt all this will find its way to the Kingman Committee. When it does it will have to resolve a question which has not arisen so far, why language awareness should be a matter for English teachers alone. Some of the best initiatives have grown out of a collaboration amongst those with a designated commitment to language (English as mother tongue, English as a second language, languages other than English, both 'foreign' and 'community' languages) and also embraced teachers of history, geography, social studies, etc. Even the fertile brain of Mr Kenneth Baker is unlikely to come up with a proposal for a committee of inquiry into every branch of the curriculum that might engage in language study. Those who want a tidy curriculum laid out in an operator's manual, should have their attention drawn to Professor Sinclair's contribution to the NCLE volume:

> Language awareness is very much a 'grass roots' movement. (. . .) I believe that the creative untidiness of the actual content of language awareness courses is in fact unrelated to the fuzziness of the cover term. They have different origins and it is a case of a useful concept happily meeting up with a spontaneous school-based perception of a need (. . .) Language awareness courses arise in different schools for different reasons, are devised by different groups and are applied at different stages to different pupils in pursuit of different objectives. There is nothing in the day-to-day teaching that one can perceive as common to all.
>
> (p.33)

I shall not go through the committee's terms of reference one by one. There is enough comment both explicit and implicit in the papers which we have gathered together in this book. I want rather to take a look at the opening fanfare which establishes the melody for all that follows.

   (To recommend) a model of the English language, whether spoken or written.

Not, we see, a model of language. A model for the English language only leaves high and dry the hopes of those of us who have seen language awareness programmes as rooted in linguistic diversity, starting with the linguistic diversity of this country. The history of linguistics is littered with attempts to create one definitive model of language which would not only account for all languages but would also capture every aspect of language no matter how rare or deviant. Saussure left us with an unfortunate legacy, for the emphasis of his model dispensed with everything that threatened good order and discipline. It was *language* on which we needed to concentrate; it was governed by an invisible social contract, an agreement to abide by the rule system of a language frozen at a given moment in time. All the rest was set aside as a matter of individual psychology which accounted for what people actually said, the way they spoke to one another, why they said this rather than that. We have come a long way since then. As early as 1929 Volosinov (trans. 1973) launched an all-out assault on Saussure's ideas, demonstrating that actual living speech was essentially a social rather than psychological matter. So powerful was the influence of Saussure and other structuralists that we had to wait until the 1960s for all kinds of sociolinguists to insist that highly abstract models cannot account for systematic relationships between social structure and language structure. We owe a great debt to M.A.K. Halliday (1978) for elaborating and making concrete that generalisation. But we can see today that students of language have gone a stage further. They are insisting that language is so complex, that there are so many of the features which can be studied from different points of view that no one model can hope to produce a scheme which will encompass all possibilities. Language resists being imprisoned in a model. Halliday himself, who has produced a complex 'map' (op. cit. p. 69) which the Kingman Committee may well find tempting, writes in a recent work (Halliday, 1985):

> It is unlikely that any one account will be appropriate for all purposes. A theory is a means of action and there are many different kinds of action one may want to take involving language. Some years ago one of the speakers at a conference began his paper with the words, 'I take it for granted that the goal of linguistics is to characterise the difference between the human brain and that of an animal'. That this should be one of a hundred goals one might readily accept; but that this – or anything else – should be 'the' goal of linguistics is hard to take seriously. (p. xxix)

Yet the Kingman Committee has been set the task of taking seriously that very goal. And Halliday is no lone figure. Wunderlich, the German linguist, offers a similar point of view.

There are so many aspects to human language and their manifestations, their individual and social functions, their psychic and physical qualities, their acquisition and history, that it is difficult, if not hopeless, to establish connections between all of them.

(Wunderlich, 1979)

The tradition emerging from Saussure set out with high optimism to reduce language to 'well-ordered', rule-governed structures and decades of assiduous industry were devoted to this end. But that kind of optimism is evaporating. Even the euphoria generated by Chomsky's concentration on syntactic structures is, as Bruner has noted, now dissipated. Linguists nowadays are much more disposed to take a modest view of their activities. Some spotted the dangers earlier than others. Hockett, in 1968, renouncing his earlier Chomskyan stance, argued that the trouble with orderly models was that they did not allow for disorderly aspects of language.

> I now believe that any approximation we can achieve on the assumption that language is well-defined is obtained by leaving out just those properties of language that are most important. For at bottom the power and productivity of language – our casual ability to say new things – would seem to stem exactly from the fact that languages are not well-defined, but merely characterized by degrees and kinds of stability.
>
> (p.10)

This position would elicit ready applause from those teachers of English who value in their pupils their 'casual ability to say new things' and who are rightly suspicious of those who want to foist on them a model which bails out the baby with the bathwater. Many of them know how long it took linguists to raise their eyes above the sentence level. For English teachers are centrally concerned with total texts, spoken or written, written composition, oral 'literature'. They know that the questions which come tumbling out are frequently ones which linguists would not claim to answer. A class is looking at or listening to a story:

- How do we know it is a story?
- What connection does it have with other stories? Other non-narrative texts?
- Does it have culture-specific features?
- What kind of cognitive processes enable us to produce and comprehend stories?
- Can we, do we, rely solely on the text in order to grasp its meaning?
- What are the differences between telling and writing a story? What are the features of oral narrative performance?

- How do events become transformed when they are narrated? Or, if you will, how does *histoire* become *récit*?
- Is there a special class of stories which we call literature? What are the criteria?
- If we know the author (fellow-student?) does that make a difference?
- What's a pseudo-author? A pseudo-audience?
- Do we accept that there is such a thing as a 'well-formed' story which, like the linguists' well-formed sentence, must conform to certain rules?
- How do we account for the universality of narrative? Is narrative transcultural as Roland Barthes claimed?
- What do people mean when they say a story is racist or sexist?
- How do we hear the silences in stories?

And much, much more. It is just because as we engage with language in the classroom we become aware of a proliferation of possibilities and questions to which the answers must remain speculative. If we want help we must look to many different sources. All the indications are that the Kingman Committee will look for a model drawn from linguistics. If it did not look elsewhere that would be a mistake. For linguists have, in spite of imperial flourishes, no monopoly of language scholarship. We have millennia of the study of rhetoric which always looked at language in action and still does.

There is still no one who can hold a candle to that greatest of contemporary rhetoricians, Kenneth Burke (1950, 1969). In semiotics and literary theory, questions of language are always at the forefront. Bakhtin's remarkable essay 'Discourse in the novel' reaches into basic questions of language and offers a theoretical base for considering conformity and deviance in language, showing them both to be always there in language use. It was Wolfgang Iser (1978), a literary theorist, who offered us understanding of how a reader makes sense of a literary text. Speech act theory came from philosophers. Discourse analysis is seen by its most eminent exponent, Van Dijk, as *par excellence* an interdisciplinary study. Readers can no doubt show how some of their profound insights into language came from diverse and surprising sources. Linguists, some of them at least, are much more ready now to acknowledge the need to collaborate with scholars in other fields and to abandon that peculiarly nasty form of academic terrorism which suggested that other perspectives were non-scientific and irrelevant. For us by contrast anything which helps us understand will be welcomed.

The brief excursion I have just made is intended to alert us to the danger of reductive models of language, which, though they may have strengths, are too limiting for our purposes. We can only hope that the Kingman Committee will not be too easily seduced and that some members will put on the table some of the work I have done no more than signpost. Language is not a well-oiled machine whose dictates we follow like zombies. It is a human creation shot through with conflict and tension. It is both a potential liberator and also what Frederic Jameson called a prison-house. Committees of inquiry must of necessity strive to be above the political battle. We cannot and must not. Jerome Bruner is uncompromising. In his recent book, *Actual Minds, Possible Worlds* (1986) he writes:

> I do not believe for one minute that one can teach even mathematics or physics without transmitting a sense of stance towards nature and the use of the mind . . . the idea that any humanistic subject can be taught without revealing one's stance towards matters of human pith and substance is, of course, nonsense.
>
> (p.128)

I hope by now that the oh-so-eminently-reasonable first term of reference begins to look at least problematic, if not a kind of nonsense. I fear the Greeks bearing a model of language.

People have been saying to me, 'All the same, the committtee may come up with some interesting stuff. You might, who knows, find youself agreeing with it.' Quite true. It has been my intention to show that we must act through an interpretation of very sparse evidence. We must construct a subtext. We should certainly not sit on our hands and wait, hoping for the best. We have been given very little cause for optimism. Moreover, we should do our best to disseminate those views which are unlikely to find expression and support in the Kingman Committee. Should it turn out that a report appears which will have us cheering wildly or merely sighing with relief, I am persuaded that will be because even prior to this publication we have created a climate in which no less was possible. If our most pessimistic anticipations are fulfilled, then we need a book like this one (and others) for people to turn to, take heart from and learn in the fraught days which will follow. We are taking our stand, addressing the precise moment but in a form more durable than the hullabaloo around the committee. We reject marching orders from an authority without title.

A few words about this compilation. Needless to say it does not cover all the ground. There was no time for that. Nevertheless, the range of viewpoints and the different themes of these papers stand solidly at the heart of current English teaching. They will show a sturdy tradition, grounded in theory and forged in years of practice, almost all of it emerging in the first place from the base, the classroom. It was created by teachers who never needed to wait for the tablets from the mountain. Even a cursory reading will reveal they are not a monolithic group reiterating compulsively a party line. Readers will be quick to see differences of emphasis and divergences but they will also see the strength of commonly held principles. It was never our intention that our contributors should constitute a harmonious chorus. I have no doubt that my own introductory piece would not command the unconditional approval of the other contributors, though I hope they will not feel I have let them down. The breadth and variety of the contributions should demonstrate that those who have misgivings about the Kingman Committee are not a clique of malcontents to be airily dismissed by a suitable label, but a set of teachers who have earned their standing in the profession the hard way. But this is not a negative and destructive text. It is not limited to critique. It also sets out an exciting set of possibilities and achievements.

I do not believe teachers will jump to it because O'Grady says. They will not starting working to the Kingman rule book the moment it arrives. They are much too canny for that. They will watch warily and manage things accordingly. Change in the classroom is a slow process and the wreckage of grand new schemes is strewn about the field or crammed into the darkest areas of stock rooms. To win assent for innovation means appealing to teachers' intellect and imagination and never flying in the face of their experience and commitment. Ruefully thumbing through tattered books, they will want to know what resources the government will throw into the ring. They already have considerable knowledge about language including the languages of government reports. So we offer them this book in the hope that it will give them views about language in schools which they can test in the same sceptical but receptive fashion with which they scrutinise all publications which purport to tell them how to do their jobs.

REFERENCES

BAKHTIN, M.M. *The dialogic imagination*, University of Texas Press, 1981
BRUNER, J. *Actual minds, possible worlds*, Harvard University Press, 1986
BURKE, K. *A grammar of motives* (1950) and *A rhetoric of motives* (1969), University of California Press
DES *English from 5 to 16*, HMSO, 1984
DES *English from 5 to 16: Responses to Curriculum Matters*, HMSO, 1986
DONMALL, B.G. *Language awareness*, NCLE Papers and Reports 6, CILT, 1985
HALLIDAY, M.A.K. *Language as social semiotic*, Edward Arnold, 1978
HALLIDAY, M.A.K. *An introduction to functional grammar*, Edward Arnold, 1985
HOCKETT, C.F. *The state of the art*, Mouton, 1968
ISER, W. *The act of reading*, Johns Hopkins University Press, 1978
VAN DIJK, T.A. *Handbook of discourse analysis*, vol. 1, Academic Press, 1985
VOLOSINOV, V.N. *Marxism and the philosophy of language*, Seminar Press, 1973
WUNDERLICH, D. *Foundations of linguistics*, Cambridge University Press, 1979

PERSPECTIVES FOR KINGMAN

HAROLD GARDINER

> Harold Gardiner taught English for 18 years before becoming an HMI in 1968. As Staff Inspector for English from 1974–79 he wrote the chapters on 'Language' in the National Secondary Survey – *Aspects of Secondary Education*, and in the 11-16 Curriculum papers known as 'The Red Books'. Since 1983 he has been participant assessor of the Wiltshire Oracy Project. He was invited to be the first President of the National Association of English Advisers in 1979.

One piece of reading which the Kingman Committee might not have on its list is a short paper called 'Language' in the 11-16 Curriculum Papers (the first 'Red Book'), written by the Inspectorate and published in 1978. It is worth recalling that the twenty or so English specialist HMIs at the time all assented to the content of that paper, although all schools of thought about the teaching of English were represented among their number. I was Staff Inspector of English then, and as I drafted the document for the critical attention of my colleagues, I was concerned to secure their support for a clear statement about what understanding of language our subject ought to enable young people to achieve as they grow into adults.

Whatever else we may wish to do, we have a plain responsibility to equip young people to live in the world which – as far as we can deduce – they will have to live in. And it is a world in which there are some very worrying linguistic ways. Then, as now, some powerful and so-say intelligent people (Chief Examiners, for example), unaware of the irresponsibility of their own language, were blaming school-leavers for the 'gross mechanical inaccuracies' and the 'barbaric' spellings of their compositions. The personnel selection people at Boots the Chemists thought then, and may still think, that two hundred 'catch' spellings out of context are an effective literacy test for would-be entrants to the firm. At that time, too, a Local Government Officer complained about the grammar of a letter written to him by a 14-year-old boy – a letter which did not contain any trace of grammatical error – and made (the Local Government Officer, that is), three grammatical errors in doing so. The point I am making is that those who want the Kingman Committee to recommend any strategy of return to the old language teaching are not, very often, a good advertisement for their cause. Teachers of English ought, indeed, to warn pupils of the existence and authority of such people, but certainly should not support their prescriptive and limiting attitudes to language and to people who use it.

Earlier, in 1972, I had been close to events leading up to the setting up of the committee of inquiry into 'the teaching in the schools of reading and the other uses of English', in the words of Sir Alan Bullock, its Chairman. There had been a NFER (National Foundation for Educational Research) report on 'The Trend in Reading Standards' by Start and Wells, and this was the match that ignited the fuse for the Secretary of State, Margaret Thatcher, to set up the inquiry. My predecessor as Staff Inspector, Ted Wilkinson, was deeply concerned that Sir Alan might find himself Chairman of a group which would recommend – to use a phrase that has since acquired general meaning – a return to Victorian values. It was thanks to Ted Wilkinson that the committee finally included so many individuals who could address the range and depth of the issues involved. There must have been six or eight who were included largely because of his insistent persuasion. And it was Ron Arnold their Secretary who, as the committee said, turned 'the views and judgements of the committee into a coherent report, written by a single hand'. We had, thankfully, 'A Language for Life' because such people were involved. What will the Kingman mix produce?

Margaret Thatcher did not get the committee she wanted, and she did not, I think, get the Report she wanted. The Start and Wells document and its findings were discredited early on, along with the Watts Vernon and NS6 Tests then in use. Within a decade, we had in their place the incomparably subtler skills of APU (Assessment of Performance Unit) testing, in English, spoken and written, and other subjects. Bullock then developed from these sentences a whole philosophy of language and learning which we should not lightly neglect:

> Reading, writing, talking and listening are associated abilities which the school should go on developing throughout a pupil's educational life. Teachers can do this only if they understand these abilities, and that means recognising them as an area which demands expert knowledge. In the secondary school it means an end to the ill-informed view of English that because anyone can speak it anyone can teach it. And it means that all teachers should be made aware in their training of the complex role that language plays in their work, whatever they are teaching. Literacy is a corporate responsibility in which the leadership should be provided by teachers with specialist knowledge but in which every other teacher shares. Standards will not be raised if the responsibility is seen as falling to a small part of the teaching population. To blame the infant teacher for every 'failed' reader is to misunderstand what reading is all about. To blame the English teacher for every mistake

a pupil makes is to misunderstand how language and learning interact. Literacy demands a continuity and community of endeavour.

My third perspective for Kingman in addition to the HMI 'Red Book' series and the Bullock Report would be the National Secondary Survey, which took teams of HMI into 386 schools and over 25,000 lessons between early in 1975 and the appearance of *Aspects of Secondary Education* (HMSO) in 1979. At the first planning meeting, Chief Inspector Miss Peggy Marshall asked me whether I proposed that we should inspect English departments in the survey or 'Language across the curriculum'. I chose the latter, and our mathematics and science colleagues looked at their subjects in the same cross-curricular fashion – certainly to the good of the Inspectorate, and, I believe, in the long term, of schools and pupils. There was a sense of experiencing the life of the school in a new and more credible way, and we began to understand how pupils 'got the message' of what they were expected to be in their pupil roles. Language, we realised, communicated about people even while it was enabling communication between them. No account of language was adequate unless it included this dimension.

And so, when I was writing the 'Language' paper for the Red Book, it was to 'the ways of the world with language' – a phrase that was intended to have a realistic and unillusioned ring about it – that I became convinced that our curriculum subject had to pay attention. The debate about 'standards' was in the air, and we would be contributing to it – perhaps even raising its level a little. These quotations trace the line of our argument:

> The conviction that language matters, but that people as language-users matter especially . . .

> English teachers' objectives need to be seen in language terms (and hence, in terms of people as users of it).

> All of us, to some extent, have a view of language as a minefield when we have to use it in unfamiliar circumstances.

> Pupils . . . may fail to develop the confidence and incentive to participate that are vital . . .

> We need to select examples of language that tell pupils what use man makes of words. He tells in different ways what he has seen and done, he gives orders, he formulates opinions and gives reasons, he enters the thoughts and feelings of others, he hurts and assuages, he creates understanding and misunderstanding.

One of the controversies that have concerned the teaching of English in recent years has been, broadly speaking, that between the 'literature' and the 'language' champions. The former worried about the place of literature in a language-centred curriculum, while the latter worried about the place of language in a literature-centred curriculum. The last quotation above implies an important role for literature. Though the paper as a whole does make much reference to language, it does not devalue literature. Though it has only one paragraph to itself, literature is very strongly present. It is 'one of the most important uses of language'; 'there is a close relationship between the response to, and the creation of, literature'; it is 'one of the most significant, memorable and deliberated kinds of language'; it 'extends our experience of language and of people as language-makers'; and 'reading a work of literature can bring a more complex range of responses into play than any other kind of reading', including the response 'which relates the vision and the intention of the writer to the language (s)he uses'.

Centrally, though, we proposed the need for a 'linguistic education' for all pupils through their 11-16 schooling. This 'education in language' starts earlier, of course. I am convinced, by observation and by people whose work I have read, and with whom I have talked, that human beings start with the ability to discover the functions, the rule-systems, syntactic, phonological and intonational, and the delights of language. It is no less clear that that ability – or the will to use it – falls into disuse. Many people dodge or opt out of using language in unfamiliar and, to them, threatening contexts. It is more often the social rule-systems that they do not properly understand, and so find alien. They opt out so often that they find it increasingly difficult to opt in. And they find that, in their secondary school years, they can opt out of language in lesson after lesson in many subjects, if they keep quiet about it. If language ceases to delight them, if it becomes increasingly difficult for them to discern, linguistically speaking, what is going on, and if their attempts to join in are judged according to criteria they do not understand, then the very purposes which they attribute to being in school may be much changed. And Kingman might note here that testing their achievement, at whatever ages might be proposed, will for such pupils be a confirmation of failure rather than an incentive to succeed.

The idea of understanding the linguistic ways of the world, translated into classroom practice, would give us an eclectic curriculum; it would have something of the 'field-work' approach to language that was indicated in the Bullock Report ('*A Language for Life*', 11.27, page 175). It would, we hoped, recover something of the wholeness of concern with language that characterised the medieval trivium, which had not only to do with grammar, but also with logic and rhetoric. How important the latter two are in our times I do not need to emphasise.

Spoken language will obviously provide a larger part of such a curriculum than it has done traditionally. Indeed, for someone given to syllabus construction, there is a fruitful prospect in turning the title, 'People talking to each other', into a course of study. First encounters; older and younger; authority and subordination; the beginnings of novels and stories; talk as argument, discussion, debate; telephoning compared with face-to-face talk; the whole field of radio and television talk, from 'phone-ins' to Robin Day's interviewing technique. The field is vast. Any number of features might invite attention – intonation, the use of pauses, for whatever purpose, 'fillers', the whole field of accent and dialect, their lexis and phonology, ways of addressing people, the linguistic expression of attitudes to strangers. There are elements of pattern *to be discovered by teachers and pupils together* in all of these. All the time, in fact, the agenda is:

> What can pupils and teachers tell each other about the language that people are using in these particular circumstances?

– 'people' being both the general and the particular, the single-minded and the ill at ease, the bewildered, the defensive, the defenceless, the authoritative, the authoritarian, and countless others.

Let me turn to metaphor. What we teach pupils about metaphor is not, I suggest, sufficient or appropriate enough to be part of their linguistic education. We may enable them to recognise the existence of metaphor, but we do not help them to recognise, and to articulate their thoughts about, its force and value in particular contexts. We learn a lot from their metaphors about writers who are at less than their best as users of language. In speeches and in journalism, very often, the metaphors reveal the weakness, the second-handedness, the simplification of the thought. By contrast, in a fine poem, the metaphors may be the strength, the created meaning, the complexity.

A number of other headings may occur to readers as suitable for the approach which we suggested in 1978. 'What pupils should know about language' could include 'how to read it'. We need more variety in the reading diet, and in response to it.

> The response needs to be more flexible than we usually imply by 'comprehension'. . . . Experience of writers' perceptions of their audience should enable pupils to recognise intentions other than the one of simply transmitting information in print, and they should be able to assent to or dissent from those intentions. We need individuals who are responsive to the printed word but not gullible – who have 'reading minds' of their own.

What we should be about is keeping young people confident and adventurous in language, and able to cope with those who have linguistic designs upon them. We ought also to be about adding to the stock of delight that language gives, and to the stock of good will that people are capable of generating through words. Our longer-term aim, extending beyond school age, is that they should be able and eager to continue their linguistic education for themselves, creating, where necessary, the opportunities for doing so.

We, of course, have been lucky. We may not have left school with much of a base of understanding the linguistic ways of the world, but we have been able to build that base since. Many do not do so. Some years ago, I heard a tape of some Sheffield 11- to 12-year-olds talking about Stevie Smith's poem, 'Not Waving but Drowning'. It did not take them long to realise that the images of the poem weren't merely maritime, they were social, and therefore linguistic. Far too many people are, linguistically speaking, too cold and much farther out than we think; far too many are not waving but drowning. A simple, even a childish wish – but simple in Stevie Smith's way – would be that all of us could be, in language terms, 'not drowning, but waving'.

A MODEL OF THE ENGLISH LANGUAGE
asking for the impossible?

JOHN DIXON and LESLIE STRATTA

John Dixon, the author of *Growth Through English*, taught for 12 years in London schools. He then lectured at Bretton Hall and was Chairman of the Schools Council English Committee as well as Director of the English 16-19 Project.

Leslie Stratta taught with John at Walworth Comprehensive, edited *English in Education* for many years and was Senior Lecturer in English in Education at the University of Birmingham.

Both have lectured extensively in this country and abroad and their current research includes investigation into examining literature and the development of writing.

1 COMMUNICATION, MEANING AND INTERPRETATION

There is a common misconception that communication between people ought to be fairly straightforward. In some contexts, it is: ask a greengrocer for a pound of apples and you're not likely to be misunderstood. However, in many contexts, spoken and written, meaning is problematic. Interpretative processes will be at work, sifting out appropriate meanings from a potential range. This is a fact about human uses of language that has to be recognised from the start.

Thus, in reading the Kingman Inquiry's terms of reference, each reader has to make his or her own construction. Perhaps we should illustrate how inevitable this is – and how fraught with difficulties.

Take the word 'model'. How should we construe this? We could interpret it as implying a skeleton outline, an inevitably simplified representation (only a first approximation?) of a highly complex human activity. And is the assumption that a definitive model is on offer (or can be defined), or is any model to be seen as provisional, constantly open to adjustment and redefinition?

We believe that any single model of 'the English language, whether spoken or written', could prove useful within limits, but will also break down when subjected to detailed scrutiny and use.

Thus, we know models that deal fairly delicately with writing but are relatively crude on spoken dialogue (and vice versa). As for reading and listening, these surely set up further demands on any model – but are they to be included in the evidence, since they are not explicitly mentioned?

Naturally, there are other words and phrases that can be construed in more than one way: let us illustrate two more, this time concerned with teaching and learning. 'What they should have been taught' could suggest the transmission of a definitive chunk of knowledge to all students by a given age. 'And be expected to understand' could imply that all children at a given age have the same cognitive ability. But perhaps 'been taught' is open enough to include exploratory investigations, in which pupils have opportunities to take some of the initiative, as they learn? Will they themselves sometimes ask the questions and set the agenda? And won't what they are 'expected to understand' – and the very form of understanding – vary with their individual maturation?

Finally, humans use language primarily for social purposes. Strictly speaking, it is not 'language' that 'works', but people who use it to do things, and in the process are constantly reshaping it.

To sum up: We have tried to give just a glimpse of the problem of meaning. Words on a page are very abstract: the reader needs to discern underlying intentions or motives. Yet intentions are not always easy to discern – and may be multiple, ambiguous, even contradictory. This is one reason why the interpretation of meanings is so often contested. Thus:

a) any model that stops short of the speaker or writer's intentions and motives manifestly fails at the first hurdle;
b) equally, a model must give some account of the interpretative processes that construct meaning and intent (and there are clear differences here between listening and reading);
c) both these components of the model depend on an understanding of the problematic nature of meanings.

2 THE NEGOTIATION OF MEANINGS

Let us turn to the classroom. A (student) teacher coming into it has to recognise a number of fundamental influences that are affecting and controlling the making of meaning.

The personal and social worlds of 11-year-olds, say, can vary a great deal. At 11 some children may still have limited experience of talking to adults outside the family, of having friends from different races (and with different home languages), of exploring interesting places with their parents, of writing letters, of reading books at home. . . . This must affect the areas (and degrees) of confidence that they bring to the classroom, in terms of their cultural experiences and uses of language.

However, the teacher has to be aware of more than that. In the course of secondary and higher education the teacher's own uses of language will have undergone a revolution: s/he will be at home in abstract discourses that are utterly alien to almost all 11-year-olds. So beside personal and social experience, maturation affects the kinds of meanings that are possible.

There is a further dimension: for many of us higher education involves a commitment to the printed word, an orientation to the exchange of ideas and experiences through reading and writing. There may be a few 11-year-olds who have already made that commitment, but most will be at home in different cognitive styles, involving much more concrete, pragmatic ways of using language. And some will necessarily depend on the support of practical activities, visuals and physical models to make sense of what school has to offer.

Finally for the moment, the teacher must recognise that words, and indeed whole utterances, take meanings from a context of use. For the 11-year-old a 'model' may mean something s/he has made with a construction kit, and not much more; for the teacher the central meaning may be the more abstract one we referred to earlier. How do we get from one to the other? Clearly, teachers have to offer a variety of new contexts that require a search for new meanings, and in so doing to develop and extend the existing frames of reference embedded in their pupils' use of language.

A cardinal error, on this model of language in use, is to assume that simply instructing children (for example in the definition of a technical term) will change the ways they operate with language to make meaning.

The main positive lesson is that teaching involves finding ways of bridging the gap between, on the one side, teachers' sophisticated, abstract ways of organising knowledge and experience and their familiarity with the language needed to express and make sense of such things, and, on the other, pupils' inevitably simpler, more concrete and less systematised ways of using language to organise their relatively limited experience.

Thus, in the classroom, meanings have to be negotiated. They cannot be imposed. And this implies that pupils will recurrently have to struggle with the unfamiliar, both in experience and language.

To sum up: Any model(s) of language should help teachers:

a) to appreciate the dependence of meaning upon context;
b) to recognise personal and social differences in using language to organise experiences (and thus to learn about one's world);
c) to take account of children's need – in order to make new meanings – for support from enactive, ikonic and notational

systems of representation, integrated with the verbal;
d) to be aware of differences in maturation, in terms of language use, and to devise teaching strategies that promote development;
e) to realise the gaps in frames of reference between teacher and pupils (and among pupils in any given class);
f) to develop ways of negotiating new meanings across those gaps.

3 LANGUAGE AND SOCIAL EXCHANGE

We have talked about the classroom as a place for the exchange of meanings, both in speech and writing. What we now want to discuss is the way that social structures, and especially relations of power and/or cooperation, determine the quality of language and learning.

In our society, many children may come to school already feeling negatively marked by their class, race or gender. They have been given the impression, for example, that their dialect, creole, or mother tongue is a second-rate kind of language – and, so far as learning is concerned, it doesn't exist. Or again, girls may have picked up the idea that they are good at language, but not in science, and are not good when it comes to competing with boys in discussion. These are tacit structures of expectation that teachers have to help pupils to resist and transform.

Within the classroom, teachers are given institutional power. (And furthermore, examination boards have gained immense power over what goes on in the classroom.) It is possible, then, for both school and board to dictate the textbooks that are used, authorise a certain kind of knowledge to be learned, and demand its reproduction in classroom and exam. Such structures of power encourage certain kinds of language use and exclude others.

To illustrate what we mean let us give an example. In a recent analysis of character questions in Literature papers at 16+, we have shown how students have been traditionally constrained to discuss characters in fiction:

a) in the form of a set of generalised traits:
b) as if a definitive, unproblematic set of traits could be given;
c) adopting an authoritative, consensual interpretation (not a personal position);
d) and asserting these things in an impersonal, quasi-objective style.

The immediate result, quite naturally, is that most students lose their own voice (and meanings), in adopting a pseudo-literary language. If this sort of process becomes typical of a subject – or a whole curriculum – horizons close down, knowledge becomes inert, and learning is reduced to the unthinking acceptance of a transmitted tradition.

Unfortunately, this kind of destructive use of power is not always recognised by teachers (or examiners) and they need to be alerted to its consequences. Quite apart from the limiting effects on education, there are longer-term implications. In a dynamic society, with a rapidly changing technology, people depend on their ability to adapt, decade by decade, in their social life and their work. And their ability to use language flexibly is a crucial factor in all this.

Naturally, what we are saying here applies equally to the work of the Kingman Committee. How can it avoid simply imposing an 'authorised' model from above, and thus producing a set of conformist practices in the classroom?

We believe that any model(s) that are proposed will need to be assessed in practice – and inevitably, in the light of that experience, be modified or even transformed. (Besides, our experience in teaching language in education courses over the past twenty years suggests to us that the research of the 1990s could well transform many of the ideas of 1987.)

To sum up: A model of language in use should alert teachers to the ways in which power and cooperation affect social exchanges – and thus the range and development of language.

4 INFORMING PROFESSIONAL DISCUSSION

Relating a model to 'all aspects of English teaching' would require a book. We must be content here with an outline of some of the principal areas that have been the subject of theoretical discussion and practical investigations in our courses for English teachers over the last two decades. (For simplicity, our main focus will be on the secondary years.)

Language and learning. English lessons involve talk, drama, writing, reading and viewing. During the sixties some English teachers began to reject the compartmentalised approach which set aside a lesson for each in isolation, and began to interrelate these activities, building from one to another the processes of thinking and imagining. This raised new questions. For example, collaborative talk in small groups turned out to lend itself to exploratory mental processes and uses of language. By comparison, writing seemed to set up opportunities for more reflective and deliberated processes and uses. Teachers started to recognise the difference between pupils' tentative attempts to use language in order to discover new meanings, as against their (more confident) movement among already well-organised ideas. Language was seen as a liberating force, yet paradoxically as a fetter.

At the same time, teachers tried to break out of the restricted range of speaking and writing demanded by classroom traditions and exams. As a result, new category systems had to be developed, which tried to recognise fundamental aspects of human communication – such as functions or purposes, levels of abstraction, reciprocal roles for speaker/listener or writer/reader, the inner 'sense of audience' – and thus the way pupils had to adapt their language as each of these changed.

Drama offered a further way of breaking the fetters on oral language. Improvisation, for example, allowed pupils to explore human issues by entering imaginatively into a wide range of roles, while learning to cope with a variety of interactive exchanges. In so doing, they revealed how much more language they had internalised than they normally used in class. At the same time, in dramatising texts they learned how to give added life (and meanings) to the bare, abstracted words on the page.

Oral and written exchange. It was not enough, however, to change strategies in teaching. Something more rigorous was required. Teachers began to scrutinize samples of classroom language. Tapes and transcripts of small group or class discussions were made and closely analysed. Fundamental errors were uncovered in traditional teaching, while at the same time we were delighted (and surprised) to discover how much many pupils could achieve when discussing on their own, without heavy steering from the teacher. At a later phase, it was belatedly recognised that writing itself could form part of a learning dialogue – the problem being a tradition of extremely crude (and often negative) teacher response to written work. So experiments began in ways of responding.

In order to investigate what was entailed in written 'competence', samples had to be analysed in detail; until recently, surprisingly, this had hardly been done. This kind of analysis led to a fuller understanding of pupils' achievements; suggested possible growing points in their work; and even hinted at developmental features. One result, today, is that teachers are recognising the value of drafting, and the subsequent talking over of drafts with and between pupils.

Still in search of real communication (and real competence in language use), teachers began to recognise that they were not the only potential audience/readers for pupils' work. For almost the first time, some pupils have begun to speak to, and write for, audiences outside the classroom – taking on adult roles. (A few even produce work sponsored by outside bodies, thus taking on a new social responsibility.)

Language and society. Outside education, the most powerful single force on our language (and opinions) is probably the media. Teachers of English have recognised for many years the need for a critical scrutiny of news, journalistic reports and advertising. Selectivity and slanting, covert persuasion, unsupported assertion, prejudice and bias – these characteristics are still only too common in the language of the press today. Analysis of these and many other features forms an excellent foundation for understanding the way people with power can use language to influence, persuade (and even control?) their fellow-citizens.

Studies of this kind lead to questions about the assumptions underlying the construction of social reality in democracies such as the UK. What constitutes news – and what is omitted? Whose voices are broadcast regularly – and whose are marginalised, or never heard? What are the predominant themes of peak hour viewing? Where do the programmes come from? Whose interests are represented, and catered for? Enquiries such as these have begun to emerge in the last decade and 'inform professional discussion'.

Language and literature. There has been a long tradition within university English teaching of studying and evaluating the representation of human experience in literature. Poems, plays and novels involve us in making moral and political judgements about human behaviour within a society. For those judgements to have any weight, there has to be close attention to language in context.

On reflection, however, it seems that literary studies in the UK have evolved in a rather piecemeal, pragmatic way. Surprisingly, there has been no major theory of reading, no organising theory of literary studies and the nature of literature. However, during the last two decades, groups of English teachers have begun to engage with a range of critical theories from Europe and North America – structuralist, psychoanalytic, reader-response, post-structuralist, Marxist, feminist. . . . Such studies are raising many new questions – the teaching of literature has become highly problematic.

What count as texts for study? Can boundaries be set as easily as in the past? Do they stop short of television programmes? What kinds of study count – exegesis, hermeneutics, ideological analysis . . .? What methods of study count – is it to be 'objective' or 'subjective' analysis; dramatic, narrative or argumentative commentary . . .? What makes questions such as these so pressing is that they probe not merely an encapsulated area called 'literary studies' but also the fundamental assumptions and structures of our culture.

These issues in higher education have naturally begun to affect teaching in schools. From a wider perspective, as we move from a print to an audio-visual culture, many theoretically interested teachers of English are very unresolved at this moment about 'literature' and the ways it is to be studied. There could not have been a more difficult period, we feel, at which to define 'a model of the English language' that would inform this 'aspect of English teaching'.

To sum up: To judge by our experience of the practice and theory of English teaching over the past thirty years (during which fundamental research has raised so many new questions), a single model of language that would 'inform professional discussion of all aspects of English teaching':

a) is probably not feasible, and certainly would be highly provisional;
b) so far as secondary teachers are concerned, would need to cover at least four major areas, viz.
    language and learning
    oral and written exchange
    language and society
    language and literature;
c) in addition, would need to cover a number of areas we cannot discuss in detail here, including:
    early language development
    language and initial literacy
    language across the curriculum
    the multi-lingual classroom
    language and culture.

5 PUPILS BECOMING CONSCIOUS OF HOW LANGUAGE IS USED

Again, this is the subject of a book. We can only consider general principles. This aspect of the inquiry seems to us to have two sides (although there are multiple ambiguities in the terms of reference).

First, every language user is conscious to some degree of how language is used, simply in the course of using it every day. One of the functions of an English teacher is to introduce pupils to new, or more complex, forms of language use and in so doing to develop their awareness of what they might do with the English language.

The other side of becoming conscious of how language is used is to engage in some form of study, reflecting on or looking closely at language the pupils themselves are engaged in using, or language being used by others.

To some extent, we have touched on both these aspects in the last section. We can only fill out these ideas in general terms.

So far as (consciously) using language is concerned we would expect pupils to have:

a) the experience of using language, spoken and written, for a wide range of functions (to instruct, persuade, inform, advise, enquire, report . . . and to make poems, stories or dramas . . .);
b) the experience of using language, spoken and written, for a wide range of audiences/readers (peers, adults known or unfamiliar, younger children . . . in addition to the teacher);
c) as a consequence, experience of experimenting in and using a range of generic styles (personal and impersonal, oral and literary . . . expressive and didactic . . .);
d) experience of listening to and reading a wide range of material produced by other pupils, by published authors, in a variety of documents, and on television.

In the course of this kind of work, we would expect pupils to become more conscious that language expresses both feeling and thought; that audiences have needs, and the speaker/writer has to move from an egocentric position to a more empathic awareness of what might be helpful (including conventional 'correctness' in the written system); that any speaker/writer can take on many roles; that recognised generic choices affect what one can and cannot achieve through language; that each role and situation calls for a decision about appropriate choices, especially in generic style and form; that attentive, empathic listening/reading enlarges the range of voices an individual can internalise . . .

Turning now to the other side, the reflective study and discussion of language the pupils (and others) are using, we find it impossible to state what every pupil aged 7, 11 or 16 should be expected to understand. No recommendation is possible, we believe.

What we can say, though, is that by the age of 16 we would hope that all pupils would have reflected on, and become *more* conscious of:

a) the range of oral uses they are trying to improve their competence in, for GCSE;
b) the range of writing functions they are trying to develop further competence in for their GCSE folders;
c) subtler uses of language in some of the literature they are reading, enacting and studying;
d) uses of language in the media and advertising;
e) choices in discourse concerning gender, race, and class;
f) uses of language in a variety of discourses (law, politics, official documents, religion . . .);
g) language as an expression of social relationships (with younger children, friends and strangers . . . and people in institutional roles, like teachers, heads, social workers . . .).

In international terms, there has been only one theoretically sound – and highly original – effort to break into this territory for 11-18 year-olds: *Language in Use*. Developed in the 1960s by a group of teachers working with Michael Halliday, this book offers a valuable basis for any future curriculum development.

What we would not wish to recommend is formal teaching about linguistic systems – a modernised version of the 19th century grammar book. A clear distinction has to be made between studying linguistic forms and studying language in use. For the latter it is essential to move beyond form to meaning and the evaluation of significance. We can see no grounds for asking any pupils to study form in abstraction from meaning and context. We can see many for asking them all to consider meaning and significance.

Besides, if the study of language is restricted to the contribution of linguistics, this would eliminate or marginalise the discussion of:

a) feeling in language;
b) attitudes;
c) logic and the rationality of arguments;
d) most structuring beyond the sentence;
e) thinking processes in oral exchange;
f) semantic complexity.

This is not to deny that a study of language in use will inevitably draw on many insights from socio- and psycholinguistics.

To sum up: Any model of the English language has to take into account:

a) a range of competences and insights that can develop in the course of the (conscious) use of language by pupils;
b) more conscious ways of understanding a range of uses of language (by pupils and others) in various contexts.

We believe that no model can spell out what every pupil should understand at a given age. And we reject any studies of language for pupils 5-16 that abstract it from contexts of use, and fail to discuss meaning and significance.

6 HOW TEACHERS ARE TRAINED

Our main experience over the past twenty years has been in directing one-year full-time courses (from Diploma to M.Ed.level) for serving teachers of English. We have also taught on comparable courses in other English-speaking countries. In our experience, the small number of teachers who have been given this opportunity are only too willing to commit themselves to the study of language in use, and to set up investigations of their own. And this seems to be the common experience of our colleagues in similar institutions.

However, access to such courses has been very restricted and is now under threat. Moreover, the emphasis in B.Ed.studies has recently been moved – at the request of the DES – from Education studies to Main subjects. Finally, most first degrees in English, while offering a firm foundation in literary criticism, cover very little of the areas we have discussed, which do seem to us a longer-term professional foundation for teaching English in primary and secondary schools.

However good the model that is finally produced, then, we ask ourselves how it will be put into practice. Only a massive extension of teacher education courses would make this feasible.

There is an important corollary. Until enough primary and secondary teachers have learnt to be active investigators of a wide range of language in use, we fail to see how it can be established what 7-, 11- and 16-year-olds are capable of. The terms of reference, viewed in this light, seem to presuppose a major investment in curriculum development projects.

Remembering the short shrift given to the last major report on English – *A Language for Life* – the moment it was published, we have every sympathy, then, with members of the current committee.

To sum up: Any model depends for its implementation on the quality of the teacher's understanding of the English language, and the way people use it. This calls for a major investment by the government in courses for teachers of English.

ACKNOWLEDGEMENTS

Among the authors that have informed our thinking, and that teachers have read and discussed on our courses, are the following:

Education: D. Barnes, J. Britton, J. Dixon, P. Doughty, A. Edwards, D. Graves, D. Heathcote, N. Martin, P. Medway, J. Pearce, W. Robinson, H. Rosen, L. Stratta, G. Thornton, J. Thomson, M. Torbe, J. Tough, G. Wells, A. Wilkinson, R. Witkin (together with publications of LATE, NATE and HMSO)

Critical and cultural theory: M. Bakhtin, R. Barthes, W. Benjamin, W. Booth, T. Eagleton, U. Eco, W. Empson, N. Frye, B. Hardy, R. Hoggart, W. Iser, C. Kaplan, L. Knights, F. Leavis, G. Lukacs, P. Macherey, K. Millett, I. Richards, L. Rosenblatt, E. Said, R. Williams

Sociolinguistics, psycholinguistics, general linguistics: D. Bollinger, D. Brazil, R. Brown, M. Coulthard, D. Crystal, M. Halliday, R. Hasan, D. Hymes, R. Jakobson, M. Joos, G. Kress, W. Labov, B. Malinowski, R. Quirk, E. Sapir, T. van Dijk, V. Volosinov, B. Whorf

Psychology: M. Argyle, J. Bruner, M. Donaldson, D. Harding, P. Luria, J. Piaget, L. Vygotsky

Philosophy: J. Austin, E. Cassirer, R. Collingwood, J. Derrida, S. Langer, C. Ogden, C. Peirce, M. Polanyi, S. Stebbing, L. Wittgenstein

Sociology: P. Berger, M. Foucault, E. Goffman, S. Hall, T. Luckman

STUDYING COMMUNICATION OR STUDYING LANGUAGE?

DOUGLAS BARNES

Douglas Barnes taught English in secondary schools for 17 years before moving to the University of Leeds, where he is now Reader in Education. His interest in the part played by language in learning led to publications such as Language, the Learner and the School, *(Penguin, 3rd edition, 1986) and* From Communication to Curriculum, *(Penguin, 1976). More recently he has published (with Dorothy Barnes and Stephen Clarke) a report on a detailed observational study of the teaching of English to older pupils,* Versions of English *(Heinemann, 1984).*

THE NATURE OF LANGUAGE LEARNING AND DEVELOPMENT

More than twenty years of research into language acquisition has established unambiguously that human beings learn the mother tongue by participating in the active life of a social group, first in the family and then in a wider range of milieux. This insight has informed the best practice of a generation of English teachers in this country, both in primary and secondary schools: the most effective learning of the mother tongue occurs when young people talk and write about topics that matter to them for an interested audience which validates their efforts to communicate by responding to the content of what is said or written. This has led to a belief that it is the English teacher's central task to create a milieu for pupils to read, talk and write about matters of importance to them. My first and most important contention is that this tradition should not be lost or impeded. In our adult lives we talk and write because we have something to say (either about the real world or about an imaginary construction), and it is the struggle to be adequate on the one hand to those intentions and on the other to our conception of our interlocutor's needs that shapes our utterances and texts. What we say and write comes out of our commitments to people, activities and purposes, and to the projects and relationships that constitute our lives. Because language is not a set of isolated skills but part of the texture of our purposive actions, it is best learnt in that context.

I do not propose to expand and illustrate this picture of the best current practice in English teaching since my main purpose is to consider the role to be played in language learning by metacognitive processes, but before doing so I should like to refer to language as a means of learning in all subjects. Partly influenced by an awareness that as readers we must construct the meaning of texts, English teachers have taken the view that much of learning is a matter of enabling and encouraging the learner actively to reconstrue his or her existing understanding of aspects of the world. This led to the movement called 'Language Across the Curriculum' which encouraged teachers of all subjects to consider whether the organisation of their lessons gave students enough opportunity to engage in the kinds of discussion and writing that would contribute to their ability to make sense of what they were being taught. This involved in part directing teachers' attention away from forms of language – spelling and punctuation for example – towards the functioning of language in learning, towards language as a means by which pupils can explore new ideas as well as towards language for the exchange of ideas. Since that time many psychologists in Europe and the U.S.A. have espoused what is sometimes called a 'constructivist' view of learning which strongly emphasises the importance of the learner's attempts to construct meanings for him or herself, and this view is currently exercising important influence particularly on the teaching of science. I refer briefly to this relatively recent advance in pedagogy in order to suggest that any advice to teachers should be framed in such a way as to preserve and strengthen these insights, which would be threatened by an emphasis on forms at the expense of functions.

JUSTIFICATIONS OFFERED FOR THE STUDY OF LANGUAGE

I now turn to the metacognitive issues. Typical justifications for the study (as against the practice) of language in schools include the beliefs that:

1 increased awareness will contribute to the pupil's uses of spoken and written language as producer and receiver;
2 it will increase the pupil's understanding of the social world in which he or she lives;
3 it will enable teachers to discuss solecisms in usage more effectively.

Whereas the first two beliefs may have some justification, I wish to dismiss the third. It is not true that to discuss (for example) the non-standard form 'between you and I' it is more effective to speak of 'the objective case' or some such general category, than to urge that in school 'between you and me' is more acceptable. It is precisely those children who most need help with standard usage who are least likely to master generalised conceptual systems at the level that would enable them to be used for guiding language use. The study of linguistic forms seems pointless to many young people, whereas they recognise the point of thinking about effective communication. (It will hardly be necessary for me to refer to the research that has shown how ineffective previous attempts to teach traditional grammatical systems have been for a large proportion of pupils. More recent systems may be more logically defensible but they are even harder for adolescents to master.)

Some study of issues that would fall into the domain of sociolinguistics should form a part of all pupils' schooling, though I would see it as more appropriately a part of a programme of general studies than a separate study in its own right. I take this view because these issues reach out beyond language to questions about the functioning of social groups, the exercise of power, the history of nations and ethnic groups in contact, in fact bear upon a wide range of social, moral and political issues that should be dealt with as a whole.

The main body of this paper will however concentrate on reflexivity and language use. Natural language use is unreflective: in whatever sense we can be said to 'know' the systems which shape our speech behaviour, that knowledge is not conscious. In learning to read and write we have to use concepts such as 'letter' and 'word' but this constitutes only the most superficial of knowledge. This leads to the question: what aspects of language would it be useful to bring to the conscious awareness of school pupils? Would the answer differ according to the pupil's age? It is remarkable that little or no empirical research has been done that would throw light upon the role of conscious awareness in language performance. Young children come to school with the ability to talk in naturalistic terms about meanings in stories and in life; what is in question is how this ability can best be extended and refined. Because language is so complex there is a difficult choice amongst the various aspects of language behaviour which might be brought into consciousness, for it is far from clear which of these would benefit performance. From other studies of skilled activity it would seem likely that conscious awareness of some aspects of language would improve pupils' uses and that others would be ineffective and even perhaps inhibiting. For example, reflective awareness of principles is useful in cognitive learning in science, when mere rote will not take the learner very far. On the other hand, in psycho-motor skills, such as riding a bicycle, reflection on the details of one's movements may be worse than unhelpful. Language appears to conflate some of the characteristics of cognitive learning with those of psycho-motor skills.

LEVELS OF CHOICE IN TALKING AND WRITING

Talking and writing, like other complex behaviours, appear to be organised in a hierarchy. As competent adults, we are highly aware of the situation we are in, the identity of the persons we are talking to or writing for, and the kind of relationship with them that we have or wish to create. We may also be aware of the effect we want our speech or writing to have upon that audience, making assumptions about what they already know and what they need to be told. This awareness of the situation we are operating in and of our own purposes is open to reflection, to discussion with others, and to refinement by conscious effort. Whenever we talk or write, our decisions at this conscious level may be said to entail choices at 'lower' levels. At the very lowest levels, the shaping of the sounds that issue from our mouths, conscious control is extremely difficult, as those who try to 'talk posh' bear witness. Even reflection upon grammatical structures is seldom part of the act of writing; the American linguist Nelson Francis once said that he had noticed that, although he spent all his professional life studying grammar, when he wrote it was the meaning he thought about and not the syntax. The control of writing is partly different from the control of speech, in that it offers us the opportunity to stop and consider, to review and rephrase.

Thus language as communication constitutes a system of systems; those at the top of the hierarchy are open to direct conscious control, whereas those lower become less and less available to introspection. They are learnt through participation in acts of communication, and in normal use they run off automatically at the bidding of decisions made at the level of meaning and conscious purpose. My contention is that the nature of this language control system should influence the choice of aspects of speech and writing behaviour to be brought to children's conscious attention. What follows is a list of the levels at which choice is made.

A Context 1 Awareness of audience, situation and relationships
2 Purpose(s)

B Message 1 Constituents of the message ('gist units')
2 Role choices (in speech, on which style, polite forms etc. depend); genre choices (in writing)

C Utterance Paragraph 1 Speech act: elicit, command, state, etc.
2 Organisation of information within the utterance or paragraph

D Forms I 1 Syntax
2 Intonation (in speech)
3 Choice of words

E Forms II Medium of production (in speech – delivery, phonology, etc.; in writing, the forms of the written medium, including spelling)

Thus if a person with a foreign accent asks me in the street the way to the university, my construal of his identity and needs (Level A) leads me to make choices of overall content, style and organisation of the message (Level B), and to realise these choices by engaging in a sequence of speech acts (Level C). The choices made at the level of speech acts are then automatically encoded at the levels of form (D and E), resulting in this example in the selection of a slower delivery than usual and so on. These choices are not made sequentially, but simultaneously within a hierarchy of control: choices at the 'higher' levels tend to entail choices 'lower' in the hierarchy. (I have formulated this example in terms of spoken communication, but with some adjustments a similar analysis can be made of the processes of generating written text.)

LEVELS OF INTERVENTION BY TEACHERS

I propose now to comment on some of the implications if teachers intervene at various levels in their pupils' uses of language, beginning with choices made at the levels of form.

Forms: Level II

It is undoubtedly possible to make speakers at least partly aware of vocal quality and some of their phonological choices: the discredited 'Elocution' showed some of the unhappy results of doing so. These highly automatic aspects of speech production probably depend more upon the reference group to which the speaker belongs (or aspires to) than upon conscious control. The influence of teachers is unlikely to weigh heavily against the norms of home and peer group. Moreover, there are problems about such everyday values such as 'clear speech'; we can only arrive at a norm of clarity by treating the language behaviour of one group of people as the proper aspirations for all, in my view an improper aim for a plural society.

Because of the slower rate at which we generate written text, it is more possible for a writer than a speaker to reflect on choices at this level. Every English teacher however will have had the experience of finding that a class in one sense 'knows' the conventions of spelling and punctuation yet fails to use them when writing. It is not easy in the classroom to generate the desire to produce conventionally accurate text without signalling to some pupils that it is the surface and not the content of the message that matters. Solutions must lie in making school communication more realistic, so that children can be encouraged to feel the pressures to talk and write appropriately that adults do.

Forms: Level I

For the skilled speaker or writer, choices made at higher levels entail choices of syntax or vocabulary or intonation. For the most part we learn to do this by participating in the everyday communication of the family and peer group, at school and at work. There is a good deal of research that suggests that teaching a system for describing syntactic structures does not increase the availability of those structures to the speaker, writer or reader. Yet it seems intuitively likely that some kinds of reflection and discussion of the details of language use does raise children's awareness and interest in their own and others' language behaviour and thus extend their abilities. (At the simplest level this can be a matter of language games, and riddles, and play on words. Later it can become the informal but detailed examination of a range of texts, including non-literary speech and writing and the students' own productions, using methods derived from literary criticism.) It is far from clear that the study of grammar can contribute to any of these functions. I have already made the point that we do not make conscious grammatical choices even when writing.

My professional duties include giving introductory courses on Language and Learning to experienced teachers and I find that when they come to me many of them conceive of language development solely in terms of extending vocabulary. Having no idea of systems of interdependent concepts, they see words as isolated from one another, from their contexts and from normal understanding of the world. (Much work in the field of semantics has also been guilty of attempting to explain semantic constraints in terms of markers attached to individual words, thus isolating the meaning of words from our general understanding of how the world is.) What is needed is a better understanding by teachers that pupils' understanding advances through the progressive use and discussion of new ideas and frames of reference, and not through accumulating extensive lists of words.

Organisation of Utterances or Paragraphs
It is possible and valuable to reflect upon the organisation of ideas within an utterance or a written paragraph, though this should be in terms of meaning and function rather than formal features. That is, if it seems useful to make pupils aware of cohesion features it should be done in terms of alternative ways of wording a particular passage, rather than through a generalising study of anaphora and so on, which would fail to make contact with the purposes of the communication. We should also beware of any return to the now discredited view that children can be taught to write at length by studying first the word, then the sentence, and so on. (Much of what follows in the next paragraph also applies at this level.)

Message Level
The structure of what we say or write is in its very nature the structure of an intention to mean; the shaping of an utterance or a paragraph cannot usefully be abstracted from the speaker's or writer's understanding of the topic and his or her ability to develop something to say about it. Discussion of the audience's needs and whether they are being fulfilled

is often valuable, but this is discussion in terms of content or style. Such discussion, though it necessarily refers to particular features in texts, need not demand that pupils first master an extensive generalised system for describing those features.

Literary criticism has long shown that naturalistic language enables us to talk very precisely about meaning and style using particular textual examples and referring to alternative means of expression. (For example, a teacher might discuss with young children what difference it made in the meaning of a particular text if 'pushed his way' was substituted for 'rushed through'.) To improve upon the naturalistic competences, what is required is developed sensitivity to a range of particular texts, not the mastery of generalised conceptual systems. Seventeen years of teaching English to secondary pupils convinced me that young people can best be helped to reflect upon their own and other people's speech and writing through modes of discussion more like the discussion of a literary work than like analysis using the conceptual systems made available by general linguistics. This is true whether or not the text is literary.

Context Level
Our knowledge of language and what it means is not separate from our understanding of the world to which language refers nor of the world in which it is used. Classroom discussion at the level of 'Context' should include some investigation of uses and users of language in our society, perhaps making informal comparisons with other societies. It is important that all citizens should understand how different language styles may prejudice people's perception and evaluation of people and events; it should be well understood that the criteria for judging language use should be appropriateness rather than correctness, and that even appropriateness may become the tool of political interests. Some knowledge of sociolinguistics would be relevant; even children of primary school age can be expected to interest themselves in why people talk differently. But any study of sociolinguistic issues should not be an end in itself but find its context in a wider awareness of people and their behaviour. This does not imply a systematic study either of sociolinguistics or general social studies, though both of these can contribute valuably to the task of extending the understanding of people and how they behave which all pupils in some degree bring to school with them.

STUDYING COMMUNICATION OR STUDYING LANGUAGE

It will be clear by now that I am recommending that teachers' efforts to encourage pupils to be more aware of language behaviour should focus primarily upon the 'higher' levels of the hierarchy. Intervention at these levels is likely to be more effective because when we talk we are more aware of people and purposes than of words and structures. Academic linguistic studies have tended to focus upon the 'lower' levels in increasingly elaborate accounts of the organisation and marshalling of systems of forms. This sophistication in university research should not be allowed to dictate the levels of language that are to be studied in schools. When we discuss with pupils how to phrase a piece of writing so that it both responds to their intentions and to the needs of a specific audience, when we talk about people trying to use language to communicate their understanding and feelings about the world whether in a literary or a more instrumental form, we are dealing with matters which are in their nature a good deal less open to systematisation, but this does not imply that it cannot be talked and written about, as literary critics have shown. Pupils of both primary and secondary ages come to school with well developed but unsystematic means for talking about people and communication; it is the business of schooling to refine and sharpen those means to the high level of precision of which they are capable, and this does not mean substituting alternative systems developed for other purposes. Describing systems of linguistic forms is not the same as understanding human communication: the two areas of study ask different questions and attempt different modes of reply.

It has been said that language is made up of three systems of systems:

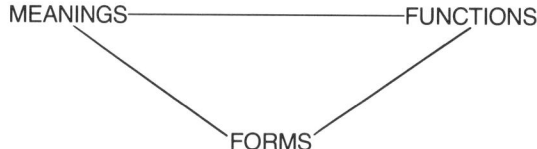

The academic study of language has resulted in a number of highly sophisticated (and competing) descriptive systems. Some of the developments in the study of meaning have not, however, been so impressive; semanticists have adopted some misleading strategies that separate the meaning of words both from the knowledge systems of which they form an undoubted part but, more dangerously, from the contexts of human interaction on which all meaning depends. The still more recent studies of how we use speech and writing as modes of social action (commonly called 'pragmatics'), although very challenging, have not progressed far enough to form the basis for a systematic study of the uses of language in context. Yet it is precisely in reflection upon meanings and functions that language study is most likely to offer valuable help to young people.

It is at present part of this country's educational policies – as expressed in the DES's *Better Schools* (HMSO, 1986) for example – to strengthen students' ability to organise and take responsibility for their own learning in a manner which is to be 'realistic', 'experiential' and 'active'. This is in part a challenge to traditional academic views of education which require the learner to submit to the requirements of an existing intellectual system until such time as he or she has gained expertise in it. For a majority of students this latter policy results in discouragement and failure. From this point of view, the study of linguistic forms would be 'academic' in the sense of requiring students to submit to a body of knowledge, much of which would seem to many of them to be pointless and academic in the pejorative sense. Pupils come to school with an existing desire to communicate and a well-developed intuitive sense of meanings and functions in particular situations, though without the habit of reflecting on them. English teaching should help them to discover that language behaviour is open to their own informal investigation, not that it is the province of experts. (It has recently been proposed that linguistics should be studied inductively, the students themselves becoming investigators of language in the community about them. Although I have some sympathy with this proposal, the history of inductive study in, for example, Nuffield science courses, gives little hope for its survival in the face of a mass examination system that does not reward the skills involved. Nor does the complete failure of the admirable *Language in Use* (P. Doughey, J. Pearce, and G. Thornton, Edward Arnold, 1971) to find any place in schools bode well for such approaches.)

Pupils should certainly 'study language' but it should be language as living acts of communication in realistic contexts, not language as idealised systems abstracted from acts of communication. One important advantage of the former is that it does not drive a wedge between English as literary study and English as language: the two address similar issues through similar means. It has sometimes been suggested that English lessons in school lack 'rigour'. Since our purpose is to help students to engage more effectively with the social world they find themselves in, we must avoid any temptation to espouse an irrelevant rigour which might actually impede them from doing so. I am not taking the obscurantist view that no systems are useful in language study, but I believe that much of what linguistics would make available (at a level which could be taught in schools) would provide the wrong kind of rigour. Moreover it would generate an unnecessary and unhelpful sense of failure in many students who are well able to learn to talk and write competently, and to reflect upon their own and others' uses of language.

A PRIMARY PERSPECTIVE

FRED FINNEY

Fred Finney has taught in secondary schools for 10 years, in primary schools for much longer than that, and is currently Headteacher of Woodlands Junior School, Ilford. He has contributed reviews to Primary Review *and is an External Examiner for the North East London Polytechnic.*

It is likely that schoolteaching destroys more genuine literacy than it produces.
Paul Goodman

> And though you probe and pry
> With analytic eye,
> And eavesdrop all our talk
> With an amused look,
> You cannot find the centre
> Where we dance, where we play,
> Where life is still asleep
> Under the closed flower.
> R.S. Thomas

The door opens and, buzzing with conversation, in tumbles, shuffles, sidles, trots, a mixture of thirty-two young bodies; male and female, from large to small, from clever to less able, from healthy to sickly; some with fluent, literate parents, others whose parents have a mother tongue that is not English; some who have had a good night's sleep, some who may have watched late television until 1 a.m.; some who have breakfasted well, some who may not have eaten since the night before. In short, your class of 10- and 11-year-olds has arrived in school.

Now, 'what, in general terms' do they 'need to know about how the English language works and in consequence what they should have been taught, and be expected to understand, on the workings of language' at age 11?

We need only look into texts of child psychology and child development to put together the expectations we might have of a typical five-year-old; so that if there are to be later 'expectations' at seven years and so on, ideally they should be grounded in the 'expectations' of where children should be when starting school. Let us look at a few of those 'expectations'.

Five-year-old children should be able to sit on a parent's knee and listen peacefully to a story in the course of which, living in a real world, they will demand some reality; their listening skills will have got them far enough to be able to follow simple instructions about simple tasks, and to be able to ask questions about those tasks; they should speak a language free of 'baby' sounds and describe experiences in sentences which follow each other in a correct sequence; the form and structure of language should be used fairly competently with rules of grammar applied and the sentences completed; they should be able to say how old they are, to criticise themselves, initiate conversations, and to make a good impression socially, in part through their language; they should be able to recognise their names in print, and to make reasonable representations of familiar objects in some sort of graphic medium.

Teachers of 5-year-old children are only too aware of how their small charges match up to these expectations, and many will have learnt through bitter experience to be prepared for a good deal less from a significant proportion of the children entrusted to their care. These children might seldom, if ever, have been read stories, in fact there might be no books in the home and they might never have seen a parent read a book; they might have been given orders, but rarely instructions, about simple tasks around the home, and they might never have been given opportunities to ask questions; they might have been positively encouraged to remain the 'baby' of the family; they might have had few experiences which are seen as worth describing; they will be able to use the form and structure of language only in so far as they have heard language used – those from ethnic minority families may have fluency in their mother tongue but have little or no English; they might be completely socially inadequate, and it is entirely possible that some will never have experienced group play; they might not even be able to recognise their own names (is that story apocryphal, of the child who thought his name was 'Oi'?).

Do these possibilities indicate more accurate, and therefore more realistic, starting points for whatever sets of objectives are to be deemed appropriate for the 7-, 11- and 16-year-old? Indeed, if this is where we start in the real world of formal education, can there be *any* possible reasonable, testable common objectives at *any* stages based on common age groups?

But, to return to our class still buzzing away. Now what? Where to start? Where to go? What is certain is that we cannot start, nor go anywhere, without language. Language is the element which pervades all learning. George Herbert Mead stated that 'out of language arises the field of mind' and that 'each individual self has its own peculiar individuality, its own unique pattern'. Few would doubt the truth of these statements as central to the role of language in education, but their implications should surely be for the consideration of teachers and those who would be teachers, and it is difficult to follow the reasoning which suggests that somehow a young learner is assisted in his learning by a 'knowledge of how the English language works'. What we know of how the English language works becomes more complex by the day, but our ability to *use* language becomes no less certain. It is significant that, no matter how many 'models' of the English language there might be, or 'models' of how language is acquired, language goes on being learned in action.

However, we *do* know that the 'model' of English based on the teaching of grammar in the way that 'an earlier generation understood the term', never was a useful model. Extensive research noted by Andrew Wilkinson shows that the performing of old style English grammar exercises leads to 'no improvement in pupils' composition' and may even 'hinder the development of children's written English'.

So our teacher of the class that tumbled in through the door some minutes ago will have no recourse to books of exercises or passages for written comprehension, but will rely on real situations arising out of the group's needs, activities and interests as a whole, and the needs, activities and interests of the individuals comprising the group. This is where the teacher starts, and where she goes is forward – *with* the children.

As to speech, the problem is to develop each child's spoken language to its optimum at each point through the continuing process of its growth; from the egocentrism indicated by Piaget to the 'world representation' of Britton. Limitless opportunities must be provided for talk of all descriptions – not at the teacher's bidding or whim, or as the result of some closely programmed theoretical framework, but the spontaneity of the monologue, conversations between children of similar or of different ages, between teacher and child or teacher and children, with roles changing where appropriate to the demands of the occasion. If children are allowed to take significant roles in discussions, making worthwhile contributions, the skill of listening will be developed to its limits. It is not difficult then, to see the value of this kind of 'conversation' across the curriculum – a conversation which could well result in *children* telling their *teacher* why they should *not* talk during story-time, or in a PE lesson, or while someone is talking. If children are to be required to know *how* their language works, they could be in danger of being like the centipede quoted by Koestler 'who was asked in which order he moved his hundred legs, and could walk no more'.

The value of positively encouraged talk, of all kinds, can be seen in its most crucial significance in schools with a high proportion of children from ethnic minority groups. One can hear, from children who two or three years earlier knew little or no English, phrases, sentences and more lengthy utterances of greater complexity than many which those of us who were trained in a foreign language for six years would begin to attempt. At home these children will converse fluently in, and continue to grow through, their mother tongue.

But our class is busy 'doing maths' and we can watch them at work, possibly in groups, in a class mathematics project, in an individual pursuit, or possibly in mathematics arising from other interests they are following. As the teacher goes among them she is making those decisions which are essential to good teaching, the first decision being the answer to the question, 'Should I, or should I not, intervene?' Having made her decision, then must come, either the nature of the intervention, or a later evaluation of the results of non-intervention. Whatever the teacher decides will have been, in a sense, dictated to her by what she sees and hears, combined with an intuitive 'reading between the lines'. What is certain is that, among the class, some will be learning 'off by heart' (whether this is the intention or no), some will be consolidating, some will be investigating and problem solving through observation, experiment and hypothesis; but no matter how carefully a teacher might prepare for one or all of these situations, it remains well nigh impossible to predict or control the path the children's thoughts will travel. Mead refers to intelligence as the ability to solve 'the problems of present behaviour in terms of possible future consequences and implicated on the basis of past experience', and it must be a very rare teacher who does not from time to time thrill to hear a child's equivalent of 'Eureka!'

As to reading and writing, children will perform these activities freely if they see a point to them, if they are given some control over the time-scale of their own progress, and if they are not made to feel inadequate. Of course we *can* help children to understand how they learn to read by using contextual, syntactical and visual clues; but would we use these terms with the children? Frank Smith's 'difficult rule (for making) learning to read easy is to make reading easy "by responding" to what the child is trying to do'. It *is* a difficult rule, difficult for the teacher, but not for the child; the *teacher* being the one who needs detailed and extensive knowledge about the complex task of reading to enable her 'to be continuously making critical and insightful decisions'.

A six-year-old girl once wrote under her picture of a little girl standing near two trees: 'This is a wood and a little girl is walking through the wood and on the tree is coloured flowers and on the other tree is coloured flowers.' When asked what she was thinking about as she drew her picture she said, 'She was getting lost in the woods and her mummy went out shopping. She never knew what time she would get back and she stayed out there for a long time. And she wanted to find her way home. She couldn't find it because there were so many trees the same.'

And a seven-year-old boy (not a great intellectual) wrote under his drawing of a river with matchstick figures: 'The river Stort is not running it is not running fast it is not running fast it is straight.' He *said* of the picture: 'There's me dad and there's me sister and there's me dog. Its going across and there was gipsy caravans up there and the dog went past them. And there was lots of dogs and they were fighting with ours. There was a bridge and when the train was coming we was busy and didn't have the dog on a lead. He was going to jump off the bridge when I stops him.'

We might ask ourselves where they had learned to write in that strange, stilted manner when their minds were so alert and full of interesting thoughts and recollections. Should we not consider whether the primitive written language in which we seem to train children is an appropriate medium from which 'the field of mind' might arise, especially when we compare it with the vitality of the same children's spoken tongue? And can we improve the quality of children's written language in any way by insisting that they know 'how the English language works'?

But the teacher of our class, for she is wise, has first given the children the mechanical skill of an easy, increasingly flowing 'hand', and then has given them the responsibility for fearlessly putting down, and editing, those words which, however few, are genuinely all they have to say; worth more than pages of imitative or repetitive drivel.

So our class proceeds through the school day. Perhaps PE will have led to some cooperative activity, which can only be made possible through the language of consultation and consensus; but the children will also have rediscovered pleasures which go beyond language.

The introduction of computers might have resulted in an explosion of writing and creativity through the imaginative use of adventure programmes, with the added bonus of the possibility of reasoned logic and argument while the children work together to solve the problems posed on the screen.

Writing of all kinds, from transactional to poetic (am I suggesting a favoured model?) could have taken place across the curriculum, and will certainly do so in the course of no more than two days; sometimes the mode will be deliberately selected, as a challenge, by the teacher, perhaps a lantern poem or a haiku; sometimes the mode will be arrived at almost by accident, or because the children have become aware, without formal instruction, of the diversity of possibilities of different kinds of writing.

Spelling will not have been neglected – recent research has led to much more effective, meaningful and enjoyable ways of learning to spell correctly – but the children will not have been afraid to write continuously for extended periods without constantly processing to the teacher for words about whose spelling they are unsure.

The children will have read quietly to themselves, and probably their teacher will have read to them another chapter of Roald Dahl's *Boy* (what discussions arise from this!) or Philippa Pearce's *A Dog So Small*; but positively **not** *Animal Farm*.

And the door opens, and with a 'See you tomorrow', buzzing with conversation, away they go.

Some of the evidence: these pieces are from children of a mixture of abilities, aged 9 to 11 years; and all are self-edited and uncorrected by a teacher. They are not presented as the best work produced by children in the school. They are simply representative.

The form of lantern poems and haikus forces an economy of language, which very often results in beautifully turned phrases and sentences:

>   A
>   fat girl
>   called Charmaine
>   sat on a chair
>   CRACK

>   It   I
>   was a   have five
>   lovely day   cats and one
>   in my house in   rabbit I love
>   May   them.

>   I   I
>   think that   like soft
>   elephants   rabbits they
>   are beautiful   have fluffy cute
>   beasts   tails

>   Go   My
>   away   friends are
>   from the door   Anne-Marie
>   you fool I hate   and Caroline too
>   you

>   Black   Calls
>   and brown   meeow
>   he's got a   at me for
>   very short tail   supper chases
>   woof.   mice

>   A girl big and fat
>   playing with a bat smash bang
>   crack goes the window

>   I stay in one place
>   and do a little dance for
>   everyone who comes

> I was in the zoo
> watching the small kangaroo
> that jumps up and down
>
> He is a good pet
> long thin tail is white and brown
> His tiny eyes shine
>
> He waggles his tail
> With all four paws on the ground
> And he has blue eyes
>
> Snow is cold as ice
> It falls from the frozen sky
> And makes me shiver

And a description moulded into a poem:

> *The Old Steam Train*
>
> The old steam train sits in the shed.
> Mice running in and out of the boiler.
> The shovel sits in the corner all by itself.
> The coal sits in the sacks, cinders and ashes
> cover the ground.
> The wheels are rusting and the whistle is dead.
> The wheels are oiled.
> The whistle is fixed.
> The wheels start turning.
> The engine starts burning.
> The mighty engine roars again.

A story written over a number of days as an exercise in handwriting – completely uncorrected by either child or teacher:

> Emma Smith was sitting at the bottom of the stairs wondering what to do. Her mother had gone out to buy some bread, so Emma was left alone in the house. She went up to her bedroom and looked inside. There lying in her bed was a prince polishing his shoes. 'Good-day prince,' said Emma. 'May I ask you what you are doing in my bed?' she asked.
> 'What do you think. I'm polishing my shoes' said the prince. Emma said 'this is my bed. Could you please get out.' 'I'm happily comfy in bed now' said the prince.

Emma was getting a bit annoyed with the stupid prince and she suddenly heard her mum's key in the front door. 'That's my mum' said Emma 'I will give you five seconds to get out of my bed. Five. Four. Three. Two. One.'

Still the prince lay there, admiring his face in the mirror. 'Your time is up. I'm going to tell my mum all about you.' The prince's face started to look worried.

'What are you worried about?' asked Emma 'Anyway I haven't been told your name yet!' 'Prince Simon' answered the prince. 'I'm also not worried. Just a bit nearvous that's all.' Nearvous in meeting my mum?' said Emma. 'Mum, I am in my bedroom.'

'I don't care' said the prince 'your mum won't be able to see me. I can turn inviseble.' That annoyed Emma because she would'nt be able to get the prince out of bed.

'Have'nt you got a bed of your own?' asked Emma. 'Yes I have' answered the prince 'but this bed is more comfortable.' Suddenly the door handle turned and in came Emma's mum. 'Hello Emma. Are you playing with your dolls?' 'She can't see him' thought Emma.

'Why is your bed, not yet made I suppose I shall have to change the bed myself' That worried the prince because if Emma's mum touched him, she would feel him. The prince was very, very worried. He did not know what to do.

Suddenly the prince had an idea. He jumped out of bed and lay on the floor by Emma's feet. Emma's mum started to make the bed and said 'This bed is warm, has someone else been sleeping in your bed?'

'Yes' said Emma 'and he's by my feet at this very moment' Suddenly the prince jumped up and opened the window and ran as fast as his legs could carry him, until he was safe back where he come from, and from then on he allways slept in his own bed.

The end.

Do these two pieces suggest the value of a child centred curriculum?

Why

Is it that the world is round
Tell me why? tell me why?
Why do trees have leaves? Why is
the sky blue? Why do cats meow?
Why do dogs bark? Why does mum do
the cooking dad, and you sit there looking?
Why do elephants have trunks? Why
is grass green? Tell me why?
Tell me why?

Why

Why don't we live forever?
How can we tell if we're dying?
When does a child become an adult?
Why do we ask questions?
How does the aircraft fly?
When do we grow?
Why do I have blue eyes and not brown?
Why are my eyes bad?
Why?

Consider the metaphor and simile in this description:

Epping Forest

Trees wavering sluggishly as if to shake each others hand. I felt excited yet I had a cold shiver down my back as if someone was watching me. When we got to the pond it looked like a puddle you get from an old pipe. Putting the net in was exciting like opening a present. And when you had to wait for the mud to clear before a cavalry of insects charge out. Madly but helplessly they try to get out the four slippry walls. Then the sqweasy sucks them up like a sweet wrapper under a vacuum cleaner. Then spat out like an unwanted sweet in a childs mouth.

When we go back from the pond we put them in little containers and watched them. I felt sorry for them after all how would you feel being picked about. The centre was nice in the room were stuffed foxs and deers and lots of wild life posters.

And the simplicity and accuracy of this observation:

Water Scorpion

The water scorpion is about 18 mm long it can grow up to 20 mm long. It breaths through its tail. When it has been under water for a long time it sticks its tail up and breaths. It eats other incects. It lives in the reeds and has four legs it is dark and light brown.

Some writing from a computer programme:

The spaceship that took us to the planet Persephone is called The Golden Hind. It was specially built to go threw comet storms and rock showers. The Golden Hind has a red shuttle attached to it with metal hooks. The Golden Hind is blue with The Golden Hind written on it in silver. The Golden Hind has four wings to keep it steady. It has two wings on its back and two in the middle. The two wings in the middle have three laser guns on each one. At the front of the Golden Hind theres another laser gun and still another one at the back. At the back of the Golden Hind theres three powerful rockets, the rockets have three speeds. 1. Normal 2. Faster 3. Boost.

And more:

I have phoned to tell you that you have been chosen out of many people to (go) on a space trip to the planet PERSEPHONE could you make it on Friday 20th. 'Oh yes certainly thank you bye.' I put the phone down with excitement.

A couple of days later it was time for the interviews and I was so nervous I thought I was going to have a breakdown. Well, I went to the Sunny Bay Hotel and I was asked loads of questions and they said they'll be in touch. Three days later I got a letter telling me I had been chosen. I was so excited that when I went out I kept shaking peoples hands and shouting 'Isn't it a happy day' and some people gave me very funny looks.

Finally a short book review:

The book is called "The Starlight Barking". It's about the hundred and one dalmations. A 'mysterious sleeping' has began and it only affects humans and other creatures except dogs. All the dogs get together determined to find out what's happening. No dog knows what's going to happen next. Soon they have to make a rather difficult choice. It's a good book, excellent to read. It'll keep you guessing from the very first page.

QUAINT MOONMARKS
On language and the growth of individuality

DENNIS CARTER

> Dennis Carter is a teacher and a writer. He is currently head of Taliesin Junior School in Clwyd. He believes in the creative potential of every pupil; in co-operation as opposed to competition; and in the massive power of words. He has written a number of articles on literature and on learning, including 'King Lear in the Junior Classroom' (*English in Education* 1986).

In his poem about the great English baroque composer, Purcell, Gerard Manley Hopkins focuses on individuality, on those things which make Purcell different or 'other', on the distinctions or traits which reveal his uniqueness; on Purcell's 'inscape'. 'Henry Purcell' is an impassioned plea to God. To Hopkins, a devout Jesuit in the late nineteenth century, Purcell, a Protestant, would be one of the damned, a heretic. Hopkins, then, pleads by celebrating the wonders of Purcell's individuality:

> It is the forged feature finds me; it is the rehearsal
> Of own, of abrupt self there thrusts on, so throngs the ear.

This individuality, evidenced in Purcell's music, is his 'divinity', a divinity which affects others with its 'air of angels'.

The fulcrum of the sonnet is its bird metaphor, the 'great stormfowl' which contains the flight of Purcell's music. This reveals his individuality which hitherto has been hidden on the pages of a musical score. That individuality is pinpointed with ornithological accuracy:

> . . . only I'll
> Have an eye to the sakes of him, quaint moonmarks to his pelted
>   plumage under
> Wings . . .

My fuller understanding of this image has its origins in my lifetime hobby of birdwatching and, in particular, in two species of birds. Birdwatching on a winter tideline you might eventually see two birds which look almost identical but are different species. In summer they are easy to distinguish but in winter difficult, until they fly. Then the patient watcher will see the difference between the grey and the golden plover. Under the wing of the grey is a black patch, under that of the golden a white one. Such small and hidden marks to denote completely different species!

I was helped to see this secret by a friend in the Dee estuary and, having consolidated this knowledge with textbooks, I was eventually able to see it for myself. Years later at college I read the Hopkins poem for the first time as part of my English Literature course. Despite the theories of literary critics and the lectures of my excellent tutors I was not helped into a knowledge of the poem. Other Hopkins poems were having a mighty impression upon me, despite the instructions about Hopkins' versification, sprung rhythm and the rest. 'As kingfishers catch fire . . .' for instance, was fitting in with and expanding my view of the universe very quickly. Hopkins' nature poems were bound to find a ready response in one so in love with nature and I remain eternally grateful to my tutors for introducing me to them. But the Purcell poem remained opaque to me.

Ten years later I was a student again on the M.Ed. Literature course at Exeter university and enjoying birdwatching trips to the Exe estuary with a friend. I re-read the poem and understanding came like a thunderbolt. The 'quaint moonmarks' are the patches of black under a grey plover's wings, patches of white under those of the golden. I began to think about Purcell writing down his notes of music, *his* marks to denote *his* music. Although the notes are part of a universal language for music, this particular group of markings in this particular arrangement are Purcell's and no other's. They are his individual markings and contain his divinity, his 'air of angels'. I looked at facsimiles of Purcell scores and found many marks which looked like new moons. Moonmarks!

In the poem the bird in flight denotes Purcell's music which transports the listener and it is this transport of joy which reveals those 'quaint moonmarks', hidden like crescent moons on the written score. At last Hopkins' words had come to me across a century bringing revelation because, after years of incubation, I now was ready. Here is a definitive example of growth of mind caused by language and it was a growth with many sources of nourishment. It took place because I was ready to fit those particular elements of the world outside me onto the growing jigsaw of my perceptions in a way which was impossible during the college course.

All of us grow like this into our culture, given the right context, by receiving such marks *from* others and by having plentiful opportunities to reveal our own markings *for* others. These markings are the sum of our inheritance at birth, our inheritance of the marks of our culture and the way we use them and interpret them. Each of us receives marks and makes marks. Everything we do, each word we speak makes a mark, even if we are unable to perceive it, let alone understand it. All of these marks constellate in different ways for different people.

So every contact children have makes its mark and all children make marks upon the reality around them. It is a two-way process with nothing getting lost or left to chance. All to a greater or lesser degree. By children's marks we shall know them, by that which is typical of them, distinctive and original in them. These marks will depend crucially upon the marks upon their individualities made by the culture which surrounds them. For teachers this is a profound, almost daunting responsibility. It means that everything which happens in school will have its effect. It means that all language, good or bad, which children write or speak, has its cause, so that planning for language growth in a school must needs be planning for the whole life and the whole language of the school. It also means that things which happen to children outside of school, and the language accompanying those happenings, have a vital place inside the school. The school is, therefore, a clearing house of experiences as well as a provider of them. School then becomes a great melting pot for language out of which new objects can be made by the children and their teachers.

The notion of the teaching of English as a single programme for all young people, irrespective of local situations, contradicts the individual nature of children's experiences, perceptions and, consequently, their living language. Furthermore, the assertion that this single programme can somehow represent a continuum along which every child will progress to be assessed at seven, eleven and fourteen implies a desire to control children's experience, perceptions and language. The intention to do these things implies that the world outside of the school and much of the world inside the school are mere incidentals to the teaching of English. Those who have such intentions would argue that an aim of the teaching is to make children better equipped with the necessary skills in English required by those two worlds. This argument is a fundamental denial of the logic of language development. Language is not naturally learnt outside of the life which it serves. A language course cannot be successful if conceived of as a sort of greenhouse or cold frame to bring along linguistic seedlings before transplanting them into the real world.

This programmatic, cold-frame approach to the teaching of English, with its systematic assessment tests, has been found wanting before, and it takes no original imagination to work out what the 'cold-frame' course will lead to next. The majority of schools will confine their teaching of English to the programme, the cold frame. Some will ruthlessly eliminate what they consider to be the incidentals, or weeds. Worse still, the programmes will be determined by those who devise the assessment materials, people remote from children and their lives at home and school.

Children will continue to develop as individuals in the wake of this new cold-frame age in English teaching. They will also develop their own language in individualistic ways. But a gaping space will open up between 'English' and language. 'English' will be school-based cold-frame words and ways of writing and talking. Language will become the sub-culture words of the child's private world outside of school. School in such circumstances becomes a separate institution from the community it serves. By framing a certain kind of language and calling it 'English' as if the other language is some sort of foreign or dialect language, it also separates the learning in the school from the great tendencies and movements in the culture denoted by the very word 'English'.

A major feature of the culture denoted by the word 'English' is the central role of the individual, whether this be the daring of great explorers or the writing of 'The Prelude'. It is ironic, therefore, that people committed to the cult of individuality should devote themselves to an approach to the teaching of English in direct contradiction to this other conviction.

It is also an approach which denies what really happens to children's language growth from birth to five. The two-and-a-half-year-old child who says, 'Read me a story, Mummy. I'm hungry for a story,' reveals an understanding of the power of words which cannot be taught by direct instruction. When that same child lies under the garden chair with two plant labels in his hand and says, 'Must connect the leads to the distributor. Then grease it,' after hearing these words once only when he observed the mending of an engine, he shows the full extent of his language mechanism for remembering and imitating.

Such invention and imitation grow out of the way of life and the way of language in the home and community. They are vital to language development. Even in a single home, however, individual children will use language differently. At 18 months one child called biscuits 'gits' whereas his sister at the same age called them 'bikbees'. The language mechanisms of the two children responded differently to the same absolute sound, spoken by the same people, the parents. How great, therefore, the variation across the whole field of language spoken and written in a single classroom in one school! How devastating to the possibilities of language and learning if the cold frame called 'English' were to be imposed.

What follows is a short chronicle demonstrating some of those possibilites, threatened by 'benchmarks' and programmes. The first concerns nine-year-old twins, one girl, one boy, who came into my class from another school on the opposite side of the country. She was bright, lively and good at getting things right. If I'd taught to an English programme with an 11+ assessment test, she would have registered a high score. Her brother, on the other hand, was lazy, acted silly and sat there grinning when referred to. The test would have condemned his English. Two children, from the same womb at the same time, arrived in my class as diverse a pair of children as could be imagined. True to expectations, the girl began to succeed in my class and the boy to fail. During our walks, however, new things began to emerge about the twins. Out of school in field or village the boy was animated. It was a common practice for the children to settle down and write about objects and places of their own choice. This became a much loved activity. The girl soon got cracking and produced pleasant little pieces very quickly. The boy would stand staring at things for long periods. Was he being lazy? Was he confirming all the reports, written and spoken, that had arrived in his wake like messages of doom? This was quite clearly not the case from the very first walk when he wrote:

Kissing-gate

Along by the kissing gate
surrounded by nettles,
blackberries are kissed
by tempted wanderers
for their lips are dark
but also delicious

The subtlety of this piece, with its sensuous richness and wit, would seem to come from the mind of an adult rather than a junior schoolchild. It has the e.e.cummings feel about it, or, perhaps, the approach of William Carlos Williams. These comparisons are borne out by the boy's entire output during the eighteen months he spent with me. Here are two further examples:

Waterfall

Watery champagne
rocketing down
surging foam
then ssshhh
the cork's back.

Landscape

Dipping dales
like dimples
catch you unawares
casting you down.
Then you're jolted up
by unsteady legs.

Such contributions to English culture would never have been made had not this boy changed schools, moving out of a programmatic approach to 'English' into an open-ended one, based upon the child and his potential.

Another boy, aged eleven, came to me one morning with this piece, written after a visit to his grandfather the previous evening:

> A large shadow falls across my path.
> I look up fearfully, I wonder.
> My heart missed a beat. What can it be?
> I hopefully look up into one eye.
> In the dim light I see a huge monster
> bending over me.
> Half man, half beast, A CYCLOPS.
> I come out of my daydream
> and realise where I am.
> My grandad's printing shop.

Yes, his grandad was the village printer and the boy found it quite natural to write about him at home and bring him, this way, into school. He also knew that I was a ready audience for this kind of witty writing with its amusing use of hyperbole. He was eleven but this piece was part of no 'benchmark'. It arose out of a group of relationships, uniting school and community and, most importantly, focused upon the child.

An eight-year-old girl had been looking at and feeling a ram's horn as part of some work based on objects brought into the classroom. She entered what can only be described as a form of meditation, behaving in a way that no programme could cause, no test could stimulate:

> A twisting, turning snake.
> Blow breath echo.
> Turning slide into the deep blue water.
> Curling walking stick.
> The crinkle cut path.
> Smooth, rough path up into
> a different heaven.
> A curled handle moves.
> Heaven suddenly awakes
> in the misty land.
> Children play on the
> trampoline clouds.
> Adults helping children
> make their invention
> so they can be born.

A ram's horn is a ram's horn, yet this child has marked for it a new set of truths from out of her own vision. Clustered around this object now are so many fragments, disparate before, but unified now. The ram's horn is different now that we have read her speculations about it. She also is different and sees the ram's horn differently. The girl has grown individually: her language, her intellect and her knowledge. The phrase 'Blow breath echo' is a new piece of English, never written before, a new harmony to add to the culture.

A child with special educational needs in an area of town with 50 per cent unemployment after hearing an actor playing Lady Macbeth as part of a project, remembered 'look like th'innocent flower, But be the serpent under't.' He had only heard those words once. Later he wrote of Macbeth and Banquo's encounter with the witches: 'That left Macbeth with thoughts rumbling in his head, good thoughts and bad thoughts.' Another child, aged 10, during a project on *Hamlet* sums up the state of Denmark: 'Everything is turning rotten. Treason grows. The curtain hides the badness. You have one face but you make two.' These are remarkable insights into Shakespeare by children in their schools. They have arisen organically out of explorations with their teachers and, in one case, actors who came in. Each example reveals great depth of understanding and the language to release it.

Language develops most effectively and richly in children out of relationships of trust in open-ended contexts. As has been demonstrated here, children are quite capable of handling even the more sophisticated and intellectually challenging ideas in their culture. They are also fully able to listen to and re-use the language that contains these ideas. In such open-ended contexts as described here, the distinctive traits of each child have a fuller opportunity to evolve. The distinctiveness of each child then feeds into the culture as developed in the classroom. The culture of the whole school community grows with the revelations of the 'quaint moonmarks' of each of its individuals. Similarly, the individuality of each child is strengthened by the self-confidence of knowing that such distinctiveness is valued by the community.

LANGUAGE IS A SPECIAL NEED

BRIDIE RABAN AND MICHAEL STRUTT

> Bridie Raban worked with the Bristol Reading Centre for 13 years before becoming a lecturer in Language, Literacy and Special Needs at the University of Reading. She was the director of the University of Oxford Special Needs Research Project from 1983-85. As well as writing and presenting programmes on reading for the BBC she has published a stream of books and articles. These include *A Question of Reading* (with C. Moon, Macmillan, 1980); *Reading* in the Macmillan Guides to Assessment series (1983); *Practical Ways to Teach Writing*, (Ward Lock, 1985); *Children Learning to Read and Write*, (CUP, forthcoming) and *Classroom Responses to Learning Difficulties* (with K. Postlethwaite, forthcoming).
>
> Michael Strutt has been a teacher of children with special needs for over 10 years. Previously he taught English in Birmingham. He is a member of the National Council for Special Education and is currently engaged in research at Ph. D. level at Reading University.

As language develops it becomes an important tool for learning. In this respect, the Bullock Report (DES, 1975) was of central importance to curriculum development in schools. The report, however, underestimated the range and complexity of contemporary research. While the report focused on language in use and on the functions language can serve, the views of Bernstein were accepted relatively uncritically and the work of Labov was dismissed in a few lines as a 'sincerely held view' (p. 54). The report gave only a superficial gloss on how to approach 'planned intervention' (p. 67) and the important debate concerning the relationship between language and thought was not considered. Support was given to the views of Chomsky without considering alternative theories and the whole area of language acquisition was treated superficially. Semantic development was neglected and the report did not live up to its own recommendation that teachers 'must have up-to-date knowledge of language development' (p. 57). Indeed, the whole section on language in the early years was full of vague generality.

The recommendation that young children should be 'bathed in language' (p. 58) is glib and unhelpful, particularly when considered in the light of Wells' research (1981, 1985a). The findings from this inquiry point out that parents who are not discriminating in the way they interact with their children in conversation do not produce 'fast-developing' children because it is quality not quantity of language input that makes the difference. This finding along with others from recent research is now influencing thinking and more emphasis is being placed on assessment in naturalistic settings, for instance, and on the role of parents (Muller, et al. 1981).

The most significant finding from Wells' research (1985a, 1985b) related to those children who showed accelerated language growth. These children were provided with adult models which were substantially different both in quantity of speech and specific conversational purposes. Fast developers received more direct requests and more short imperative utterances. They received a higher proportion of utterances which picked up or extended the topic of the child's previous utterance or ongoing activity. A high quantity of questions requiring a yes/no answer also seemed significant.

Some of those who were 'bathed in language' did not make fast progress which would suggest it is not quantity alone that is significant. No differences between normal and accelerated development were found to be related to utterance length or syntactic complexity. Modifications which took account of a child's communicative intentions seemed to be most important for fast development. It is suggested, therefore, that adult contributions should encourage reciprocity and support the child's contributions. In contrast, an adult style that is domineering or didactic is unlikely to be helpful, because adult expansions do not have the primary function of 'teaching' the child. They may perform a modelling role but their principal function is to negotiate an interpretation of the child's utterance.

In an attempt to determine the importance of environmental variables, Wells (1985a) has investigated two possible explanations for a common sequence of development of meanings, forms and structures in children's language:

1 that the order in which learning occurs will be determined by the relative frequency with which items within systems are heard by learners in the speech that is addressed to them;
2 that the order in which learning occurs will be determined by the relative cognitive and linguistic complexity of items within systems.

Both explanations receive strong support from the data. However, it would seem that the influence of input is enabling rather than determining. Cues from the child's comprehension are likely to increase the complexity of speech rather than the other way round. Wells concludes that although adult input may have a facilitating effect, it is the nature of the interaction between adult and child which dictates the course of language acquisition.

In classrooms, the more attention-seeking and less inhibited child may be unsuccessful in achieving conversational interactions with teachers, for the teacher does not wish to reinforce behaviour which may adversely affect group management (Beveridge and Hurrell, 1980). Indeed teachers, in encouraging attention to task, are often discouraging communication. Approaches to language development which do not pay attention to helping children to use language in socially appropriate ways may well be useless.

Harris (1984) has shown that language teaching sessions in special schools can produce different types of interaction between teacher and child depending on classroom organisation. For instance, Brinker (1982) found that group sessions are better for the occurrence of varied and unpredictable intentions and verbal eliciting was higher in individual sessions. Spontaneous communications are important because they allow children the opportunity to attempt to control an interaction and to judge whether they have been successful in conveying their meaning. The teacher is seen to have a more important role than providing theory-based strategies for intervention, or using packaged schemes. More valid forms of intervention can be produced by developing existing classroom activities which create those genuine social interactions most beneficial to the chimdsen&s!language development.

Increasing attention has been placed on the contexts in which language develops. Particularly important are play situations. Play situations are likely both to encourage cognitive growth and provide a degree of structure to teacher-child interactions without becoming over formal or teacher-directed. McConkey (1984) has pointed out that children must be active investigators and confident experimenters if they are to become competent language users.

More attention is being focused on the pragmatic functions of language. The social function of language, pre-linguistic communication, intentional communication, the physical context of the situation, and the rules of discourse and speakers' social relationships to receivers are all seen as important. Children must be able to communicate efficiently and effectively, using language that is appropriate to the context of its use. Clearly, language cannot be taught as a unitary skill. The rules of language must be induced by the child from real experiences and real interactions. The teacher may wish to manipulate the environment and these interactions, but the imposition of structure robs the child of initiative. Working without the structure of a language scheme, however, risks bewildering the teacher.

Teachers in special schools rightly consider that language development is central to the curriculum. Many of the children in their charge are poor communicators, some with mild and many with severe language difficulties. In addition, even those with mild language difficulties often have difficulty in coping with higher levels of learning. Children's mechanical reading ability, for instance, often outstrips their comprehension. Many teachers in special schools feel that because language is so delayed, specific efforts must be made to teach it. Often the assumption behind such teaching is that the language of slow learners is deficient. Furthermore, it is assumed that language can be explicitly taught.

Behaviourist techniques are also based on the assumption that language can be explicitly taught and these techniques lie behind much of what teachers and therapists do in their efforts to 'shape' children's language behaviour. They will use imitation and reinforcement of elicited structures and will use structured programmes that 'unpack' the language acquisition process and attempt to build it up step by step.

Behaviourist approaches mushroomed in the 1970s. Mowrer (1984) identified more than 200 language programmes using such approaches and these have all been available to teachers and therapists. However, the change in direction towards an emphasis on the semantic and pragmatic functions of language in the late 1970s was one which educators found difficult to accommodate. Increasing the emphasis on children as active negotiators of their own meanings, on language as a process of reinvention and on children as rule formulators and hypothesis testers has meant a decline in the legitimacy of behaviourist methods, although there remains a lack of understanding as to what to put in their place.

Behaviourist techniques are context free and they may be applied to any aspect of syntactic, semantic or pragmatic development. They do, however, distort the learning process if they reduce the learner to a state of passivity which is incompatible with current understanding of how children acquire language. In addition, there is no clear evidence of such programmes effectively teaching complex language structures. As Rutter (1980) has pointed out, there is also the problem of applying theories about language learning in the school context to more general situations requiring appropriate spontaneous use in varied contexts.

Primary considerations in deciding upon how to provide for these children's language development include the following questions:

- Do children with learning difficulties form a coherent group as regards their language development?
- Is their language development characterised by delay or specific deficits?

De Villiers and de Villiers (1978) have reviewed the evidence relating to these questions. In phonological development, Down's syndrome children differ from normal and retarded children. However, the development of semantic relations was found to be similar for normal and all retarded children, including those with Down's syndrome. In terms of syntax and grammatical development the language of retarded children is delayed but still in keeping with their mental age. In short, most studies fail to reveal any substantial difference between normal and retarded populations as regards language acquisition besides general developmental delay.

It is widely recognised that there are cognitive prerequisites to language which are acquired particularly during the sensory-motor stage of development. It is not, therefore, surprising that children with learning difficulties should suffer a delay in language development. The fact that cognitive development in slow learners follows a similar sequence (Weisz and Zigler, 1978) would suggest the likelihood of a similar sequence of language development between normal and slow learning children. There may, however, be a degree of linguistic impairment due to specific cognitive limitations. Limitations of production span, sequencing ability and short term memory may be significant and may be responsible for the kinds of linguistic structures that can be comprehended and produced. In production, for instance, longer sentences may be broken down into more manageable 'chunks' to increase communicative competence. Indeed, Graham (1980) has argued that the effectiveness of some language intervention strategies may be due as much to improved attentional and processing strategies (particularly short term memory) as to the acquisition of new linguistic structures and vocabulary.

In considering language delay or language deficit it is important to bear in mind that functioning may be delayed or deficient at one or more levels. The studies previously cited have concentrated their attention either on surface structure or form of utterances or on what are assumed to be the cognitive underpinnings of language. These cognitive elements may affect either the complexity of syntactic form or the development of semantic relations, that is the content of language. It is also important to recognise another aspect of development – the use to which language is put. Some children may not develop appropriate uses of language, they may ramble repetitively or associate ideas in a tangential manner without regard for the listener. Such children may not be able to choose the appropriate register of language on a specific occasion and may cause embarrassment.

Although children with learning difficulties may have some specific processing deficits, the balance of evidence suggests that the pattern of their linguistic development is the same as for normal children and this is likely to be the case for nearly all children to be found in special schools for severe and moderate learning difficulties. However, in a survey of language provision in special schools in one local authority, Strutt (1986) concluded that the general language policies adopted by these schools were inconsistent. The schools in this survey revealed little agreement over the main problems facing the children in acquiring and developing language and the relationship between language and the rest of the curriculum was generally vague and uncertain. Where such a relationship was recognised there was little understanding of the nature of this relationship. This uncertainty was also confirmed by an inspection of the curriculum documents.

All the schools for children with severe learning difficulties that were visited during this survey were in the process of adopting the Derbyshire Language Scheme (Knowles and Masidlover, 1982). This scheme is a combined scheme of assessment and remediation based on the language skills of normal children. The emphasis is on initial assessment and subsequent development of comprehension, building up to expressive communication within game-like contexts. The scheme takes account of several strands of recent research. For instance, it stresses the importance of child initiatives in joint activity with adults and the importance of motivation without artificial reinforcement. There are no language drills and teachers are urged not to correct the structure of children's speech but simply to model and expand children's utterances.

This scheme uses play techniques and 'role reversal' which allows the child to initiate language more easily. Behaviourist techniques are countenanced in difficult circumstances, as is repetition with older children, so long as this is not seen as a rejection of the child's attempts to communicate. The emphasis is on constructing as normal a language environment as possible while maintaining structure through the use of games which are likely to elicit particular exchanges or linguistic structures and make repetition of such structures more likely. The scheme has a strong semantic base and it attempts to teach the relationships between objects and people within the teaching setting.

The Derbyshire scheme, like other schemes, provides no evidence of its own effectiveness. Its adoption by schools is, therefore, an act of faith. The scheme is impressive in its carefully structured format and comprehensive range of suggested activities for teachers. Assessment procedures are, however, very time-consuming. The greatest strength of the scheme is the emphasis on developing real, meaningful communication in structured settings or 'eliciting contexts'. Masidlover (1986, pc) has, however, expressed his concern that the packaging of materials may lead teachers and therapists to misuse the scheme. They may well use the scheme to target utterances, to rely heavily on behaviourist methods and consequently lose any real 'communication'. The extent to which this may occur was evident from the school visits.

It was clear from the visits to these schools and classrooms that the heads and language co-ordinators were not fully aware of the guiding principles of the scheme. Activities were more teacher-directed than they should have been and in two schools the language sessions were rigidly time-tabled. There was a tendency to work towards fixed behaviourist objectives and to rely heavily on imitation and repetition. There was an over-concern with superficial, surface features of language and a belief that the Derbyshire scheme's strength lay in its detailed analysis of the acquisition of structure.

It was observed that when a school's policy was translated into practice in classrooms it seemed that even more of the scheme's guiding principles were lost. The sessions observed were teacher-directed and didactic, they relied heavily on imitation techniques and reinforcement and the language produced by the children was often less elaborate than that which they produced in spontaneous speech.

In the schools for children with moderate learning difficulties, structured approaches to language teaching were not used in any consistent way. In these schools there was a bewildering variety of schemes in use, many of which conflicted in their philosophy and approach to language teaching. In one school visited there was an emphasis on language 'enrichment' and the use of stimulating first hand experiences to motivate the children to talk. A further school used a wide range of language schemes, including *Concept 7-9* (Wight et al., 1972) and suggestions from Shiack (1972). 'Experiential' enriching language activities were considered important though it was felt that more structure was necessary for the younger children. In most of these schools there was a tendency to talk more about literacy and reading schemes than about spoken language development. However, no consistent picture emerged from the survey of these M.L.D. schools.

Of all the language sessions observed, one is remarkable for its simplicity and effectiveness. Three children between the ages of seven and ten were taken by the class assistant to the medical room. The forty minute session involved the recounting of a story ('The Picnic') which the assistant made up as she went along. She involved the children as characters in the story and used a verbal hesitation technique to allow individuals to supply words or complete sentences. She also stopped to ask questions, 'What can you see in the forest?', 'What will we play?'. Children could bring in their own ideas and the story would continue in a way which would accommodate the children's contributions. Clearly, the children enjoyed this activity and the classroom assistant displayed considerable skill in maintaining the story and the children's interest over a long period. There were no picture stimuli and this made it easier to tap the children's own experiences. In this way a sensitive interchange between narrative and personal experience was evident.

The local authority itself had no overall policy for language work in special schools. Individual schools were, therefore, grappling with the problem in their own ways. Teachers' understanding of the process of language acquisition and development was often found to be sketchy and in most schools there was little or no awareness of recent developments in research. Throughout, it was clear that the more complicated the scheme the less likely it was to be fully and appropriately implemented and this was the case with the Derbyshire scheme. There remained the tendency to focus on surface features of language rather than on underlying meanings and although some schools mentioned the importance of language in use, there was little evidence that this was being incorporated into the curriculum for younger children. The role of parents was marginal and speech therapists were restricted to specific areas of expertise.

Various strands can be drawn out of the findings of recent research on language acquisition and development which teachers and therapists must take account of. For instance, language functions are not insular in nature and it is impossible, therefore, to divorce semantic development from the development of syntax, both these being contingent upon pragmatic functions which either generate or mould development. Language is essentially for communication and it is impossible to consider the utterance apart from the message. Indeed, Bates and MacWhinney (1979) have pointed out that certain grammatical patterns can be discovered only in the context of communication because they are functional in nature. Language is an active rule-formulating process, it is self-regulating and in this sense children 'select' their own learning goals and proceed at their own pace. Because of this, certain language forms may be available in the input at an early age but will not appear until later in the child's development. The challenge for the teacher and the therapist is to attempt to simplify the learning task without distorting its basic character.

Johnston (1985) summarises some basic principles of instruction:

- Language teaching should fit the child's social purposes and emerging meanings.
- Teachers must take account of non-verbal knowledge and communicative intentions.
- Teaching should also pay more attention to messages rather than concentrating on more formal properties of language.

There are few signs that young children think much about talking, it is an automatic process. Therefore language rules are likely to be learned more quickly in the context of communication. Given that children with learning difficulties do not appear to learn language efficiently in normal contexts, it would seem most appropriate to use focused linguistic input to narrow the child's search for order and to simplify the task of extracting rules. This would involve a reduction of demands on linguistic processing such as attention and memory and this requires sensitivity to the child's level of linguistic development so that teachers and therapists are aware of the input they are providing. Hackney (1984) has found that teachers do this automatically, not just according to the age of the child but also according to the level of mental retardation. It is, therefore, not necessary to take children away from practical and social activities, rather to establish the physical, communicative and linguistic environment in which the child can learn. The play situation is particularly important in this respect for it allows language to grow as a social activity.

Those who argue that such an approach has been tried in schools and that such children do not learn in an 'enriched' environment should bear in mind the evidence from Tizard et al (1980) and Wells (1985b) which suggests that classrooms are linguistically relatively impoverished when compared to homes, for instance. However, the dilemma for teachers remains as to how to control the interaction sufficiently so that a 'facilitating' environment is maintained while at the same time ensuring that the child can retain the initiative. It is the adult's style that determines the child's role and there is no simple solution to this problem for it is in the nature of communicative interactions to be fluid and for there to be an ebb and flow of control.

Professional accountability has led teachers to seek simple, manageable, short-term remediation strategies that concentrate on overt behaviour and surface structure rather than attempting to understand how children acquire language. One must finally face up to the question of whether it is indeed possible to teach language. If teaching is taken to mean the imparting of knowledge or information about language, then language cannot be taught. One cannot use language to talk about language to a child who is only just learning it and Jones (1981) reminds us that attempts to apply direct instruction to developmental processes are likely to produce contradictions. However, certain guiding principles are clear:

- Avoid teacher-directed, time-tabled language sessions.
- Pay less attention to structural complexity as an end in itself.
- Abandon schemes and approaches that are essentially behavioural.
- Recognise the contribution that children make to their own development, allowing them more control over the expression of real communicative intentions.
- Recognise the role of parents in facilitating language development in relation to approaches within the school.
- Attempt to increase the socio-interactive and cognitive processes that underlie language acquisition and development and to extend pragmatic functions.
- Pay more attention to the context of the situation and attempt to sustain, as far as possible, a naturalistic linguistic environment.

This approach will require teachers to argue against simplistic notions of accountability in language teaching. Ultimately, it will require an act of faith, but one no greater than that which has underlain the adoption of current schemes. The difference will lie in the fact that a new approach would be more flexible, more responsive and allow children to sustain motivation and initiative in their own learning.

REFERENCES

BATES, E. AND B. MACWHINNEY, 'A functionalist approach to the acquisition of grammar', in E. Ochs and B. Schieffelin (eds) *Developmental Pragmatics*, New York, Academic Press, 1979

BEVERIDGE M. AND P. HURRELL, 'Teacher responses to severely mentally handicapped children's initiations in the classroom', *Journal of Child Psychology and Psychiatry*, vol. 21, 1980, pp. 175-82

BRINKER, R.P., 'Contextual contours and the development of language', in M. Beveridge (ed) *Children Thinking Through Language*, London, Edward Arnold, 1982

DEPARTMENT OF EDUCATION AND SCIENCE, *A Language for Life* (The Bullock Report), London, HMSO, 1975

DE VILLIERS, J.C. AND DE VILLIERS, P.A., *Language Acquisition*, Cambridge Mass., Harvard University Press, 1978

GRAHAM, N.C., 'Memory constraints in language deficiency', in F.M. Jones (ed.), *Language Disability in Children: Assessment and Remediation*, Lancaster, MPT Press Ltd, 1980

HACKNEY, A., 'Perceptions of the development of handicapped children as revealed in teacher-child interactions', *Special Education: Forward Trends*, vol. 11, no. 3, 1984, pp. 19-22

HARRIS, J., 'Encouraging linguistic interactions in special schools', *Special Education: Forward Trends*, vol. 11, no. 2, 1984, pp. 117-24

JOHNSTON, J., 'Fit, focus and functionality: an essay on early language intervention', *Child Language Teaching and Therapy*, vol. 1, no. 2, 1985, pp. 125-34

JONES, M., 'Environment and communication: a review', *Special Education: Forward Trends*, vol. 8, no. 4, 1981, pp. 22-24

KNOWLES, W. AND M. MASIDLOVER, *Derbyshire Language Scheme*, Ripley, Derbyshire. 2nd edition, 1982, (Private publication)

MCCONKEY, R., 'The assessment of representational play: a springboard for language remediation', in D.J. Muller (ed.) *Remediating Children's Language*, London, Croom Helm, 1984

MOWRER, D.E., 'Behavioural approaches to treating language disorders', in D.J. Muller (ed.) *Remediating Children's Language*, London, Croom Helm, 1984

MULLER, D.J., S.M. MUNRO AND C. CODE, *Language Assessment for Remediation*, London, Croom Helm, 1981

RUTTER, M., 'Language training with autistic children: how does it work and what does it achieve?', in L.A. Hersov and M. Berger (eds), *Language and Language Disorders in Childhood*, Oxford, Pergamon, 1980

SHIACK, G. McG., *Teach Them to Speak*, London, Ward Lock, 1972

STRUTT, M., 'Language in special schools for children with learning difficulties: A study of theory, policy and practice in one English Local Education Authority, unpublished M.A. thesis, University of Reading School of Education, 1986

TIZARD, B., H. CARMICHAEL, M. HUGHES AND G. PINKERTON, 'Four year olds talking to mothers and teachers', in L.A. Hersov and M. Berger (eds), *Language and Language Disorders in Childhood*, Oxford, Pergamon, 1980

WEISZ, J.R. AND E. ZIGLER, 'Cognitive development and retarded and non-retarded persons: Piagetian tests of the similar sequence hypothesis', *Psychological Bulletin*, vol. 86, no. 4, pp. 831-51, 1978

WELLS, C.G., *Learning Through Interaction*, Cambridge, Cambridge University Press, 1981

WELLS, C.G., *Language Development in the Pre-School Years*, Cambridge, Cambridge University Press, 1985a

WELLS C.G., *Language Learning and Education*, Windsor, NFER, 1985b

WIGHT, J., R. NORRIS AND F.J. WORSLEY, *Concept 7–9* Leeds, E.J. Arnold, 1972

SOME LESSONS FROM LANGUAGE MONITORING

A personal view

DENNIS BROOK

Dennis Brook worked as a teacher for 13 years and has now been English Adviser for Derbyshire for nearly 16 years. He was a founder member of the National Association of Advisers in English, and for seven years he was the Association's Vice Chairman. He is joint Chairman of the English Advisers' working party on oral communication and has had some influence on the establishing of the National Oracy Project. He has been a member of the APU steering committee for the last four years and he was also on the SEC Working Party which produced draft criteria for GCSE English.

THE BACKGROUND

In 1975, the Bullock Committee recommended that a system of monitoring be introduced which would employ new instruments 'to assess a wider range of attainments than has been attempted in the past and allow new criteria to be established for the definition of literacy'.[1] The Committee recognised that existing definitions of literacy were inadequate, that more and more demands were being made of the linguistic resources and repertoires of more and more of the population, and that anecdotal and folk memories would continue to assert a golden age of achievement somewhere in the past if baselines, founded on a more adequate view of literacy, were not established and if standards were not monitored over time. Much of the evidence presented here is culled from the important work of the Language Monitoring Team at the NFER working as an agency of the Assessment of Performance Unit. However, other studies undertaken in the past 10 years, some published more recently than others, have also monitored aspects of language performance and are yielding evidence which points in similar directions.[2] These studies are all founded upon the evaluation of the products of classroom activity (the APU exercise samples coursework as a central feature of the monitoring of writing). The APU Language Monitoring Team has also devised a functional and linguistically coherent assessment framework to facilitate the analysis of the evidence emanating from the new test instruments. These instruments are themselves founded upon sound linguistic principles. The other studies cited are also linguistically informed.

A LINGUISTICALLY COHERENT VIEW

Language is used for a wide range of purposes, in a variety of contexts (it is always context bound) and for a variety of readers or audiences, according to whether the use is writing or speaking. The speaker is able to adjust what he has to say and how he says it according to the responses and reactions of the audience. The audience can actually help the speaker to express ideas more effectively if it is supportive and sympathetic and can be destructive of the speaker if hostile. In writing, the reader is more distant and, in order to communicate ideas and feelings successfully, the writer has to consider the needs of the reader, to fashion or anticipate the reader's responses to what is being expressed, and to master the demands of the writing code. As we shall see, the differences between the speech system and the writing system are significant influences upon pupil performance. These factors, taken together, make considerable demands upon the pupil as a writer.

The communicative force, and the ultimate success of what we say or write, depends upon establishing a clear understanding of the task in hand and of the requirements of the task – the purpose, the circumstances, to whom it is addressed. This understanding shapes the selection of content, its organisation, the appropriateness of the style or the tone adopted, the lexical choices made, the forms and structures used. The functions determine the forms. The pressure to make meaning forces the writer or speaker to draw upon his linguistic reservoir 'to find some words/for sounds and things'.[3] By using language to grapple with experience, by defining and wrestling with the task, by extending the range of purposes, by tuning to and experimenting with the 'voices' of others, the writer or speaker extends his linguistic repertoire. It is from perspectives such as these that the APU Language Monitoring programme has developed and the findings should be evaluated.

STANDARDS

The findings of the APU Language Monitoring surveys present a very different view of the performance of children as writers at the ages of 11 and 15 from that often featured in the press. If we were to accept a popular view of literacy, then there are grounds for satisfaction. In *The Assessment of Writing – Pupils Aged 11 and 15*, Janet White tells us:

> About 3 per cent of each age group, excluding those in special schools, are in great difficulty with writing.
>
> About 60 per cent of children's writing receives impressive marks in the middle range, indicating that this work is interesting and legible:

- a majority of 11 year olds (70 per cent) receive marks of 3 or above (on a 5 point scale) across the range of analytic marking categories;
- a majority of 15 year olds (60 per cent) receive marks of 4 or above (on a 5 point scale) across the range of analytic categories.[4]

The surveys have shown that even those who have great difficulty in constructing a text have achieved some control over the written language.

> For example, most letters are formed according to a regular pattern; enough words are either in standard spelling or systematically misspelt to enable a rough interpretation of subject matter; there is some understanding of the function of upper and lower case letters; sentence marking and paragraphing are present in rudimentary form.[5]

> For the 15 year olds in this group there is little time left for them to improve before they leave school and it is likely that they have developed negative attitudes to writing and negative attitudes to themselves as writers. However, it should be acknowledged that the vast majority of children are well beyond 'the stage of incomprehensibility in writing'[6] by the age of 11. We know that about 50% of the pupils in the APU surveys produce writing "which is judged to be middle of the range or slightly below".[7] This writing is legible, has few grammatical errors and "shows responsiveness to the task set".[8]

The popularist view of writing is all pervasive in the results of the APU surveys on attitudes to writing and in other studies undertaken between 1979 and 1987. There is abundant evidence in *Aspects of Secondary Education* (HMSO 1979) and in the, as yet unpublished, research report *Writers in the Making*[9] that the writing curriculum for pupils, when all their writing is considered, is not dominated by unfettered creativity, in which the elements of grammar and orthography are neglected for self-expression. Indeed, the picture is remarkably traditional. Pupils perceive writing as being primarily about presentation, surface features and grammatical accuracy. They receive messages that spelling, length, layout (neatness) and grammar matter most. It is possible to question what they mean by 'grammar' but there are certainly huge numbers of decontextualised exercises in their books to indicate that teachers do give considerable attention to 'where' and 'wear' and 'were'; to 'there' and 'their'; to 'of' and 'have'; to the apostrophe; to the full stop and capital letters; to paragraphing; to those features which are thought to be the hallmark of the literate. It is not surprising that spelling, punctuation 'grammar' and neatness take precedence in the minds of pupils over content and organisation. Planning, drafting, editing, attention to style, the making of lexical and syntactic choices are not seen as essential activities of the writer's art. Very few pupils of 15, in the *Writers in the Making* survey, considered the needs of the reader to be significant.

In the face of such evidence, it is difficult to see how the often prescribed folk remedy of going 'back to the basics' can have any credibility in helping to raise standards. Spelling and grammatical accuracy are important and they are taught but they constitute only part of the writer's needs. As a model of language to inform teachers and help pupils, the 'back to basics' remedy is clearly wanting. In reality, the writing curriculum has never abandoned 'the basics'. To achieve higher standards much more attention has to be given to the '*how*' of writing rather than to the 'what'; consideration and time must be given to the process in order to improve the product. This means reducing the volume of writing set in order to fashion the meaning.

SOME SIGNIFICANT FINDINGS

There are four significant findings in the APU writing surveys which should inform teacher understanding of the linguistic needs of children and the process of writing. They point the way towards improvements in performances. Those findings are:

- the ability of pupils to write well depends upon understanding the specific features of the task set and no task is uniformly difficult or inherently easy;
- spoken language influences the writing of pupils at both 11 and 15;
- the literary 'genre', valued by English departments in secondary schools, has a marked influence on the writing curriculum of the schools and tends to devalue other writing;
- negative attitudes to writing are associated with poor performance.

The latter finding reflects the still prevailing prescriptive approach to error.

THE TASK-SPECIFIC NATURE OF PERFORMANCE

If the ability of the pupil to write 'purposefully and well'[10] depends upon the specific demands of the task, and if no task is uniformly difficult or inherently easy, then it is no longer helpful to talk of a generalised ability in writing for the vast majority of the population. Only at the extreme ends of the spectrum, the most able and the least able writers, is it possible to make valid generalised statements about performance. For the majority of the school population, the problems which children have are task-specific. Just because a child has difficulty with one task, it does not mean that he has difficulties with others. When we consider the vast range of possible tasks, purposes and readerships, together with the subtlety of language and the myriad of possible solutions, then the momentousness of this finding for teachers and for assessors becomes apparent.

For the teacher, it argues the need to expose pupils to a wide variety of tasks, for different purposes and readerships. It requires investigation into the nature and demands of the task set in order to discover what constitutes successful performance on the task and how success might be achieved. By raising this awareness of the demands, the teacher establishes frames of reference so that the pupil might tackle similar tasks on future occasions with confidence. This might involve exposure to a wider range of written models (this is discussed more fully later). It is a matter of 'in my beginning is my end'. When setting forth, a teacher should give glimpses of the ends but should recognise that there are many possible routes and ends. The variety of routes and ends depends upon the task and the purpose; some purposes yield more variety than others. We are good at suggesting beginnings to pupils but less good at helping them to map routes or to visualise destinations. This is not a formulaic or behaviourist view of writing but sees writing as a craft in which individuals need guidance and personal attention, preferably from those who write or who know what it is to 'wrestle with words'.

For the examiner, it casts doubt upon the reliability and desirability of judging performance on the time-honoured list of writing tasks in a single examination. It points to a system of coursework assessment, where teachers and schools are organised in consortia using a linguistically sound assessment framework, where teachers have to justify their criteria and standards to others, and where Examining Boards validate the results. For those devising grade criteria, staged assessment or even benchmarks, it casts doubt upon the feasibility and validity of producing a single list of criteria which embraces all purposes or on which standards can be determined. It was the task-specific nature of performance, more than any other issue, which perplexed the SEC Working Party on English grade criteria and which, ultimately, drew the most severe criticisms. To be credible, grade criteria have to take account of the complexity, variety and individuality of the performances of pupils when they are using language for many purposes and in a multiplicity of situations. Criteria should reflect the complexity of the mix and register any variations in performance caused by variation in the task. Such complexity is difficult to record in a form which teachers can use. The temptation is to impose a generalist formula which assumes that there is a facility with writing 'irrespective of what is being written'.[11]

Once we move down the path of reduction, the criteria devised rest upon a linguistic arbitrariness which reduces the wide range of purposes and gives especial status to one form of writing, like 'expressive/ narrative', over all others. Consequently, when teachers read the grade descriptions attached to the new GCSE English syllabi, they find them unworkable because the work before them does not fit into the guiding model as the model is inadequate. If there are enormous problems in describing criteria for the GCSE to accommodate the range of tasks and purposes, how much more complex will it be to formulate benchmarks at different age levels, with ever-increasing gaps in mental ages and ever-widening experiences of life, living and language as children grow! The activity conjures the image of people trying to trap linguistic butterflies, the fittest of which flutter away.

SPEECH AND WRITING

The writing of children aged 11 and 15 shows evidence of the influence of speech. Different tasks focus different aspects of the problem of learning the distinctions between the speaking and writing systems. Space allows us to illustrate only one task-specific problem and to account for a range of other factors.

On reflective and discursive tasks, where the pedagogy of necessity relies upon the discussion of issues and where rhetorical forms are evident, there is difficulty in transferring what is heard into writing. Frequently the topics are of a wide-ranging nature and children do not have the information to write a balanced account. The pedagogy concentrates on content, usually by class discussion, sometimes (and more successfully) by group discussion. In general discussion it is difficult to 'own' the ideas and many proceed by assertion and the assertions not only reflect, improperly, what was said but also the cadences of how it was said. There is little distancing from the material so that connections or sub-ordinations can be made. Without attention to connecting or sub-ordinating ideas, cohesion is lost. In tasks in the advocacy mode, not a necessary way of proceeding in reflective or discursive purposes, some children struggle to find the appropriate 'voice' to address the imagined reader. In searching for the voice as a writer, they write as a speaker.

To make meaning, the speaker can use many techniques which include gesture, tone of voice and repetition. The speaker organises thought in more extended forms, in sentence paragraphs rather than in sentences, and it is common to find the use of simple co-ordinating devices like 'and' and 'then' to elaborate the idea. The speaker may also assume shared knowledge with the audience and where the shared knowledge does not exist, the speaker and the audience are free to negotiate new positions. For the writer the situation is more challenging. The writer cannot assume shared knowledge with the reader and has to anticipate the reader's needs and responses. Gesture and intonation are not available as spontaneous devices and tone is difficult to create. Children tend to print in capitals for emphasis. Repetition, unless used judiciously, is irritating to the reader and simple co-ordinating devices suggest that the writer is talking to an ever present friend. To organise thought, the writer has to co-ordinate or sub-ordinate ideas with sophistication.

On yet another level, writing is much more open to scrutiny; grammatical inaccuracies, errors of punctuation and spelling are fixed for all to see whereas speech 'goes whistling down the wind'. Some children find handwriting difficult. Moreover, when the speaker of non-standard English becomes a writer, the 'voices' which habitually go through the head do not necessarily correspond with the forms of standard written English. Verb agreements, demonstratives, personal and relative pronouns may not be used in standard ways. Double negatives are commonly used in speech but are solecisms in writing. These are only some of the non-standard forms encountered. For many children, learning to use the writing system is like wandering through a minefield. It is essential to teach the differences between the speech system and the writing system sensitively. We should teach about varieties of English, including standard written English, in the context of language in use and show how those varieties function and relate to each other. This calls for a fundamental rethinking of notions of correctness and of approaches to error, otherwise the walking wounded will languish.

MODELS OF WRITING

When schools were asked to supply coursework samples of writing to the APU team for analysis, the materials offered were predominantly literary in kind. Writing is seen to be that which the English department values and to which the English department gives status. Similar findings came from Peter Medway's survey *What Gets Written About*.[12] In his survey, fictional stories and personal accounts of experience (autobiographical material) account for some 36 per cent of the sample. When poems, plays, descriptions, fictional documents relating to stories and book reports were added, 79 per cent of the writing analysed called for an aesthetic reading. Both pieces of research found little non-literary writing in evidence. The APU found that the least familiar forms of writing in schools were reporting an event witnessed, summarising reasoning, writing practical instructions, describing objects in technical terms, discussing a problem and suggesting solutions. It is clear that there has been some neglect on the part of English departments in teaching the more utilitarian purposes and in presenting good models of such work.

The position should not be wholly a matter of surprise. The central purpose of the work in English is to give children opportunities to use language to represent the world to themselves and others. Through language – listening and talking, writing and reading – they are able to discover what elements in their experiences are unique to them and what they share with others. Literature is an important means of extending and defining experience and offers a 'third space' in which life and living can be discussed and evaluations made. If subject English did not offer these opportunities, it is hard to see where in the curriculum the linguistic, cognitive, affective, social and aesthetic could, together, be handled so powerfully. The models which have informed English teaching from the early 1920s until the publication of *Language in Use* in 1971 have been largely informed by a literary or a child-focused perspective. The models of English given to children are of narrative fiction, from the bedtime story to A-level English Literature. It is small wonder that 'imaginative' writing is preferred by so many and, in spite of task-specific variations, they seem to succeed in this form.

There is a case for children to be exposed to the cadences of non-narrative prose; teachers tend not to read this aloud. However, the ear needs to be 'tuned' to reports, to descriptions of processes, to historical accounts, to varieties of discursive and reflective writing. It is also necessary to discuss the task, as we have seen, and the ways in which it might be tackled; to discuss appropriateness and outcomes; to observe how others have sought to solve the problems. English teaching needs to give more attention to the utilitarian, non-narrative purposes but within the framework of context of use. English cannot be expected to provide all the 'real' contexts for those purposes so readily as colleagues, who are daily demanding non-narrative language use, or employers, who value the instrumental. On the one hand, there is an overwhelming argument for schools to develop a writing policy embracing more purposes and to which *all* teachers contribute. On the other hand, there is a need for discussion with employers to establish what the schools can reasonably do and what employers accept as their responsibility. School-leavers cannot arrive in employment ready made for *all* writing demands, given the task-specific nature of performance and the context-bound nature of language. Language is learned in the using.

The significance of the APU Language Monitoring has not yet been fully understood. These ideas derive from study of the APU reports over the last four years and from discussion with members of the team. They also derive from a long association with the *Language in Use* group. We owe a debt of gratitude to those who have steered and carried through the Language Monitoring programme. We also owe a debt of gratitude to the *Language in Use* team, whose work, some 15 to 20 years ago, produced materials and perspectives more innovative than any in the field of English since the 1950s and whose approach will become increasingly important. We owe an especial debt of gratitude to Geoffrey Thornton, whose knowledge, vision and teaching contributed so much to the language debate and whose recent, untimely death diminishes us all.

REFERENCES

1. Department of Education and Science *A Language for Life* (The Bullock Report), HMSO, 1975, p. 513
2. The studies which the writer has in mind are:
   Gubb, Jenny, Gorman, Tom and Price, Eurwen *Writers in the Making*, NFER, (as yet unpublished);
   APU Language Monitoring Reports, HMSO;
   Harris, John *et al. Writing across the Transition*, Sheffield LEA contribution to the National Writing Project;
   Medway, Peter, 'What Gets Written About', in *Writing of Writing*, ed. Andrew Wilkinson, Open University Press, 1986.
3. Macbeth, George 'A Child's Garden'
4. White, Janet *The Assessment of Writing*, NFER-Nelson, 1986, pp. 8-9
5. *Ibid.*, p. 11
6. *APU Primary Language Report*, HMSO, 1982, p. 100
7. White, Janet, *op. cit.*, p. 14
8. White, Janet, *op. cit.*, p. 14
9. Gubb, Gorman and Price, *op. cit.*
10. White, Janet, *op. cit.*, p. 8
11. SEC Working Party Report on the Draft Grade Criteria in English, 1986
12. Medway, Peter, *op.cit.*

LANGUAGE OR ENGLISH?

The needs of bilingual pupils

CAROLE EDWARDS, JENNY MOORHOUSE, SUSAN WIDLAKE

Carole Edwards has a B.Sc. degree from St Andrews university and has been a teacher for 15 years teaching a range of subjects including Science, English, Mathematics and English as a Second Language. She has been a Head of Department in a multicultural comprehensive school and is currently Head of the Language Support Service in the London Borough of Redbridge. She jointly runs an R.S.A. course in Teaching English as a Second Language and gives lectures on teaching second language learners to read and second language acquisition.

Jenny Moorhouse has a B.A. degree from Manchester university and a M.A. in Linguistics and Language Teaching from York. She has been a teacher and translator in Indonesia and Head of English as a Second Language in comprehensive schools in Bradford and Redbridge. She is at present an advisory teacher with the Redbridge Oracy Project and is involved in the R.S.A. course in Teaching English as a Second Language giving lectures on linguistics and assessment procedures for bilingual pupils.

Susan Widlake has a B.Sc. degree in psychology from London University and has taught English as a Second Language in both primary and secondary schools. She is currently a senior teacher in the London borough of Redbridge Language Support Service. She jointly runs an R.S.A. course in Teaching English as a Second Language and gives lectures on bilingualism and supporting second language learners in the mainstream.

English is the national language of Britain and the language of wider communication. As such it is an essential prerequisite for successful participation in British society. There are, however, other languages of Britain which are the first languages of small but significant linguistic minorities. These languages, though ignored by the Kingman Committee's guidelines and terms of reference, are equally valid for communication and are essential for the cultural and linguistic vitality of the linguistic minority groups and a source of potential enrichment for society as a whole.

The DES document *English from 5 to 16* pays very little attention to the language development of bilingual children in Britain. Paragraph 1.5 states that ethnic minorities may need special provision and paragraph 3.12 states that 'The language children bring with them from their home background should not be criticised, belittled or proscribed. The aim should be to extend their language repertoires. This should include enabling them to use the grammar and vocabulary of Standard Spoken English when that is appropriate if they do not already do so.' There is no mention in the document of bilingual children's first language acquisition or indeed of their second language acquisition. The terms of reference for the Kingman report do not suggest that this report will deal with these issues in any depth.

In this chapter we examine the role of the other languages of Britain both in their own right as vehicles of communication and as part of group and individual identity and as an aid to the successful acquisition of a second language i.e. English. We also examine other factors influencing second language acquisition and the implications for teachers and teaching.

ESL LEARNERS IN BRITAIN

Most teachers in multicultural schools will come into contact with bilingual pupils at different stages of learning English as a second language. There will be obvious beginners who understand and speak very little English. There will be some who have been learning English for two or three years and who are fluent in everyday conversation but may need support for learning new concepts through the medium of English and for developing English literacy skills. Others will be fully competent in spoken English but still not fully competent in reading and writing skills. Some bilingual pupils will be competent in English on a par with their monolingual peers. Most of the bilingual pupils will be fluent in their first language – unless they have been discouraged from using it – and some will also be literate in their first language.

This chapter is concerned primarily with those bilingual pupils who are still acquiring English as a second language and have not yet developed competence in English on a par with their monolingual or competent bilingual peers. Much of what is considered and proposed is, however, also relevant to all bilingual pupils and to monolingual pupils as language is constantly developing.

THE FIRST LANGUAGE

A teacher was recently heard to comment on a radio report she had heard that morning in which Professor B. Parekh had advocated some form of bilingual education for linguistic minorities. Her comment was: 'That's ridiculous. It would only encourage it.' What was 'it' that she feared would be encouraged? Presumably she was subscribing to the 'common sense' view that spending any time using the first language would interfere with the acquisition of the second, that using another language would be detrimental to the children's educational attainment and that the sooner they stopped speaking these other languages at home, or anywhere else, the better.

The barely-thought-out assumption behind this view is that monolingualism is the desirable norm and that it is our job as teachers to *replace* the first languages of these children with English as quickly and effectively as possible. The facts that, historically and globally, bilingualism is the norm and that children do not need to lose their first languages in order to acquire a second, are not considered at all by many teachers, some of whom even advise parents to stop using their first languages at home so that their children can concentrate on learning English.

The 'common sense' view also advocates that the sooner children from linguistic minorities begin learning English the better. Those who start learning it in the nursery or infant school are assumed to have the best chance of success. They can pick up spoken English from the other children, learn through the medium of English, and by the time they transfer to junior school they should "know" English. If by this time they are behind in school work, notably reading, they may be offered remedial help. The real cause for worry according to this view is the older children coming into school with no knowledge of English or as some have even been heard to describe it, 'no language'!

These 'common sense' assumptions raise some interesting questions:

- Is it true that the younger children are introduced to English the better?
- Is it true that by the end of their infant education, children who spoke little or no English on arrival at school, can be assumed to have 'learnt English' and can be taught and assessed in English on a par with other children?
- Would offering an education which used both the first language and English be detrimental to academic achievement?
- Will the other languages of Britain survive if they are not taken up by mainstream education?
- Is it desirable for us as a society to move towards monolingualism?

We believe the answer to all these questions to be a resounding 'No!'

First of all, it seems obvious that if children are taught in a language they do understand, they will learn more than if they are taught in an unknown language. So, if we want young children to learn important concepts such as early mathematical concepts and reading skills, we would do well to introduce them through the *first* language which will for some be the *only* language, since many children, although born in Britain, spend their early years learning to communicate in the language of home and have little experience of English prior to starting school. The Bradford MOTET project showed that children educated bilingually (in Punjabi and English) performed better on tasks with higher conceptual content after a year than those educated through English only. Both groups showed a similar level of proficiency in English (Fitzpatrick, 1987).

If children are given the opportunity to develop their first language to an advanced level, to learn to read and write in it and to develop important concepts through it, they will have little difficulty in transferring these skills to a second language. Schools in various parts of the world have adopted such an approach, using the first language exclusively for a number of years and establishing literacy in it. The second language is introduced later, first as a subject and then as the language of learning in other subjects. Bilingual children educated in this way have been found to achieve a higher standard of English literacy than those educated only in English as a second language, even though the latter have had more exposure to English. (Gale et al., 1981; Rosier & Farella, 1976).

This also applies to older pupils in the early stages of learning English as a second language. For example, a learner who is introduced to concepts such as 'force' or 'magnetism' in the first and stronger language will more easily be able to understand and express the concepts in a second, weaker language. Similarly, a learner who already possesses literacy skills in one language will more readily acquire literacy skills in a second language than a learner who is illiterate in the first language, and has therefore not acquired such skills as skimming, scanning, 'reading between the lines' etc. in any language.

Cummins (1984) suggests that this transfer of skills and concepts from one language to another is due to a single proficiency underlying the development of the higher level language skills required for cognitive and academic achievement. Once this 'Common Underlying Proficiency' (CUP) is developed in one language, it is easily transferable to any other language.

Perhaps then the fears of the teacher we quoted are unfounded. Perhaps encouraging the development of the first language would produce children who are better learners generally and more proficient in English oracy and literacy than if we discourage or ignore the first language.

In contrast if children are introduced to skills and concepts through a language they do not understand, their progress will be impeded and it may take them many years to catch up. True they will acquire basic fluency in English by mixing and communicating with their English speaking peers and teachers but they may not so easily acquire the higher level skills required for cognitive and academic achievement. A second language learner can, according to Cummins (1984) develop surface fluency in face-to-face communication in a second language relatively quickly. He uses the term 'Basic Interpersonal Communicative Skills' (BICS) to include phonology, basic syntax, oral fluency and sociolinguistic competence. The length of time required to acquire BICS will depend on the language environment in the classroom as well as on factors in the individual, but on average would be about two to three years. However, it takes at least five to seven years for a learner to acquire Cognitive and Academic Language Proficiency (CALP) through a second language. This is the ability to 'manipulate language in decontextualised academic situations' (Cummins, 1984) and is the foundation of literacy. It is the CALP skills which are manifestations of the Common Underlying Proficiency described above and which develop more effectively and efficiently through the stronger language.

Thus we have in our Junior and Secondary schools ESL learners who appear fluent because they have acquired BICS in English, but who, having been educated initially in their weaker language, are still developing CALP. Cummins himself admits that the BICS/CALP dichotomy appears oversimplified and needs refinement. Nevertheless, the distinction is a helpful one as it goes some way towards explaining why apparently fluent ESL learners are still not achieving on a par with their peers.

So far we have focused on first language maintenance as an aid to second language acquisition and to learning. It is, however, important in its own right as an embodiment, symbol and expression of individual and ethnic group identity and culture. As Fishman (1977) says:

> Language is the recorder of paternity, the expressor of patrimony and the carrier of phenomenology. Any vehicle carrying such a precious freight must come to be viewed as equally precious, as part of the freight, indeed as precious in and of itself.

If we ignore and devalue the first languages of linguistic minority groups we are ignoring and devaluing part of those people and their culture. This is likely to lead to a feeling of low self-esteem and rejection by the wider community. In such circumstances linguistic minority groups may withdraw into themselves and maintain a separate and segregated identity or they may assimilate into the dominant culture and lose part of their own identity and culture. All in all, the non-maintenance of minority languages is not conducive to cultural pluralism and potential enrichment for all is lost.

The Swann Committee rejected arguments in favour of bilingual education, principally on the grounds that to implement it, minority children would have to be segregated. They feared that this might highlight differences and have a detrimental effect on race relations. Some teachers in multiracial schools have noticed that although majority and minority children are educated side by side, this physical proximity does not necessarily lead to contact. Racial name calling and other forms of racial harassment go on in schools which have been multicultural for years and pupils in the same class may know nothing about each other's backgrounds and cultures and remain in segregated groups. To argue that this can be counteracted by failing to maintain minority languages is tantamount to advocating a return to the assimilationist views of the 1960s. Furthermore, even if members of linguistic minorities did give up their languages, colour would still distinguish them from the majority and the racism would continue. Positive anti-racist education is required and without it all our efforts are in vain.

The minority languages of Britain should not be allowed to disappear. Monolingualism is not superior or preferable to bilingualism and society can only benefit from having bilingual, biliterate people in it. This is frequently acknowledged with regard to European languages but the same status is not accorded to Asian and other minority languages. The horizons of all our children would be widened by the opportunity to learn other languages with the advantage of native speaker models to help them. This would lead to greater understanding of lifestyles, cultures and religions and to contact through shared experience. Only through such positive measures will people come to accept that all cultures and languages are equal and have equal rights to be valued and maintained.

THE SECOND LANGUAGE

All languages are equal. Behind that linguistic truism lies a social fallacy. Although all languages and language varieties have equal potential for expressing concepts, ideas, thoughts and emotions in an equal degree of depth and complexity, they are not all accorded social and political equality. For those living in Britain the language of power is English. A degree of fluency and literacy in English is required for social interaction in the wider community, for economic survival and for coping with the demands of everyday life in the wider community. It is also required for access to education, employment, the media, and positions of power and influence.

If those for whom English is a second language are not to be disadvantaged, we have a duty as educators to ensure that they are given every opportunity to develop competence in English. Fluency and literacy in English will not in itself lead to ethnic minority groups and individuals gaining power and influence, but it is a necessary prerequisite in our current society.

In trying to ensure that all bilingual pupils become competent in English we need to ask ourselves:

- What is involved in being able to understand and use a language effectively?
- How are these skills most efficiently and effectively acquired?

- What are the implications for English as a second language learning and teaching?

A language does not consist of a quantifiable and finite body of knowledge to be broken down into discrete sections and taught systematically to the learner. It is a highly complex, dynamic and creative system with infinite possibilities, which can be acquired by learners through exposure, use and interaction. Nor is language a neutral tool of communication in a social and political vacuum. It is a powerful force influencing and influenced by the setting, purpose and participants in communication, expressing and encompassing identity and culture.

Acquiring competence in a language therefore involves not only the ability to understand and produce correct sentences using a range of vocabulary, but also the ability to use language appropriately in a variety of settings, for various purposes and with various participants.

Canale (1984) has analysed competence into:

Grammatical competence – mastery of the language code or system.
Sociolinguistic competence – mastery of appropriate use and understanding of language in different sociolinguistic contexts.
Discourse competence – mastery of how to combine and interpret meanings and forms to achieve unified text in different genres by using (a) cohesion devices to relate forms and (b) coherence rules to organise meaning.
Strategic competence – mastery of verbal and non-verbal strategies to (a) compensate for breakdowns in communication and (b) enhance the rhetorical effect of utterances.

These components develop in conjunction with and alongside each other, not separately, and although learners need to acquire competence in all four areas, they do not need to be consciously aware of them, i.e. knowing how to use a language does not necessarily involve knowing explicitly about language.

In a society heavily dependent on books and written information, learners need to develop competence in both oral and literacy skills. They also require both Basic Interpersonal Communicative Skills and Cognitive and Academic Language Proficiency if they are to cope adequately in both everyday face to face communication and in more cognitively demanding communication involving higher order discussion and literacy skills (Cummins, 1986).

As ideas about what is involved in language competence have developed from emphasis on language as a system to the view of language as a tool of communication in society, so ideas about how both first and second languages are acquired have developed from a narrow behaviourist view to an interactionist view involving the environment, the learner and the interaction in which the learner is involved.

For many years environmental factors were thought to be of paramount importance in both first and second language acquisition. The application of behaviourist learning theory to language acquisition suggested that language was a set of habits acquired through imitation and reinforcement, stimulus and response, reward and punishment. In learning a second language, old habits interfered with new habits. If the old habits were different from the new habits, there would be negative transfer and errors would occur. If the new habits were the same as the old habits, then positive transfer would take place. Thus by contrastive analysis of the L1 and L2 it would be possible to predict areas of difficulty for the learner.

Mentalist views attacked behaviourism and accorded greatest importance to the learner in language acquisition. Chomsky proposed the idea of a Language Acquisition Device present in every person. For this device to work the learner required access to language input although the input served only as a trigger and did not shape the process of acquisition. The learner built up language competence by 'hypothesis testing' and 'successive approximations'. In this more creative view of language acquisition errors were regarded positively as an essential part of the developmental process for both first and second language acquisition.

Both behaviourist and mentalist theories are now regarded as inadequate and incomplete explanations of how language is acquired and a more eclectic view has emerged which regards language acquisition and development as being a result of interaction between the learner and the environment.

> Language acquisition derives from the collaborative efforts of the learner and his interlocutors and involves a dynamic interplay between external and internal factors. (Ellis 1985)

Research has shown that a variety of learner-related and environmental factors influence both first and second language acquisition. Here we comment briefly on factors influencing second language acquisition.

a) *The First Language*
The second language learner is not an empty vessel to be filled with English. To behave as if that were the case and ignore or discount the cognitive and first language skills the learner brings to school, is to assume a deficit model in which the ESL learner may be judged unfavourably against fluent English-speaking peers. Even worse the learner's first language may be regarded as a hindrance to the acquisition of English and its use discouraged or forbidden.

As has been discussed in the previous section the first language plays a very positive role in the development of a second language in that skills acquired in one language can be readily transferred to another and bilingualism can lead to cognitive advantage rather than disadvantage. The first language can also be used to facilitate the development of cognitive and linguistic skills in the second language.

b) *Input and Interaction*
Obviously language input is crucial for language acquisition and whatever the quantity and quality of the input, some degree of acquisition will take place. However, for effective and efficient acquisition, the learner needs what Krashen (1985) refers to as 'Comprehensible Input'. Input is made comprehensible by:

- use of already familiar structures and vocabulary
- use of concrete referents (pictures, objects etc.)
- a 'here and now' orientation
- use of familiar topics and concepts
- inclusion of the learners' own background and experiences
- adjustment strategies.

Adjustment strategies have been found to occur naturally in normal interaction, both between mothers and young children acquiring their first language and between native speakers of a language interacting with second or foreign language learners. These strategies include:

- use of alternative forms
- paraphrasing, expansion and explanation
- word-coinage
- gesture and mime
- pausing
- repetition
- prompting
- simplification and shortening of utterances.

Although these strategies work well in small group and one-to-one interaction, they do not work so well in a classroom one-to-many situation as teachers tend to adjust their speech to the middle range of English competence in the class.

The main prerequisite for the successful use of these strategies is the motivation to communicate. Both learners and interlocutors are going to be more willing to use adjustment strategies, to improvise, make guesses and persist in the negotiation of meaning if they have a real need or desire to communicate. The use of such strategies is not so much prompted by attempts to learn or teach the second language as by attempts to build relationships and share information, thoughts and ideas.

The interaction which takes place allows second language learners to form hypotheses about language on the basis of the input received, to try out the hypotheses in their own language output and to modify the hypotheses on the basis of further input or feedback. However, negative feedback such as overt correction of errors has not been found to be very helpful and can in some cases inhibit communication (Dulay, Burt and Krashen, 1982).

Second language learners need to interact with a variety of native speakers or competent English models in a variety of situations and for a variety of purposes in order to develop sociolinguistic competence. However, peer group models are especially important and are thought to have more influence on language acquisition than either teachers or parents (Dulay, Burt and Krashen, 1982).

c) *Attitude*
Attitude also has a part to play in second language acquisition. Learners are likely to acquire a second language more easily and effectively if they wish to identify with and participate in the second language speech community and if they feel accepted and valued in that community (Giles & Byrne, 1982; Schuman, 1978).

Second Language acquisition may be impeded (though is unlikely to be prevented) by feeling psychologically or socially distanced from the second language speech community, by feelings of rejection or negative attitudes and by feeling that their home culture (including language, religion etc.) is not valued or, even worse, despised. Feelings of anxiety, "culture shock", lack of confidence and low self-esteem are also likely to impede acquisition. As well as impeding acquisition because of these psychological and cultural factors, non-acceptance and negative attitudes also lead to a decrease in the amount of interaction between second language learners and members of the target language speech community.

d) *Motivation*
Motivation too is important. A learner's motivation may be instrumental (e.g. for getting a job) or integrative (for participating in the target language community). Integrative motivation has been found to be most conducive to language acquisition and the greatest motivation of all is simply a desire to communicate, a need to get meaning across and the pleasure derived from doing so (Gardner and Lambert, 1972).

Thus English will be most effectively and efficiently acquired in natural communicative settings through comprehensible input in interaction with fluent peer group models, in an atmosphere where the learners feel accepted and valued and where their first languages are used and encouraged.

SOME IMPLICATIONS

If the preceding arguments are accepted there are various implications for teachers and others involved in education, some of which are considered below.

The Other Languages of Britain Should be Maintained
If the other languages of Britain are to be maintained, the education system must find ways of incorporating them, even if we are not to have full bilingual education. Some primary schools have bilingual teachers allowing at least some pupils' first languages to be developed and used as functional languages of learning. Some secondary schools offer minority languages as an option either exclusively for speakers of those languages or for all pupils. Others have "language tasting" courses where pupils learn various languages for a term or half a term and then may select which language or languages they want to learn. However, schools offering any of these are still relatively few and greater efforts should be made to train and recruit bilingual teachers.

While the decision-makers argue over these issues, teachers can at least encourage first language maintenance. First, we can reassure parents that communicating with their children in their first language will neither diminish their children's chances of becoming fluent and literate in English nor prevent academic success. We can also encourage parents to read to their children in their first language, a vital experience until recently denied because attractive story books in other languages were not widely available in this country.

Finally, we can encourage attendance at minority language classes which may be held outside school time – and hope that education authorities will at least provide facilities free of charge.

Children Should be Encouraged to Use their First Language in School
In school we can create an atmosphere where the ability to use another language is seen as an asset. Many teachers have succeeded in doing this even without knowing any of the children's first languages themselves. Children can listen to stories in their first language either on tape or told by parents or older pupils, sometimes accompanied by music, mime or dance. Dual text story books can be provided or children literate in their first language can write their own for others to read.

Older pupils who arrive in this country fluent and literate in their first language but with little or no English should be encouraged to communicate and discuss their work with others who speak that language and to write notes in their first language. As teachers, we should not be too worried that we cannot 'mark' work written in the pupils' first language. Whatever they write will be for their own benefit rather than ours and it is preferable that notes are made in a language they do understand, than that they copy notes in English which they do not understand. As their English develops they can write in English with the help of teachers or peers while still continuing to write in their first language as and when they find it appropriate.

All Children Should Develop Language Awareness
First of all, we as teachers must be aware of the first languages and

language skills of pupils in our classes but this can only be done if the atmosphere is positive. Children will deny knowing any language other than English if they feel that there is a negative attitude towards their first language.

We should also be on the lookout for any opportunities of making pupils aware of languages and language varieties other than standard English and of showing that all languages and dialects are equally valid for communication. Although use of standard English is demanded in some circumstances it should not be presented as a superior language or dialect. There are increasing resources available to help teachers develop such an approach through various topics and curricular areas and those who have tried it have noticed improvements in the self-confidence and involvement of the children from ethnic minorities.

Children need to develop an awareness of how different languages, varieties and registers are used depending on medium, setting, purpose, function and audience. In this way they can become aware of the power of language to inform, persuade, express emotions, etc. We do not, however, subscribe to the view put forward in the DES report *English from 5 to 16* that children need to develop the metalanguage of language. Knowing how language works and how to use language does not necessitate knowing metalanguage for talking about language and knowing the metalanguage does not ensure knowing the language. An Israeli boy who said "English is a very hilly language. Hebrew is more flat and I don't put all the hills in English yet," clearly had an awareness of intonation and stress, although he had never heard the terms in either Hebrew or English.

The Best Environment for the Acquisition of English as a Second Language is in Mainstream Classrooms
Educationally, if we accept that the curriculum in our schools is the best curriculum for children, then it should be accessible to all children. The Swann Report (1985) rightly recognises

> the limitations on the breadth of curriculum which a language centre or unit can offer and the inherent injustice of denying any pupil access to other subjects until he or she has mastered English.

A mainstream classroom should provide a more stimulating and motivating learning environment than either a language centre or a withdrawal group and should give children who are acquiring English as a second language equal opportunities with their peers for cognitive skills to develop.

Linguistically, research suggests that language is most effectively acquired in a natural learning environment. The mainstream classroom provides a potentially more appropriate environment than the withdrawal group and also provides fluent peer group models to provide input for and interaction with the second language learners. The greatest motivation for acquiring a language is the desire to communicate and this too is more likely to occur in a mainstream classroom in the context of other learning than in a specific language learning context.

It is socially divisive to segregate English as a second language learners from their peers for specific teaching. They should have equal opportunities with other children for social interaction and building up relationships with peers. Withdrawing children gives the impression to their peers that they are inferior and need to be 'taught to read and write in order to catch up'. This deficit model should not be encouraged – a view supported by the Swann Report.

English as a Second Language Learners Should be Supported in the Mainstream Classroom
It is not enough to place English as a second language learners in the mainstream classroom. Children who are not being educated in their strongest language need to be supported in learning while they are acquiring their second language. Ideally, they should be supported by bilingual teachers who can support first language development as well as using it as an aid to developing the second language. Failing that they should be supported by an ESL specialist who can analyse the linguistic demands of the classroom and make the curriculum more accessible by breaking down tasks into manageable units, providing concrete referents, etc. The ESL teacher can also devise tasks and techniques to develop ESL learners' understanding and use of English through the context of other learning with the focus on meaning not form. This is more conducive to second language development than the withdrawal group where the focus tends to be on learning the language rather than on acquiring the language through learning.

Mainstream Teachers and Support Teachers Should Work Collaboratively for the Benefit of All Pupils
When a support teacher works alongside a mainstream teacher, the two teachers should plan and work together to provide appropriate activities for all the children while ensuring that the learning of the second language learners is supported. In the initial stages the teachers should discuss:

- their expectations of collaborative teaching
- their perceptions of the pupils' needs
- organisation for teaching
- suitable working groups for the pupils
- division of workload and responsibility
- teaching methods and approaches
- learning aims for the class
- support for the English as a second language learners
- including the experiences of all the pupils and using them as a resource

- appropriate anti-racist resources.

Being aware of each other's aims and expectations and developing appropriate activities and techniques together will be beneficial to the cognitive and linguistic development of *all* pupils and will ensure some support for ESL learners in lessons where the ESL support teacher is not present.

Pupils Should Work Collaboratively
Collaborative learning is valuable in all classrooms and is particularly effective for ESL learners. Collaborative learning is where pupils work together sharing experiences, exploring ideas and co-operating in the carrying out of a task, thus developing both conceptual and linguistic skills. Working in collaborative groups enables a second language learner to contribute and express ideas in the secure environment of the small group rather than in the more intimidating full class situation. It also involves more of the interaction which is so important to language acquisition and allows for negotiation of meaning, leading to a greater likelihood of comprehensible input. Working collaboratively gives pupils opportunities to develop such abilities as making sense of information, posing questions, giving opinions, commenting on the opinions of others, supporting their own views, predicting, hypothesising, reasoning, deducing and reporting, etc. When engaged in collaborative activities, pupils work co-operatively rather than competitively. They develop skills in adapting language for different purposes, effects, situations and audiences and develop social interaction skills such as turn-taking, maintaining discourse and listening to other people's points of view.

Pupils in the early stages of learning English also benefit from collaborative groupwork even though they may not initially contribute. Such pupils may remain silent for quite a long time. It is important that they are allowed to do so while they absorb some of the rhythms and patterns of English and begin to internalise their own rules. Learners in the 'silent period' should be encouraged to participate in practical activities and to listen in collaborative learning tasks but should not be pressurised to speak.

For collaborative learning to take place effectively care must be taken both in the grouping and in the devising of tasks and activities. Groups should contain both native English speakers or proficient bilingual pupils as well as the English as a second language learners requiring support. It is helpful for pupils in the early stages of learning English to be in the same group as a speaker of the same first language. When constructing tasks, care must be taken to ensure that collaboration is required to carry out the task – six children sitting at the same table, but each doing their own tasks, is not necessarily collaborative learning.

Oracy and Literacy Skills Should be Developed Together in a Communicative Context
Listening, speaking, reading and writing are best developed alongside

one another in the service of real communication and learning rather than "taught" as separate skills. Discussing what they have read or are going to read and planning what they are going to write is especially important for second language learners. Through discussion they can be helped to become aware of a sequence of ideas and the development of an argument, to develop skills of predicting and questioning, to distinguish subtle meaning, to understand cause and effect relationships, etc. The input provided from participating in discussion and from reading will provide models for their own language output in both reading and writing.

When teaching English as a second language learners to read it is important that they do not learn to read by decoding signs into words without understanding what they have read. A phonic approach is unsuitable for teaching English as a second language learners to read as words are introduced because they are phonically regular and may not therefore be familiar or on familiar topics. Many reading schemes are also unsuitable as the language used in them is neither the English we speak nor the English we find in 'real' books.

The essential prerequisite for developing reading skills is motivation. The pupils must want to read what they are given whether for pleasure or information. They should be introduced to 'real' story books from a very early age. The teacher can read the book to a child first, then gradually let the child take over the reading of the book. A similar approach can be used with older English as a second language learners although suitable books are more difficult to find. Learners can produce their own books by telling the teacher what to write, then illustrating the book if they wish and reading their own book.

It is also important to have a range of non-fiction books available related to ongoing topics so that the learners' reading materials are related to both their learning experience and the development of their spoken and written English. Second language learners benefit from active collaborative reading tasks such as prediction, sequencing, cloze, information transfer and tasks which demand a variety of reading strategies such as skimming, scanning, reading for detail and reading between the lines.

In developing writing skills, second language learners need ample opportunity to plan and discuss their work with a teacher or peers before writing it. Like all children, second language learners need to write first drafts of their work in which they are concentrating principally on content. Once they are satisfied with the content, they can edit their work with the help of a teacher or peer from the point of view of grammatical accuracy, choice of vocabulary, punctuation and spelling.

The collaboration can be extended beyond the preliminary planning stages to the writing itself, i.e. one piece of writing can be produced by each pair or group.

Second language learners in the early stages of acquiring English will probably make numerous errors in their writing. Many of these can be eliminated by techniques already mentioned such as talking before writing, collaborative writing and drafting. Nevertheless, errors will still occur. Correction of these errors in the final piece of written work will have little effect on the future correctness of the pupils' writing. Errors should be regarded as developmental and will progressively disappear as the learners' English develops provided that learners are given opportunies to discuss their work and have access to good models of written English through their reading.

Care Should be Taken in the Assessment of Bilingual Pupils
Assessment of bilingual pupils' English language skills needs to be made in order to:

- assess pupils' overall proficiency in English in order to ascertain which pupils need support;
- diagnose pupils' English language support needs so that appropriate tasks and activities may be devised to meet those needs;
- monitor pupil progress (and thereby monitor and evaluate the provision made).

Commercial tests are not particularly helpful in this area as they bear little relationship to the actual demands of the school curriculum. It is more useful to use descriptive categories and checklists which allow pupils' English language skills to be assessed and monitored in the classroom by observation of the pupils in the process of communication and the analysis of the product.

Ideally pupils' first language skills should also be assessed to give a more complete picture of their skills. In schools where bilingual teachers are not available this is not feasible unless parents or older pupils are involved. However, teachers can at least make efforts to find out whether pupils are literate in their first language and the extent to which they use their first language and with whom.

Where second language learners are thought to have learning difficulties it is essential that they are assessed in their first language as well as English. Even where learners appear fluent in English, verbal sub-tests in English may still not be appropriate as learners may have good surface fluency but not yet have acquired the more cognitive and academic language skills. The use of non-verbal sub-tests to diagnose learning difficulties should be avoided as although they are not language-based and therefore appear to be ideal for second language learners, such tests are not valid for use on pupils from a culture other than that on which they were normed (Cummins, 1980). Again observation of pupils in class and use of a checklist of non-linguistic skills is more useful.

The Ethos of the School Should be Anti-racist and Reflect the Multicultural Nature of our Society

Supporting children's second language acquisition as described here can only be really successful within the context of a school where racism is not tolerated.

The atmosphere of the school needs to be such that racism is countered. The school should recognise and cater for pupils' religious, dietary and dress requirements. Notices and displays should reflect the fact that we are living in a multicultural society. The teaching and learning styles in the school should encourage collaborative work amongst children. The pastoral system in a school should meet the specific needs of ethnic minority children, and the form/class teachers should be aware of the cultural, linguistic and religious backgrounds of the pupils in their classes.

A school should have an anti-racist statement agreed by the staff of the school. Such a statement would state clearly the staff's view on racism and how racist incidents are to be dealt with.

The staff of a school need to ensure equality of opportunities. Every effort should be made to make sure that children are not grouped in a way that is likely to hinder their progress e.g. a child being placed in a remedial Maths group because of his/her limited use of English. It must be recognised that many tests are not culture free and militate against certain groups of children.

The curriculum should be anti-racist in approach and children should be given an historic perspective which is not ethnocentric. The children should learn about the roles that different ethnic groups have played in our society. Reasons for migration should be explained and children should have the opportunity to discuss cultural and linguistic diversity.

Links with different community groups are important. Ethnic minority parents should be actively encouraged to join in the life of the school, and provision should be made to communicate with parents whose mother tongue is not English.

Resources in a school should reflect the fact that our society is multicultural. Racist materials should be avoided or countered and every effort should be made to buy anti-racist materials. Children should be encouraged to discuss bias and prejudice in reading materials.

CONCLUSION

The failure of the Kingman Committee's terms of reference to make any mention of either the other languages of Britain or the teaching of English as a second language in schools is indicative of the low status accorded to both the languages and their speakers.

In this chapter we have focused on the role and importance of the first language and on factors influencing the successful acquisition of English as a second language. We conclude that:

- The other languages of Britain should be maintained and encouraged. They are valid vehicles of communication and learning and part of group and individual identity. They are also a valuable aid to English as a second language acquisition and a source of potential enrichment for monolingual English speakers.
- Support should be provided for English as a second language learners within the mainstream classroom enabling English to be acquired naturally and effectively in the context of other learning through interaction with peers. Thus the emphasis is on meaning not form.
- As argued elsewhere in this book, age-related objectives are inappropriate tools for measuring children's ability to use English. They are particularly unsuitable for bilingual children who, at seven, are often being educated in their weaker language.
- All schools should strive for a multicultural, anti-racist ethos showing equal respect for and value of all languages and cultures and avoiding ethnocentric attitudes or approaches.
- All teachers should receive initial training in understanding first and second language acquisition and the role of language for the individual and society. This understanding is valuable for all teachers, not only those in multicultural schools. Teachers in all-white schools need to develop language awareness both in themselves and in their pupils as they are all part of the wider multilingual and multicultural society.
- Specialist training should be given to both bilingual and ESL support teachers dealing specifically with bilingualism, second language acquisition, multicultural and anti-racist education and implications for both teaching and assessment in multicultural schools in Britain. Many TESOL and TEFL courses are not a suitable training ground for ESL teachers.
- In-service training should be provided for teachers with bilingual pupils in their classes so that they can support the learning of their pupils when the support teacher is not with the class.
- The model of language should be a communicative one and teachers should be aiming to develop the ability to use language accurately and appropriately in a variety of settings and situations, for a variety of effects and purposes and with various participants. Both teaching and assessment methods should reflect this model and emphasis should not be placed on discrete language items or metalanguage.
- Finally, although this chapter has dealt specifically with the needs of bilingual pupils learning English as a second language, the model of language we accept and the methods and techniques suggested for developing oracy and literacy skills are in many ways appropriate and beneficial to all pupils, a conclusion supported by many class and subject teachers. Thus, these proposals are conducive to the development of bilingual pupils' language skills within the mainstream classroom.

BIBLIOGRAPHY

BAETENS-BEARDSMORE, H., *Bilingualism: Basic Principles*, Multilingual Matters, 1982

CANALE, M., 'On some theoretical frameworks for language proficiency' in Rivera, C. *Language Proficiency and Academic Achievement*, Multilingual Matters, 1984

CUMMINS, J., 'Psychological assessment of immigrant children: logic or intuition' in *Journal of Multilingual and Multicultural Development*, vol. 1, no. 2, 1980

CUMMINS, J., *Bilingualism and Special Education: Issues in Assessment and Pedagogy*, Multilingual Matters, 1984

CUMMINS, J., 'Wanted: a theoretical framework for relating language proficiency to academic achievement among bilingual pupils' in Rivera, C. *Language Proficiency and Academic Achievement*, Multilingual Matters, 1984

CUMMINS, J. AND SWAIN, M., *Bilingualism in Education*, Longman, 1986

DES *English from 5 to 16*, HMSO, 1984

DULAY, H.; BURT, M.; KRASHEN, S., *Language Two*, Oxford University Press, 1982

ELLIS, R., *Understanding Second Language Acquisition*, Oxford University Press, 1985

FISHMAN, J., 'Language and ethnicity' in Giles H. (ed.) *Language, Ethnicity and Intergroup Relations*, Academic Press, 1977

FITZPATRICK, F., *The Open Door*, Multilingual Matters, 1987

GALE et al., 'Academic achievement on the Milimgimbi bilingual education programme' in *TESOLQ*, vol. 15, 1981

GARDNER, R. and LAMBERT, N., *Attitudes and Motivation in Second Language Learning*, Rowley, Mass. Newbury House, 1972

GILES H. AND BYRNE, J., 'An intergroup approach to second language acquisition' in *Journal of Multilingual and Multicultural Development*, no. 3, 1982

KLEIN, GILLIAN, *Reading into Racism*, Routledge & Kegan Paul, 1985

KRASHEN, S., *Writing*, Pergamon, 1984

KRASHEN, S., *The Input Hypothesis: Issues and Implications*, Longman, 1985

PEAL and LAMBERT, 'Review of the relationship of bilingualism to intelligence' in *Psychological Monographs*, vol.76, no. 27, 1962

PERERA, K., *Children's Writing and Reading*, Blackwell, 1984

ROSIER and FARELLA, 'Bilingual education at Rock Point: some early results' in *TESOLQ*, vol. 10, 1976

SCHUMAN, J., 'The acculturation model for second language acquisition' in Gringras, R. (ed.) *Second Language Acquisition and Foreign Language Teaching*, Arlington: Center for Applied Linguistics, 1979

SKUTNABB-KANGAS, T., *Bilingualism or Not?*, Multilingual Matters, 1981

SMITH, F., *Reading*, Cambridge University Press, 1978

The Swann Report: *The Report of the Committee of Enquiry into the Education of Children from Ethnic Minority Groups*, HMSO, 1985

The Thomas Report: *Improving Primary Schools*, ILEA, 1985

WALLACE, C., *Learning to Read in a Multicultural Society*, Pergamon, 1986

WILLEY, R., *Race, Equality and Schools*, Methuen, 1984

LANGUAGE AND GENDER

ROS MOGER

Ros Moger has been a teacher for 14 years. She is now an Advisory Teacher with ILEA and an active member of LATE/NATE.

A man and his young son were in a car crash. The father was killed and the son, who was critically injured, was rushed to hospital. As the attendant wheeled the unconscious boy into the operating theatre the doctor on duty looked down and said, 'It's my son!'

What was the relationship between the doctor and the boy?

This little riddle has been used at the beginning of a number of articles about language and gender and I've brought it out again because, no matter how familiar we are with it, it still manages to make us work hard as readers. That word 'doctor' has a very strong resistance to the image of a woman and an even stronger resistance to the image of a mother. To make sense of the story we have to eradicate the male image and consciously superimpose a female one. This process reminds us that the making of meaning is a complex business. The vocabulary and the discourses we draw upon are culturally determined and the meanings we make are shaped by the cultural context in which we operate. The puzzle of the story hinges on the gender assumptions embedded in the English language. The word 'doctor' resonates with maleness for socio-historical reasons and even though our personal experience may tell us that there are plenty of women doctors about, we still have to struggle with the meaning. In helping our pupils reflect on language and in encouraging them to take control of language, we have to engage in an exploration of the way meanings are made. Such an exploration will inevitably lead us into discussion of the gender assumptions which infuse our language and which, in turn, construct us as women and men; for that is the other side of the riddle. If the word 'doctor' signals maleness, how is a young woman to conceptualise a career as a doctor? Language not only embodies cultural assumptions, it also plays a part in shaping them.

It is that interrelatedness of function, social context and meaning which has made language such a central issue in any discussion of gender and education. In the English language the available terms for women: 'girl', 'lass', 'lady', 'mistress', 'whore', 'spinster', are not simply referential. They do more than name. They carry values and status reflecting the gender and class relations of our society. In using these terms uncritically we can affirm those relations. For example, it still surprises me to hear colleagues addressing groups of girls as 'Ladies'. With its connotations of class and Victorian codes of propriety, the term takes on an ironic tone in the context of a large urban comprehensive school for girls. As teachers, it is important for us to listen to our own language as well as that of our pupils; to reconsider language that may place constraints on the expectations of our pupils and to question many of our accustomed modes of address, praise and rebuke.

In the classroom there are many ways in which we can discuss and investigate language and its influence on girls and boys, women and men. At the most basic level we can compare and analyse those 'naming' words: bachelor/spinster, tart/stud, mistress/master, actress/actor. We can look at the use of adjectives as applied to one or other sex: bossy/authoritative, powerful/domineering, determined/stubborn, positive/assertive.[1] We can, with care, explore the language of the classroom itself and particularly the language of abuse exchanged by young people, rooted as it is in a powerful cultural fear of female sexuality.[2] We can observe and discuss the language of small children and the books they read, the songs they sing. We can look at novels, newspapers, advertisements and television and unpick the gender assumptions we find there. We can explore the language of the school, its assessment systems and its public exams.

Work of this kind is relatively easy. Pupils are generally very ready to discuss language in this way because they are able to draw on what they already know. They quickly become adept at 'reading off' gender assumptions but that in itself is not a particularly constructive piece of learning unless it is placed within a coherent framework of an English course which makes language and its relationship to society central to the English curriculum. Only then can our pupils use the knowledge they have and explore its full implications. Only then can they move beyond 'pleasing the teacher' with appropriate responses and make the knowledge really their own by being able to stand back from it and place it in the context of other things they know about language.

Language isn't a static system. It is constantly being adapted, changed and even abandoned. At an intuitive level our pupils often understand this better than we do and, for their own purposes, they are quite prepared to appropriate and rework language mercilessly. However, this intuitive understanding is made more useful to them if they know something about the origins and growth of language so that they can appreciate the possibility of change. Change isn't always straightforward, of course. The generic use of 'man' continues to be defended in professional and social circles. The provocative interjection of 'Man is a mammal who suckles his young' shocks but rarely convinces. The tantalising paradox of 'Madam Chairman' still fails to unnerve determined opponents of 'Chairperson' and 'Chair'. Ridicule is never far away. Those wonderfully fictitious tabloid stories about 'Loony Left' councils insisting on 'person-covers' and 'chalkboards' serve to remind us that there is always something important at stake when people get worked up about words. Change is possible because meanings are not fixed. They can be contested and renegotiated, but this is often a long and painful process involving much indignation, particularly when the power relations of class, race and gender are at stake. The dominant institutions of our society have a tendency to fix meanings and give the impression that they are incontrovertible and common sense. For example, the terms 'strike', 'trade union', 'private', 'public', 'welfare state', all carry dominant meanings when they are used by the media and these meanings feed into our understanding of industrial relations, education or health care. The word 'feminist' has had its meaning so firmly fixed that many women find it necessary to preface remarks with 'I'm not a feminist but . . .'. Many of us, of course, have become skilled in oppositional reading when we sit in front of the television screen and in that sense we can individually negotiate meaning, but at an institutional level it is much harder.

However it does happen. The use of the word 'black' instead of 'coloured' is one example of such change. Gradually the language of the committee meeting, the workplace, the trade union is shifting to acknowledge the other half of the population and in the English classroom there is always plenty we can do to encourage our pupils to challenge words and suggest alternatives, helping them to be aware of the dynamic nature of language. But turning words upside down, reversing genders, supplying new words for old; all of these activities need to be taken on in a context of a broad and informed study of language. We need to look beyond individual words because human interaction isn't simply a matter of reading meaning from those words in isolation. Meaning is produced through the particular organisation of words into utterances and the meaning of one utterance will depend on its relationship to others. It is the discourse itself as much as individual words which contributes to social relations. Significantly, the discourse available to men is one in which gender and sexual identity appear to be absent. Men are 'people' or 'humanity' or 'mankind', whereas women can never appear as non-gendered. If they are to appear at all they have to be represented as 'women'; they have to be written into the discourse quite consciously. This is a particularly crucial point when dealing with those discourses of power – the medical profession, the legal system, parliamentary government and even the teaching profession. I cannot be the only teacher to read through my new conditions of service wondering if I could defend my non-compliance on the grounds that the document is addressed only to my male colleagues. These discourses marginalise and exclude women from the start, whilst men can appear to be non-gendered. When we are alerted to the duplicity of the non-gendered subject we cannot fail to notice all those curious contortions which occur in the media: 'lady writers', 'lady lawyers' and, of course, 'lady doctors', bringing us right back to that unfortunate car accident.

English teachers have been drawing attention to gender issues for a very long time. Ten or fifteen years ago classroom work may have been contained within units on 'Inequality' or 'Women' and the main concern may have been to redress the balance with more books by women or more books featuring strong female central characters. We have come a long way since then and many teachers aim for a much more integrated approach so that an awareness of gender issues informs all their teaching, through from the choice of books and materials and the questions asked of texts to the expectations of male and female pupils. We still have a very long way to go for, as many of the examples used above indicate, the focus has been mainly on gender in relation to *girls*. There are very sound reasons for this emphasis but there is a clear need to ask searching questions about gender in relation to *boys* and *men* for language reflects and constructs them just as significantly. Such questions should not be asked in isolation, however, but should be just one more aspect of a continuing investigation of language and its role in our society.

NOTES

1   There have been a number of studies of language and gender but one of the most useful reference books is still *Words and Women* by Cascy Miller and Kate Swift, (Penguin, 1979)
2   Sue Lees' book *Losing Out – Sexuality and Adolescent Girls* (Hutchinson, 1986) is very valuable for its discussion of the language of abuse.

LANGUAGE IN THE SECONDARY SCHOOL

DAVE GILBERT

Dave Gilbert is Head of English at Heathfield High School in Congleton, and has worked with NATE groups across Cheshire. He makes occasional contributions to the Education section of the Guardian, *usually in the form of verse letters.*

The attention which secondary schools have paid to language has generally been in the field of literacy, especially the first two of the three Rs. Rarely a week passes without reference from some quarter or other to 'poorer' standards of literacy. This, at least, identifies it as important. What is so depressing is that so much of the opinion expressed is based on purely subjective judgement, often making comparisons with the past because people tend to believe that things were better then than they are now. The truth is that things are not so much 'better' or 'worse' but they are 'different'. English is a dynamic language: over the years it has grown and moved with the times. As society changes it places new demands upon the language and it would be surprising if general usage did not also alter to accommodate and reflect these changes. Language lives in so far as it is used, and definitions of 'literacy' must allow for this.

The Bullock Report (1975), in its search for 'A Language for Life', provoked valuable and timely consideration of how language works in schools, focusing thought positively on the complexities and possibilities of language as a vehicle for learning. Significantly, it recommended that the skills of oracy should be recognised and encouraged in schools, and the variety of purposes which language serves should be reflected in the work expected of pupils. Perhaps the most important result of all that followed Bullock was the clearer appreciation that language is the major medium for both teaching *and* learning. Successful learning requires not just coming to terms with the *subject matter* but also the *language* that the situation demands. For this reason, all teachers in the secondary school, not just English teachers, should be more conscious of their responsibility for the development of the child's language.

THE RESPONSIBILITY OF ALL TEACHERS

Many more teachers are now aware of the fact that educational failure is often the result of linguistic factors, yet there is still so much more that can be done by them to compensate for this.

It is easy for a subject teacher to forget about the pupil's experience of language. In the secondary school pupils bounce at speed from one discipline to another all demanding a complex variety of language skills, usually in the written form. Whatever their potential, pupils too often find themselves unable to handle the language which processes of analysis and impersonal comment require, yet it is the use of this kind of language that has traditionally made up such a large part of pupils' working lives in the secondary school.

Subjects have different specialist vocabularies, or they use 'familiar' words in a different sense: the word 'image', for example, would be used differently by the teachers of physics, art and literature. But the difficulties which the secondary pupil faces have less to do with awkward vocabulary than with the abstract and impersonal 'register' of much subject teaching. Some teachers may throw out at the pupils the long, technical words of their subject in the hope that some of it sticks, but this can make the teachers sound superior and if the pupils have not been prepared for the terms they will in turn feel inferior and lack confidence. To borrow a term from the world of computers, language in the secondary school has to be 'user friendly'.

As far as possible the teacher should endeavour to explore the new vocabulary of a subject *with* the children. The teacher can help by focusing pupils' attention on new words and on the spelling and meaning of terms or phrases, which includes encouraging a class to say these out loud. It takes no more than a moment to draw attention to words, but if pupils are encouraged in this way to 'discover' new language it is more likely to stick. Reinforcement by pointed use of the terms or using wall displays will also help to draw attention to the importance of acquiring the appropriate language for that subject. Simple games using these terms, like wordsearches, should not be ignored either, especially with younger pupils. They all contribute to breaking down the mystique of new language. They allow pupils to be active in their exploration of that language instead of merely passive (and often confused) receivers of it, with the end result being more effective learning.

What about written language? It is all very well a teacher saying, 'James Ford cannot write his geography assignments', but how often does the teacher then consider the language difficulties James Ford may be having? The requirements of written language skills for examinations are varied. Specialist teachers must take some of the responsibility for exploring those skills of planning, drafting and organising as they relate to their subject. The language demands of subjects are often very precise; the writing up of a scientific experiment, a geography field study, a CDT design submission, all require different skills and different ways of writing, and all need to be featured throughout a pupil's course. The teacher has to be aware of the importance of writing as a mode of learning and not merely as a mode of assessing learning.

The type of writing that comes first to children is the expressive, that nearest to spoken language. A great deal has been done to demonstrate that impersonal writing does not come easily or early in the child's use of language, yet so much that we demand in secondary school insists on such transactional writing with little encouragement or opportunity, unless in English, for expressive response. This is to fail to utilise the language that would readily allow pupils access to a subject as well as making them feel that there was room for their opinions. Of course, it is still desirable in the long term to arrive at the 'appropriate' style required for that subject, but it would be more user friendly to invite pupils through their own language first.

So much of the writing that secondary pupils do, and they do a great deal, tends to be a re-presentation of teacher or text book language. What is needed is to encourage a greater variety and balance of opportunities for written language. Language being used implies the presence of particular speakers and writers, who have in mind particular listeners and readers and a precise set of circumstances that provide the context for what they write. Particularly in the light of the broader criteria of GCSE, subject teachers can no longer use exams as an excuse for the rather stale traditional diet of 'notes' and 'essays'. The importance of display work, peer group 'criticism' and feedback, response to positive teacher praise and marking are but some of the ways in which pupils can be encouraged to explore and use language with a purpose. Without balance and variety a pupil's opportunities for experiencing and even more of using the language s/he needs will have been restricted.

What is important in writing is equally true for spoken language. Talk can be noisy in a classroom, it can appear undisciplined and may suggest to an anxious teacher who is worried about the thin walls dividing his classroom from the next, that it is best avoided. But talk is too important to be so dismissed. After all, it is the form of language likely to be dominant in our pupils' lives, and it is the natural form of communication for problem solving. Yet how often do subject teachers go straight to the written task without utilising the valuable opportunities for group discussion, group problem solving and reporting?

Opportunities should be provided for children to make full use of talk in a variety of contexts. Not only does it help and further learning, it also develops important perceptions of the social uses of language. It is encouraging that so many GCSE subjects now stress the importance of assessing problem solving through talk. Understandably, teachers not used to this may be worried about how you actually go about assessing talk. It is not easy, but there is a strong case here for teachers to be given the time and opportunity to develop cross-curricular links and supports. English teachers would certainly welcome the opportunity to assess their pupils' talk in situations away from the usual context of the English lesson. But equally, by being given the chance to see their pupils in different situations, all teachers could benefit from a clearer appreciation of the potential of talk and acquire the confidence to make more effective use of it in their lessons. Perhaps, eventually, teachers may actually even learn to talk less themselves and listen more. That really would be progress!

All that has been mentioned so far may seem like stating the obvious. It is, for it is the obvious that teachers, constantly racing against time, bells and course deadlines, tend to overlook. But it does reflect the need for all teachers to provide an appropriate context for language use. Such contexts must take account of the demands of technical language, the variety of written and spoken tasks with a clear and defined sense of audience, and reinforce the common principles of the importance and the interdependence of language skills. This implies much about the importance of classroom management and layout in the secondary school – the right environment will encourage the right language. The way desks are arranged will either encourage or discourage purposeful talk and pupil-centred learning. The way in which wall displays are used, be it to encourage peer group appraisal or to reinforce subject skills or terminology, will help establish a firmer language consciousness amongst pupils. Naturally, the lesson format and user friendliness of the teacher's language will hold it all together.

The Bullock Report emphasised that all teachers needed to be more aware of the potential of language. The role of language as it relates to the learner is a shared concern which spans all subjects, and it has been encouraging for some teachers to find that problems they thought were specific to them or their subject are in fact shared by others. Despite the many successes of groups in schools across the country, much of the initial momentum of language across the curriculum has tended to get bogged down by the countless changes and demands that teachers have been swamped with in the past few years. A clear understanding of language is essential if we are to foster effective learning. Teachers need and deserve the time and encouragement to explore it fully.

WHAT ABOUT THE ENGLISH TEACHER?

All that was mentioned in the last section applies to the English teacher as well as to those teaching other subjects, but the teacher of English does have a special concern and relationship with the development and use of language in the secondary school.

Thankfully, the GCSE National Criteria for English have now stated openly that 'English is to be regarded as a single unified' subject. Good English teaching is about developing self-expression *and* communication by drawing attention to the varied possibilities of language in use. It must never be seen as just a 'service' subject, there to teach the 'basic skills' of 'correctness' alone. English teachers are concerned with *what* a pupil has to say and write, and *how* s/he expresses it. Naturally, we are all concerned that our children become fluent and flexible in their writing, able to use their imagination and develop their experience. In this respect there is a strong case for instilling an appreciation of the technical skills of written communication, for it furthers communication and can also improve the self-image of the communicator.

Instead of exercise work, which has little or no worth in its own right, be it for spelling, punctuation or grammar, we should create the right context which requires deliberate attention to technical accuracy. Our aim should always be effective communication, and the conventions of spelling, punctuation and grammar are the tools that can help to get us there and *not* ends in themselves. Exercises which encourage out of context dismantling of words, phrases or sentences do not help. Appreciation of technical accuracy comes through real situations and writing which has a clear purpose. Using literary and non-literary material it is possible, by guiding pupils' attention, to promote understanding of technical accuracy. By looking at style, structure of sentences, vocabulary used in others' writing, perhaps using the novel the child happens to be reading, s/he may then appreciate and assimilate more. Not to do so is to miss an opportunity.

Diagram 1 breaks down the aspects of technical English that one English department hoped pupils would have considered by the end of their third year in secondary school. The department required a strategy which would provide practical ways of targeting pupils' particular needs. The inner circle identifies the concepts while the outer circle provides *some* suggested ways of tackling them. The diagram attempts to encourage more flexibility in the department by illustrating how the teaching of technical skills can be linked to the wider contexts of 'real' situations. There is an obvious emphasis placed upon the pupil's responsibility, and on the need to be in situations which require attention to accuracy. This language consciousness is largely intuitive and does not develop easily through prescriptive tasks (e.g. exercises).

Ultimately, much of the English teacher's work on technical English is often responding to an individual's problem – few classes all exhibit the same problem – so methods and materials cater for this. There are many successful spelling strategies for instance. Take the 'Look, Cover, Write,

DIAGRAM 1

Check' strategy,[1] a proven way of encouraging successful spelling and, as is necessary, tailored to the pupil's needs. Far better than the Friday torture of the spelling test!

In the early years especially, language must be fun to explore and use, *not* a doggedly routine and repetitive study. There should always be a very obvious *audience* for whom pieces are written and correctness required. Encouraging this type of correctness is much more useful than placing emphasis on an isolated and often futile 'exercise' type of accuracy. It is also important to establish opportunities for using 'private' language, note-taking and drafting for instance, that tends to demand less rigid accuracy than the more formal 'public' language does. Our aim then, as English teachers in this context, is to establish the motivation of the pupil to *want* to use *appropriate* language correctly: wall displays, magazines, passing work on, letters to newspapers or organisations outside school, simulations, all enable technical skills to be seen as important.

Unlike most other subjects, there is a flexibility about the subject of English which defies a clear-cut list of facts to be learnt; it is not a linear subject. The development of a child's awareness of his or her language potential does not entail the learning of a body of facts *about* language. It is, rather, a process by which pupils come to understand more fully than before the nature of their own experience as users of language. The teacher of English especially, must play to the needs of pupils; whilst being responsible for the development of a child's self-awareness through the very necessary personal involvement afforded by expressive and poetic language, teachers should also aim to promote the child's wider consciousness of the scope of language in general in a way which will carry over into and from other subjects.

DIAGRAM 2

Literature and language are inseparably linked in the study of English. Literature is frequently the most common source material used by the English teacher because it provides easy access to the familiar styles of language known to the pupil and also gives pupils the opportunity to experience a variety of characters and their language. There is an interrelation between literature and language that has no clearly defined boundary, as can be seen in Diagram 1, where so many of the references for language 'study' are directed to literature. However, there is also the more precise 'study' of literature which could well be seen as a particular example of language in use. Like so many other specialist subjects, it has a body of specialist terms and concepts for the student to assimilate. Diagram 2 may prove useful to show how this specialist language might be introduced in a user friendly way. As with the first diagram, it aims to encourage the personal involvement and enthusiasm of the pupil by encouraging exploration of the language within a precise context and with a clear sense of audience. It tries to identify the concepts that pupils might reasonably be expected to have encountered by the end of their third year as a basis for years four and five. Method and content would, of course, vary according to pupil needs and ability, but the outer circle offers *some* suggestions of how to introduce these literary concepts in an entertaining and varied way.

CONCLUSION

It has not been within the scope of this short piece to look at all aspects of language in the secondary school, nor specifically at all the varied encounters with language in English. But the principles behind it are important and some of them should have come through here.

If the pupil is to make clear and useful sense of the language encountered in the secondary school, then s/he must be able to see the full potential of language *in use* across all subjects. The only way that this is possible is for all teachers to have a full and informed understanding of how language contributes to both teaching and learning.

REFERENCE

1 This strategy is described in Margaret Peters' book, *Diagnostic and Remedial Spelling Manual*, Macmillan, 1975.

DEFINITIONS OF ENGLISH

SHROPSHIRE NATIONAL ASSOCIATION FOR THE TEACHING OF ENGLISH

A DEFINITION OF ENGLISH

The proper business of English is fundamentally the processes of language. Language never happens in a vacuum. It must be *about* something, and it must be presented and received in a certain *form*. Language has no abstract existence. Its reality is always in a particular utterance, which serves a particular purpose for the presenter and the receiver, whether or not either party is conscious of the purpose, and whether or not the purpose is the same for each.

People learn their mother tongue (and, ideally, other languages too) in use and in context. Babies learn to speak by conscious or unconscious imitation of adults, and by a powerful unconscious ability to infer and internalise generalisable structures and conventions from particular utterances. This ability is in operation very early, long before a baby pronounces words. Understanding of characteristic intonation patterns in English sentences, or of the conventions governing conversation between two people, begins to develop soon after birth.

Five-year-olds have extensive experience of and fluency in their spoken mother tongue. Almost none of this ability has been achieved by instruction and correction; almost all of it has been achieved by experience and experiment. Even in cases where parents draw children's attention to an 'imperfect' utterance, and offer and reinforce a 'correct' (i.e. adult) alternative, children are unlikely to take up that offer until sufficient experience has persuaded them of its usefulness. In fact, too much instruction and correction, particularly if children begin to feel anxiety about language as a result, will do more harm than good.

The achievement of literacy is best understood as an extended and specialised use of children's existing linguistic ability. The written language, it is true, has significant differences from the spoken. But children beginning to read and write are not being introduced to a set of symbols and conventions which bear no relation to their previous learning. Children who successfully become literate are those who come to understand – again, consciously or unconsciously – analogies between forms of language in speech and writing. A child's own name has a form, spoken and written. A story may be told, read or written. A word, a phrase, a sentence, a whole passage, which has meaning for children in speech, which they have come to understand as doing certain jobs in certain contexts, may exist also on the page or the supermarket shelf or the television screen, and will mean the same thing or something very similar. It is that realisation, that recognition of a relationship between speech and writing, which is the significant act in the process of becoming literate.

In this process, the role of instruction and correction is greater than in the process of learning to speak. Writing is a more artificial, historically much more recent activity than speaking; and children cannot normally be expected to attend to the learning of writing all their waking hours as they can be expected to attend to speech. The physical skill of making letters and words on paper generally needs to be taught, for instance, although there is plenty of evidence of children learning to write without such conscious instruction. But experience still plays the major part in literacy learning, and instruction and correction the minor. These proportions remain true throughout the rest of children's development as readers and writers, into adolescence and adulthood.

Mature writers, with an independent voice and impressive control and repertoire, have got to that level of competence mainly as a result of countless experiences, through reading, of how writing is done, countless experiments, more or less successful, of trying it themselves, and a continuous, varied experience of the spoken language. Of the many possible reasons why too many of our children fail to become competent and confident readers and writers, four are more likely to apply than any others:

1 the relationship between oral and written language has not become clear to them;
2 they have not had sufficient experience of the written language, through reading, through being read to and through their own attempts at writing;
3 an excessive concern with instruction and correction, in particular a negative attention to superficial failings as the major or only teacher response to their efforts, has undermined their confidence and taken away valuable time which should have been devoted to the experience of the written language;
4 their schooling has not often enough provided them with real purposes for reading and writing.

Competence in the use of English develops, then, as a mutually affecting process in which talking, listening, reading and writing help one another. The teacher's job is to provide contexts which will call forth increasing powers of expression and of comprehension from the learner; contexts which, by being interesting, worthwhile, diverse and relevant to the learner's needs and development, have a good chance of producing outcomes which have those qualities too. To divide the four language modes from one another, to teach them in isolation, is bad practice because it ignores what we know about how children's language ability develops. To take any of the language modes, and split it into sub-skills to be learned separately and eventually put together to produce the real thing, is bad practice for the same reason, and for another reason also. In the analysis of language, it is always possible to propose categories, to introduce distinctions, to sub-divide, in order to make the analysis clearer and more precise. However, the analysis of English whether learnt by children as a mother tongue or as a second language, does not precede the production of English. Analysis of language is a very interesting area of study to some who are generally already fluent producers of language, but it does not make for better readers, writers, talkers and listeners. Repetitive attention to certain isolated parts of English (an activity which may not deserve the term 'analysis') before, or worse, instead of, extensive experience of English, is an unproductive and arid way for children to be spending time.

ARGUMENTS AGAINST AGE-RELATED OBJECTIVES

A rejection of age-related objectives does not arise from an optimistic belief that children will simply develop as users of the language as a result of unplanned exposure to it. It is not that we prefer vagueness, but that we are sure that there is a better kind of planning. The planning comes in the provision of 'contexts which will call forth increasing powers of expression and of comprehension from the learner' mentioned in our definition of English above. It is with this positive responsibility in our minds that we offer three arguments against objectives at 7, 11 and 16.

First, the setting of age-related objectives misunderstands the nature of development in English. It is not that English has no purposes. It is that children, as soon as they begin to use language, are employing and developing a whole range of competences. Certainly the complexity and variety of the material children read, for example, will increase between 5 and 16, as will the complexity and variety of children's written sentences and texts, and certainly discussion topics appropriate for 16-year-olds are likely to be different from those appropriate for infants. The tasks with which children are engaged will change, but they will be drawing on experience, language and meaning which they have received, and turning that into active competence, in a way which is common throughout their schooling.

The second objection is that it is easy to say that, at a given age, most children *should* be able to do a range of things. Whether or not a child *can* do something, however, depends enormously on the context in which the something is attempted. All 11-year-olds, for example, will, in some contexts, be able to express feelings and ideas accurately in speech. In other contexts, more demanding or less familiar, there will be a great disparity of accuracy of expression, and the variables which produce that disparity are many. A teacher is not enabled to help pupils improve the accuracy of their expression in speech by the general injunction that accuracy of spoken expression is desirable by 11.

The third objection is that, whatever disclaimers are made in advance, age-related objectives will be used by some teachers as skills which must be taught discretely and as such. Children develop as users of language in the course of doing things with language. Our positive responsibility is to plan what those things will be.

THE DEFINITION IN PRACTICE IN ONE SCHOOL

We conclude with an extract from the policy document of an English department in one Shropshire secondary school. It is intended to exemplify two principles: first, that a general definition of English must be translated into the working experience of each school where English is taught and used; secondly, that it is possible to describe in some detail the characteristics of English as it will be encountered by learners and teachers, without resort to age-related objectives. The document as a whole includes syllabuses for each year, a section on assessment and plans for future development in the department. This extract, one example among many, implies the kind of planning which is the positive responsibility of all of us.

WILLIAM BROOKES SCHOOL ENGLISH AND DRAMA DEPARTMENT POLICY DOCUMENT

A AIMS AND OBJECTIVES
   Our general aims (not in order of importance)
1. To stimulate students' *involvement* in language, developing an awareness of its powers as an expressive/communicative medium and to generate a desire to use it appropriately in a variety of forms, and for a variety of purposes.
2. To develop a *sensitivity* to words and the structures of language and to enable students to use this sensitivity in their own writing and in response to the writing of others.
3. To develop the *reading ability* of our students to enable them to understand, appreciate and evaluate both factual and fictional reading material appropriate to their age group and beyond, and to develop ultimately into autonomous readers.
4. To develop our students' ability to *listen carefully* and *speak fluently* and appropriately.

5 To ensure that students have mastered the *basic conventions* of written language: spelling, punctuation, grammatical structure, etc.
6 To develop in each individual and class an awareness of the value of *disciplined work* necessary for progress in English and to develop the study skills necessary for such progress. This involves the ability to work on their own as well as working constructively with others in small groups or whole classes.
7 To help students learn to *value themselves and others*, sharing each other's work in an atmosphere of mutual respect.

The department and the community
The department makes a considerable contribution to the communicative and cultural life of the wider community (both within the school and outside) (a) by the regular production of a monthly newspaper containing news, discussion articles, quizzes, humour and imaginative writing; (b) by the periodic publication of collections of imaginative writing for sale; (c) by the production of plays which are open to the general public and often to local primary schools; (d) by co-operation in the holding of an annual live arts festival at the school each spring; (e) by regular theatre trips and the use of visiting theatre groups. These contributions are an integral part of the role of an active English department in a rural comprehensive school.

The place of English in the curriculum
English occupies a unique and central place in the curriculum of any school, having a dual function which derives from the dual nature of language itself, as both the medium of thought (basic to the emotional and intellectual growth of the individual) and the medium of communication. We do not see English in the role of a 'service' subject, merely responsible for monitoring and developing accuracy of language skills for use in other content areas, but we do recognise the importance of subject English in developing listening, speaking, reading and writing for use across the curriculum. However, we regard ourselves as partners with all other teaching staff in the school, and parents at home, in achieving these goals. The unique role of English as a curriculum subject resides in its concern with language as an expressive medium in the widest sense, taking as its starting point a felt experience (e.g. the reading of a poem, the watching of a play or film, participation in drama improvisation or simulation) and exploring, through a concentration on language, the fuller understanding or expression of the meaning of that experience.

In this process we seek to educate the sensibility of the student, enhance the ability to discriminate between and evaluate the forms of expression that they encounter, and be self-critical about their own language use. This is a far more complex matter than the mere teaching of 'technical' accuracy (spelling, punctuation etc.), although this is clearly part of developing successful communication.

Objectives in more detail
While recognising the organic nature of growth in English which is inextricably linked to personal and social development, we welcome attempts

to define clear objectives for English teaching. Age-related objectives seem to us misconceived, as Bullock and, usually, HMI acknowledge, but in general terms we accept the need to clarify what skills and abilities students should develop during the secondary years, through work in English.

Listening
- The ability to listen carefully, and with concentration, to instruction, informational material, exposition and discussion, in order to be able to participate fully and with understanding in collaborative activities.
- The ability to distinguish different styles of language appropriate to different purposes and audiences, and to evaluate critically what is being said.

Speaking
- The ability to speak with fluency and confidence in appropriate styles in a variety of situations and for a range of purposes (including narration of real and imagined experience, argument and persuasion, description and explanation, improvisation and drama).
- The ability to be sensitive to an audience and modify speech according to the audience's needs.

Reading
- The ability to read autonomously, and for pleasure, whole books of some complexity and length, including imaginative literature.
- The ability to understand what is being read, including the ability to distinguish tone and detect inference, in a way that leads students to evaluate critically the truth and value of what they read.
- The ability to use reference material and informational texts for a variety of purposes, so that students further their own knowledge and broaden their interests.

Writing
- The ability to write in a range of styles appropriate to different purposes and different audiences. Such a range should include:
  a) Narration – both personal and imagined experience
  b) Description – of places, people and things
  c) Persuasion
  d) Argument
  e) Exposition and explanation, including the explication of literary texts.
- The ability to use a variety of types of written form (including the letter, the article, the script, the story, the poem) appropriately.
- The ability to write as an aid to learning and to conveying information accurately (e.g. to summarise, make notes and construct tables, charts or diagrams where appropriate).
- The ability to use a range of language structures and devices for stylistic variation and effect (e.g. complex sentences, imagery).
- The ability to exercise sufficient control over spelling, punctuation, paragraphing, legibility and layout for writing to be easily comprehensible to, and appreciated by, the reader.

B SOME COMMON APPROACHES AND ATTITUDES

It is clear that the key to effective teaching of any subject lies in effective classroom methodology. English teaching requires a degree of intimacy, trust and involvement between teacher and pupil, and between pupils within the class, to be effective. While each teacher's style will be unique, we share the following strategic approaches and attitudes which are common to the team as a whole.

1 *The experiential core*

At the core of most successful lessons lies an experience which may be individual, but is often shared with others in a group or whole class. The experiential core can arise from a work of literature (poem, prose, play script, film), from involvement in the exploration of ideas through the medium of drama, from participation in a simulation or discussion with others arising from their own experience, from exposure to another art form (music, a picture or a photograph), indeed from an indefinite range of possible sources. This experiential core is crucial for the success of the lesson because it is this which creates involvement and the consequent desire or need to use language, either to make sense of the experience to oneself, or to communicate it to others. It is important to remember that whatever medium we explore in, the starting point must be related to the pupils' own experience and perceptions, even though our aim is to go beyond them.

2 *The centrality of drama and oral work*

Each class in the first three years is timetabled to have one double lesson a week in a room suitable for drama. This reflects our shared belief in the value of drama as a means of developing language skills and understanding experience through enacting it. A shared drama experience, often as a whole class with the teacher also in role, can become a vital focus for subsequent activities, as well as being important in itself.

Oral work should have a central place in English lessons. In a variety of kinds of enquiry (for example the study of texts, the solving of a problem or the discussion of a controversial issue) pupils learn through interaction with others, and develop their powers of oracy in doing so.

3 *The importance of drafting in written work*

It is unreasonable to expect pupils to get writing right in one draft. Just as professional writers would go through several drafts before producing a finished copy, and would often discuss different drafts with others, so our pupils should be encouraged to do the same. The teacher is an important collaborator in this process of editing, but need not be the only one, and pupils should be encouraged to discuss the work in progress together. It is often helpful to use competitions, or appearance in the school newspaper, as additional incentives, offering a wider audience, to persuade pupils of the need to produce more polished drafts of their work. We should seek for real audiences whenever possible.

4 *Encouraging autonomous reading*

While the use of class readers is important in providing a shared experience of a novel or play, the practice of reading the book aloud (in parts, or with the teacher or a selected pupil reading) does not necessarily help more reluctant readers to become autonomous readers for pleasure. It is crucial that we actively promote the borrowing and buying of books on a purely individual basis too. This is done in several ways: by the use of the library collection of books (especially paperback fiction) which can be borrowed; the use of at least one lesson a week with classes in the first three years for private reading; the active participation by the teacher (who needs to be familiar with as much children's literature as possible) in helping pupils choose appropriate books and recommending books to them; and the regular visits by both the County Librarian and local bookshop staff, who recommend new books and sell books to pupils on the school premises.

While we may never make all our pupils enthusiastic readers, we can produce a reading community, one where reading is seen as a normal and habitual source of pleasure, interest and information.

5 *Mixed-ability teaching: the class, the individual and the group*
We believe strongly in the use of mixed-ability groups to give the best opportunity to all students to develop in a rich and natural linguistic environment. However, we recognise that such grouping needs to be carefully handled in order to cater for the needs of all the children. To teach the whole class together all the time, using the same materials for all, is not the way to achieve the goal of giving the maximum opportunity to everyone. Sometimes, however, to teach the whole group together is important to achieve class identity and to provide a shared experience of literature, drama and discussion. We try continually to utilise the methods of whole-class teaching, group work, pair work and individualised learning, and never concentrate exclusively on any one method. Group work is excellent for discussion and for setting different tasks to different groups of students. When setting written work an effort is made to give a choice of assignments, of varying levels of difficulty, to cater for individual needs and preferences, although students may need to be guided to the best assignment for them. In the fourth and fifth years it is particularly important to ensure that higher attaining students are guided to more demanding literature.

6 *Resources*
The need continually to develop resources is a natural corollary of mixed-ability grouping. No one teacher can be expected to produce the range of materials needed for mixed-ability classes, and so the sharing of this workload is essential. Members of the department are encouraged to keep adding to the department's resources, which are available for all. We recognise however that it is often difficult to use directly materials prepared by others, and that it is in the sharing of ideas that the most profitable teamwork occurs. For this reason we have developed the notion of an 'ideas file' on the teaching of literature. A similar file of drama structures is in process of being developed, and all members of the department are encouraged to submit successful ideas to be shared by others.

A BIRD AND THE CHARABANC

Three decades of children's knowledge about language and about literature, and about what language and literature exist to serve

ANDREW STIBBS

> Andrew Stibbs is now a Lecturer in Education at Leeds University, having taught in schools for 19 years. He has written books and articles on literature teaching, children's literature and assessing children's language.

I was returning from the pub with the two next oldest members of my cricket team when, in a bout of paralinguistics, Cooky unsurprisingly puked.

'Spit . . . Nohohholoholohohohoahahahahaaaananannnnn. Yeu knohohohohohohooooooowww – in that booooooooooooooooooooooooooooook yeu read us.'

'Sure to be gobdsmackedness, 'tis that story,' said Tim. 'That kid that ate 17 oranges. In that Spit Nolan book. That book you read us in the second year.'

O literature – parable, apophthegm, balm, remembrancer, emetic! A lifetime's work was vindicated: I'd always told them it would comfort them in direst moments. *'Spit Nolan'! Spit Nolan!* Spit Nolan! Never mind that the book's not called *Spit Nolan*, that neither is the kid who ate 17 oranges, and that we're not told that the kid who ate 17 oranges puked. Cooky was an active and re-creative reader, and we may infer the hero vomits after the tale's narrated events – vomits in the *histoire* rather than the *récit* as anyone would know but only one with the explicit knowledge about jargon'd say.

Years before I'd read *Spit* to Tim and Cooky, as years before that to Marie. Now Cooky was redismembering the inferably vomiting narrator of its companion tale in Bill Naughton's *The Goalkeeper's Revenge*. (There's a story of a baker in there too. He loads his half a loaf with arsenic. Fortunately, the accidental recipient is so ungrateful that he throws it down a grate.)

Whatever happened to the oranges, there in the allotment Spit Nolan came back to me as surely as Cooky's eight pints. Ways and whys I'd read him to Cookys and Tims (and Maries) of three generations signpost how English teaching has changed around me and bring back all I'd learned about language – from literature, from life, and from pupils like Cooky and Marie (and Larry).

Marie's was the first class to which I'd read the tale of Spit and his ambiguous pals (Chick, Duckett, Haddock – all creatures of two elements). It's a story of a pre-war working class trolley champ with one lung – weedy Spit with his Oedipal disability! Spit with his Cuchulainy skill! Spit with his apart and secret education! Spit the Wise Child quoting Marx without quoting marks! Spit the romantic of the rows, carrying his lostladylove's cryptic emblem!

I was in the first generation of unwittingly theory-laden English teachers in unselected secondary schools. Zealous, intolerant, self-righteous, arcadian, insular and bigoted, our beliefs predisposed us to schoolteaching, and we carried on the English Civil War through culture. And in my case, to Liverpool, leaving the dilettante metropoles to their usury, estate agencing, managing, executing, broking and jouissance, wrongly confident that we would bury their candyfloss, before Mr Toad was driving the charabanc of education. Blame a book.

Knowledge about Language didn't feature in our Cause's programme. It was implicit in Roundhead English that the canon embodied Fine Thoughts which, when we made them explicit, would infect a reader already sensitive enough to recognise them. But it was the canon-writers' fancy to hide their Fine Thoughts in case histories, so that only the winks and nudges of we 'critics' could expose them to the readers.

I found this place on the map where, according to the blamed book (Pedley's *The Comprehensive School*, Penguin, 1963): 'The teachers have bravely picked up the gauntlet carelessly tossed down by an affluent society' (p. 63).

Alec and I turned up for interview and each of us (for this was 1963) was offered a job upon the threshold. I accepted mine only after I'd insisted on an hour's tour, a tour on which I tried to decipher the cries and signs from the windows, and make sense of the language which was directed at me – language of which I had no knowledge. At the end of that tour, I'd picked up many a tossed-down gauntlet and enough scores for a career of settling.

My pupils were those children I'd been taught about. Children 'with no language' or at best 'restricted codes'. Bleasdale, Russell, Dodd, Hatton, McGough – names like that they had. I was shut off from them by a monstrous great dike of inexperience,* untrained in their dialects, genres, or social usages. Through my first year my more experienced

---

* On the monstrous great dike of Chesil Beach, of which Larry read, the pebbles increase in size as you go east, because storms which drive the shingle eastward are strong enough to move all the stones, whereas storms which drive them west can only move the smaller ones.

neighbour could be heard crying 'I can still hear somebody talking' above the massed Kopspiel and the dull steady roar of breaking furniture. You can too? But if you want *me* to stop talking, to get on with Alec's, Spit's, Marie's, mine, whoknowsbut yours and Cooky's Tale, you must learn enough from these digressions – or rather these deferring of their fates – to want to learn their stories. Only the insensitive charabanc goes directly.

In these early 60s, Alec and I went in for pastoral, with Newsom's third Neglected Quartile – destined to leave as 4 Progress, 4 Enterprise, 4 Challenge, 4 Technical, 4 Service, 4 Retail, and 4 Manual, the equal-eleventh streams. These were the classes for whom traditionally, knowledge about language had been 'How to Fill in a Job Application Form'. I hear your anachronistic hollow laughter.

Were they grateful? Knowing their language would be developed by use in purposive and social contexts, we ran courses called 'What's it all about?' We tidied the graveyard and fished prams from the streams, and we took them out to make films. I packed Marie and all in my mini and they used their language to complain, embarrass, and make jokes at my expense. When we halted at the crossings, they opened the windows and complained to old ladies: 'Dis dirty old fella's kidnapping us, missus. Get de police!' My giving them 'the real prospect of a long rewarding climb to a satisfying and community life' (Pedley p. 73) fixed the UK in its slump. So rewarding was our dock-trip that Marie's redirected expurts stopped the bus's long climb back to school. Who knows that she was not the cause of the current vindictiveness which might want her likes to know about subjects and objects rather than about Spit.

How unlike Spit, for whom 'You own nothing . . . except those things you have taken a hand in.' (p. 24), was Marie with her 'Yer underdearm, sir! We wus gunna gidem t de penshunners!' Can you see her cunning mocking face by means of this language? It would help you to hear her voice in these paper signs. But there is risk. Suppose the face you see is not the one I see? Then her words will surprise you. Reading, like chess, sex, cricket, education itself – these are all games of exchange, patience and mutual searchings out; all such entail risk. Games too of sporadic progress; no ticking off of regular signposts at 7, 11 and later, but rather progressing in the same way as Spit rode *Egdam*, 'he coaxed *Egdam* over the tricky parts, swayed with her, gave her her head, and guided her'. (p. 28).

I say nothing of the Strike Marie caused, for that is my neighbour's story: how he was reading *Treasure Island* at the fateful hour and, having locked the door, went down still reading, like a dutiful captain, trampled underfoot as his reluctant listeners charged for those same first floor windows in which I'd seen the signs, willing to risk injury to escape Great Books it's true, but also to head for the local newspaper office to air their grievances – sign of their knowledge of the power of the written word.

Our neighbour counselled me and Alec to get our pupils to write by 'imagining they're victims of disaster'. Since we mudel our lives on what we read – says Phyllis Rose (*sic*) in *Parallel Lives*, ensuring she's a self-fulfilling profit to we who read her – what would that mean for Marie and co? Alec, better trained than me, helped me through. One of his two tips was: 'Read 'em this story about the last ride of a trolley-riding champ who's only got one lung.'

> Spit was right out of the Wheelwright's Shop. Indeed he 'spent most mornings . . . searching Enty's scrapyard for good wheels' (p. 21).

With precocious responsibility, he rebuked his noisy followers: '– folk want their sleep' (p. 26). Such was his tact that he accepted Chick's ominous cemetery rose so as not to disappoint him: 'Ee, wot a 'eavenly smell!' (p. 26). (I wonder if Spit, who must have been about 11, knew the 'subject' of that verbless sentence, and whether that was the subject of his utterance.) He rode his trolley with a delicacy as unostentatious as the memento of his renounced tubercular love, and an economy equal to that of his language, until the lumbering adult-engineered machine of the publican's son knocked him off the tracks and under a deconstructive charabanc.

We, of course, anticipated as Marie could not that Spit was doomed. 'The British Queen' would be his tanist. Its thundering technology, engineered by adults and ridden by the publican's red-faced son would crush the riddled *Egdam* and Spit's instinctive delicacy. (Heroes must die in defeat for their survival is patheticer than we can fear. We require the mercy we don't expect; innocent Maries want the justice in which they will be disappointed. The rose fartelled.)

So, hoping its anti-industrial discriminations would rub off on my Noble Savages, I read *Spit Nolan* to my eleventh stream, and invited them to find in it a romantic celebration of their own rude doomed virtue.

I did it differently then, Hegelianly mating chastened Leslie's British Queen with the backward *Egdam*. But now I see the engineer (like the butcher, the Baker, the publican and the grocer's daughter) was clearly winner – as clearly as did Spit – and I vainly wait disintegration of his lumbering product from its internal contradictions.

'Spit Nolan was a pal of mine,' says the fictional narrator, about the tale's eponymous subject. (And what's the subject of that? Knowledge about Language would say 'Spit Nolan', but knowledge about language might say it was the speaker, or death.) Marie Burns was a pupil of mine. 'Marie' – we'll now agree you know her too; 'was' – we refer to a past (maybe the same as Spit's creator's?) and so to Marie's unpresence; 'a' – she had been only one of my pupils, as have been Cooky and Tim; 'pupil'

– I created her and I see through her; 'of mine' – less jealous than 'my' but doubled and deferred. Even in the nuts and bolts of language lie possibilities which no 'knowledge about language' can schematise.

Marie – she who started Britain's decline by stealing so much from the docks on our form trip, she who caused the local church to need reconsecrating after we went to count the Dead of Two World Wars, she whose verbal persecution of Lewis's Santa Claus led to the withdrawal of the occasional holiday which in its turn caused the Grotto Strike which made the national dailies – Marie could not believe that Spit had died, for the story mixes one genre Marie knew about – the comic book – with one she didn't, and children, in their innocence, can't hear the youthbird's song in the absence of its sound.

Ten years later, at the time of that Bullock Report whose recommendations about – among other things – knowledge about language have still not been implemented by the parsimonious philistines, I read *Spit Nolan* to Cooky and Tim and Co. By then the radical force in English teaching was sociolinguistic – urban and demotic. We discussed Spit's Theory of Property, wrote Instructions for Building Trolleys, and collected slang words for trolleys – one of theirs and one of mine. It was Cooky's enthusiasm for Spit which led me to read Naughton's *Late Night on Watling Street* with them in the fourth year. That's about language: the lorry-driver who lies about killing the policeman is sent to Coventry by his mates – who nonetheless will not split on him. Is there a knowledge about language which explains lies and different forms of silence?

In the 60s I praised the story's realism but questioned the 'neatness' of its ending and the apparent superficiality of its rose- and bird-metaphors. I deplored the superstition I found in the fate of the rose, and had not even noticed that Spit was compared to a bird till Marie (not always a penshunner) wrote her 'Elegy for Spit Nolan':

> He lies there
> Blood everywhere
> Without a care.
> He asked who won the trolley race
> You won Spit.
> No I did not.
> The bird that went so fast
> His wings did drop
> And fell so fast.

I hadn't noticed the bird.

Knowledge – testable, definable knowledge – goes in for small focus (that small focus that sees the wood, not the trees). But we come to the wood from the trees, as Larry came to read from the book to the chapter, from chapter to page, from page to paragraph, from the paragraph to the word and from the word to the phoneme. Of which I shall speak more hereafter. And as I was to come to the knowledge of musical notes from a knowledge of 'music'. And when we get down to the wood, the word, sometimes the focus finds the twig's a bird, and the bird takes flight. The letter – the phoneme: 'o' for instance. The letter 'o' is a vowel, children. As in 'know', in 'love', in 'rose', in 'bogey', in 'story', in 'stop'; (in 'l ve', in 'r se', and 'b gey' for that matter). It is a cry, it is a hole, it is a whole, it is an absence, a zero which becomes infinity when it's doubled.

Marie knew more than me, for there is more to knowing than knowing about, or even knowing how. There is the knowing you do not know you know, like Spit's instinctive delicacy, or Marie's intuition for the binarities of the bird and the charabanc, or her misintuition of Spit's Oediness, his Cuchery and his Marxism.

Having failed to learn to play the piano at 7, 11, or later, I learned to play it at 40, because by then, still knowing nothing *about* music or pianos, I knew what a piano could *do*, what music sounded like, and what it was like to behave like a pianist. I learned by playing Beethoven (to *my* satisfaction – or rather to my excitement), not the Old Macdonalds of the piano-primers. I learned the use of eyebrows. I learned to play so that my hair grew. I learned to let the music play me. Only later would I try to be note-perfect.

That's how Marie's classmate Larry (Holborn 'reading age' 7.6) learned to read, not on the remedial readers he was given but ('clearing it without a pole') on the *Moonfleet* I was, with Roundhead arrogance, reading them, because he wanted to know how it ended, having begun like this:

> 'The village of Moonfleet, lies half a mile from the sea on the right or west bank of the Fleet stream. This rivulet, which is so narrow as it passes the houses that I have known a good jumper clear it without a pole, broadens out into salt marshes below the village, and loses itself at last in a lake of brackish water. The lake is good for nothing except sea-fowl, herons, and oysters, and forms such a place as they call in the Indies a lagoon; being shut off from the open Channel by a monstrous great beach or dike of pebbles, of which I shall speak more hereafter.

But *Moonfleet* goes on to crawl into caves, teeter on cliff-edges, break into tombs, disturb ghosts, find and lose great wealth, fight for life, and come home at last to the circler's arcadia.

Myth, 'sea-fowl, herons, oysters', 'underarm', 'The bird that went so fast/His wings did drop', 'Folk want their sleep', Kopspiel, z ro, paralinguistics and silence – King'smen have their work cut out!

Now knowledge about language comes from all the languagings we've ever read or heard or thought or said – Scouses, Creoles, the language of the Rev. J. Meade Falkner and his like, and the deceptive simplicities of 'Spit Nolan was a pal of mine'. All these experiences are the pebbles of which a great dike's built. Such 'knowledge about', and 'knowledge how' and 'knowledge that' can't be prescribed, because we've all had different language experiences – because we've all had different lives? As Miroslav Holub says in 'A Boy's Head':

> . . . it just cannot be trimmed
>
> I believe
> that only what cannot be trimmed
> is a head
>
> There is much promise
> in the circumstance
> that so many people have heads

At which, because texts, like Spit, have shapely and timely pseudo-endings, let this text enter the web of its own readings which sustain the readings of itself and thereby change its reading and its having-been-read, like a dog chasing its tale, and returning to its own . . .

REFERENCES

FALKNER, J. MEADE, *Moonfleet*, Edward Arnold, 1898
NAUGHTON, BILL *The Goalkeeper's Revenge* and other stories, Harrap, 1961; Puffin, 1968
PEDLEY, ROBIN *The Comprehensive School*, Pelican, 1963

OBJECTIVES FOR LANGUAGE LEARNING

PAM CZERNIEWSKA

Pam Czerniewska's particular interest is in children's language development. As an Open University lecturer for eight years, she produced a number of study texts, television programmes and audio-cassettes on different aspects of language and literacy. From 1980-83, she was a director in a New York literacy programme teaching young adults to read and write. Currently she is director of the National Writing Project.

Why is it that setting objectives for language learning has proved so difficult? Why does each attempt to establish a language curriculum, a policy for developing children's language or just a checklist of desired language achievements seem merely to highlight the divisions in teaching approaches, to create confusion instead of consensus?

Clearly, such a complex question will have a complex answer to which I can only hope to make a partial contribution. But some of the thoughts and examples below may help to explain why language learning objectives have, in the past, failed to provide a common framework within which teachers can develop teaching strategies. Most of the examples are drawn from the School Curriculum Development Committee's National Writing Project. While there is a consequent emphasis on writing, the underlying principles can apply to all aspects of language learning.

To set the scene for my argument, and to root it firmly in practice, here are some examples of language learning:

Two Shropshire reception class children, Fiona and Neil, were invited by their teacher, Sheila Hughes, to help each other write, once a week, starting with stories about their favourite colours. Fiona wrote her story herself with the teacher providing some spellings; Neil dictated his story for the teacher to write. Each text was accompanied by a picture. Each week they exchanged books and made comments which the teacher wrote underneath. These are some extracts:

Week 1

Fiona wrote: *I like black because I have a toy black dog and I have always wanted a real life black dog.*

Neil commented: *She could have made it better if she'd put legs on the dog.*
Neil wrote: *I like yellow wallpaper and I am going to ask my dad if I can have some.*
Fiona commented: *He should have put 'wallpaper' at the end of his story.*

Week 2

Fiona wrote: *Red makes my Mummy happy. She had a red Renault 5 car and there is a lot of room in the boot.*
Neil commented: *She should have put spokes on the wheels and two lights front and back.*
Neil wrote: *This is a red lorry and I like it.*
Fiona commented: *He should have said where the lorry was going and why he liked it.*

By week 6

Fiona wrote: *The bear is trying to get some honey out of a tree. He looks very cuddly but really he is dangerous.*
Neil commented: *Drawn a bigger tree. It is a good story.*
Neil wrote: *My teddy bear is sitting by a tree thinking about doing something naughty.*
Fiona commented: *Ears and paws on the bear. I would like to know what naughty thing this teddy was going to do.*

In a Dorset school, Vivienne Miller's class of six-year-olds had finished writing books for younger children. A visit to the school library to look at book covers led to the children discovering that books often talk about and include photographs of the author on the back cover. And so, by the end of the day, with the help of mirrors, there appeared self-portraits and descriptions such as:

Helen Gilber is 6 years old. She likes writing things about animals. Helen thinks making friends is important.

Hana Kempster is 6 years old and she likes fairies but she has not seen one yet.

These are impressive demonstrations of young children's language abilities. Their achievements include the use of complex language in both speech and writing: '*I would like to know what naughty thing this teddy was going to do.*' Not only are there examples of complex grammatical structures but also sophisticated acknowledgements of the structures appropriate to the writing task. Note, for example, Helen and Hana's use of the third person to talk about themselves: *she likes fairies but she has not seen one yet.* Furthermore, all four children show an ability to talk about the language act they are performing. Fiona, for example, points out and corrects Neil's language when she notes his omission of 'wallpaper'. (Most adults would accept this ellipsis and perhaps Fiona's objection reflects the style of early reading materials.) Fiona, and later Neil, show an ability to reflect on a story's worth. The two six-year-olds are clearly able to take on the role of author and talk about themselves in that light.

I begin with these two examples because they seem to raise fundamental issues for any attempt to set objectives for language learning and specific learning outcomes for different age groups.

What objectives have Fiona, Neil, Hana and Helen achieved?

Here are three objectives taken from the DES's recent (and controversial) *English from 5 to 16* (1984).

In their writing children should:

- Write descriptions in which the salient features are conveyed clearly.
- Write accurate descriptions of people, places and things.
- Have some ability to adjust the form, content and style of writing to the nature of the task and the needs of the reader.

They seem to fit appropriately with the pieces of writing looked at above. But that creates a problem because these objectives came from different sections of the document. They are, respectively, objectives for 7-year-olds, 11-year-olds and 16-year-olds!

It's a problem which is implicitly recognised in *English from 5 to 16* by the repetition of similar objectives for each age group with just a few amendments to give the impression of difference:

- Set down directions and instructions when there is a clear purpose for doing so (*7-year-olds*).
- Frame instructions and directions clearly (*11-year-olds*).
- Frame instructions and directions clearly and succinctly (*16-year-olds*).

What this demonstrates, quite simply, is that language learning is not linear. Except for a few one-off learning achievements like alphabetic knowledge and letter formation the essentials of language are returned to over and over again, each visit resulting in more sophisticated language use. Thus, over the years, Fiona and friends will revisit the question of how to write stories, descriptions and autobiographies, how to comment on another's work, how to write succinctly and so on.

This cyclical view of the language learning process has radical implications for the development of age-related objectives, implications which should help policy makers struggling over paper exercises in stylistic ingenuity. It involves looking at language not simply as a body of knowledge which can be split up into smaller nuggets of knowledge according to the size of the child, but as something that is constructed in interaction with the teacher and the task. Put another way, somehow we need to prevent the language bits (e.g. writing instruction) being divorced from what we know about learning and what we know about the social practices of language.

THE CONSTRUCTION OF LANGUAGE BY THE LEARNER

Any account, model or set of curriculum guidelines for language needs to acknowledge the role played by the learner in language construction. Children are not linguistically empty vessels to be filled with bits of language at specific points. They come to the language tasks set by schools with a considerable knowledge of speaking, reading and writing developed through their active explorations of the language around them.

The construction by the child of how to write and how writers behave can be seen in the pre-school child's early attempts at literacy. Parents, nursery teachers and full-time researchers can produce many examples to show how children are involved in working out the organisation and uses of written language. Ferreiro and Teberosky (1979), Clay (1975), Goodman, Y. (1986) and Goodman, K. (1985), for instance, in their observations and interviews have recorded how, long before schooling begins, children can distinguish what is and what is not writing and can generate rules such as: a word must have at least three letters; letters should not be repeated; word length is related to the size of the object it represents, (so an adult's name will be longer than a child's). Such deviations from the adult rules provide telling insights into language learning. Ferreiro and Teberosky write about a child who wrote OIA for 'cat'. When asked to write 'kittens' he produced OIAOIAOIA. It might not be the way that most languages have decided to represent plurals but it seems a possible and sensible solution. Naturally, these early rules are later abandoned and new ones created as children discover more examples of how, why and where writing is used in their culture, a process which continues into adulthood.

These examples of children's learning about writing are paralleled in the way children learn to speak and learn to read. Examples abound of young children's ability to generate rules of spoken language, rules which they couldn't have got directly from the adult. There is the familiar use of non-adult plurals: 'foots', 'sheeps', or the overuse of -ed endings: 'goed', 'runned', 'comed' which show how active children have been in listening to the language about them, developing hypotheses about its structure and drawing conclusions. Another endearing example is the child who announced after school that he had been *have* all day, a construction derived, presumably, from the instructions to be good and to behave.

In reading, too, it can be demonstrated that the child is no passive recipient of text whose interpretation will await instruction in phonics or word shapes. Young pre-school children will often 'read' a book before they can recognise all the individual printed words, substituting grammatically and semantically acceptable words for unknown ones.

This is not the place to develop a general theory of child language and literacy. The examples serve to make the point that children are always trying to make sense of what is going on around them. They are active participants in the language learning process and this participation would be oddly distorted if children were expected to get little bits right before they move on to the next bit, for instance, to write simple sentences correctly before trying to write a story. Such a procedure would be ignoring the child's learning process and the social contexts in which language occurs.

LANGUAGE LEARNING IN CONTEXT

It is often emphasised that language is a social fact, its construction being determined by both the immediate context, e.g. who's speaking or writing to whom and their relationship to each other, and the wider context, e.g. the power relationships between certain groups. This culturally embedded view of language appears to be put to one side in setting language learning objectives, with little reference being made to the fact that what is to be taught about language will be radically affected by how it is taught.

Some comments from children about writing can illustrate how the school context can affect their efforts to make sense of literacy. Pupils of all ages have been asked questions such as: *What's important about writing?* or *Which piece of writing pleases you most and why?*

The many answers included:

- *I like writing because if we could not write we would have nothing to do in school.*
- *The worst thing about writing is copying off the board.*
- *I write for my teacher to prove I can write.*
- *I don't like writing because I get flat bits at the end of my finger.*

More positive comments are also heard:

- *Writing is important to us, it helps you learn.*
- *When I'm in a good mood I enjoy it.*
- *What the teacher says about my writing matters to me.*

While answers vary greatly, comments that have been made in practically all classrooms are that neatness, punctuation and spelling make writing good, that teachers are the main, often sole, audience and assessors of writing and that writing takes up most of the school day.

These are rarely the intended perceptions for pupils to arrive at. They will have arisen when the teacher's aim was to develop children's ability to, say, *write simple stories of reasonable coherence* or to *expound an argument or thesis*. But because such aspects of language cannot be separated from the classroom context in which they occur, it can easily happen that from the child's point of view the aims were *to provide the teacher with neatly written texts*.

Again, while the examples come from writing similar examples could be given for reading and speaking. If the language learning objective is, for instance, *to develop children's appreciation of the pleasures of reading*, a completely different objective will be achieved if materials are limited to reading schemes and competence assessed by word recognition tests. Similarly, an aim for oral development might be *to develop discussion skills* but if the children are in rows facing the teacher and the topic is unrelated to the children's experience the pupil-defined objective will be far removed from the teacher's.

LANGUAGE ENTITLEMENT

Where does this take the considerations of language learning objectives? The examples above have shown, I hope, the inadequacy of any list which assumes that language can be arranged hierarchically or otherwise into age related categories, and/or that language can be seen as an autonomous area distinct from the contexts in which it is used. This inadequacy appears to be recognised by HMIs in their *English from 5 to 16: the Responses* (1986) in which lists of objectives are replaced by 'illustrative examples' of language experiences to be provided and 'broad indicators' of expected pupil outcomes.

Street (1986) makes a useful distinction between an autonomous model of language and an ideological one. The former, he argues, represents the 'Great divide' in which literacy is studied 'in its technical aspects, independent of social context'. The ideological model, on the other hand, sees literacy practices as 'inextricably linked to cultural and power structures in a given society'. The argument leads us beyond this article's discussion of language learning objectives into questions about the cultural values embodied in the language taught in school and the effect such values have on different children's access to language and literacy.

What seems to be indicated is a new focus for language teaching goals which moves the emphasis away from itemising decontextualised language abilities to be learned towards establishing the contexts in which language should be developed. What is needed is the creation of contexts in which the full range of language, both spoken and written, can be exploited and developed and in which the learner plays a central role.

In practice, and again with a focus on writing, a context-centred set of objectives might look like this.

> All children need to be provided with opportunities which will reflect writing as an important, purposeful, interesting and enjoyable process and which allows them to be actively involved in the development of their abilities in different literacy practices.
> Within this broad framework specific opportunities need to be created which will allow children to experience:
>
> *The nature of writing.* Writing should be seen not as some unitary skill, but rather as a set of cultural practices each with its own conventions and demands. Thus the writing done for a television script is very different from the writing of a newspaper article or from, say, a recipe. These variations need to be recognised by teachers and introduced to children. With older children, discussion of the demands of different writing will be appropriate. This complexity of written forms needs to be related to children's oral and reading experiences. The development of listening, talking, reading and writing abilities are closely related. Children need to read examples of what they are asked to write; they need to use their oral language experience as a basis for their writing (especially in the early years) and they need to look at the differences between the language modes.
>
> *The behaviour of writers.* Learning to write is not simply a matter of practising different written forms. It involves learning about writers and the difficulties they have: deciding what to write; employing the written structures and conventions; revising what has been written and evaluating its effect on the reader. Above all, the learner needs to develop a sense of self as writer. Opportunities for such development can be provided by the teacher writing with the pupils, by adults or older pupils working with or alongside learners and by visits from published authors.
>
> *The process of writing.* While the final outcomes of writing instruction are important, equally important are the procedures which lead to the finished product. Attention needs to be paid to writing strategies before, during and after writing. Thus, all

learners should experience different strategies for *pre-writing* such as brainstorming, group discussions, plans and such like; for *during-writing* such as drafting and discussions about progress with peers or potential readers, and for *after-writing* such as editing and publishing. Through such experience of the writing process, learners will recognise that writing can be assisted by collaboration with others. The skills for handwriting, spelling and punctuation will be introduced as essential parts of the writing process, their refinement following the development of a text's meaning.

The purposes and audiences of writing. The effective development of children as writers entails writing activities which the learners recognise as purposeful and which have an audience other than the teacher. Opportunities need to be developed to ensure that a range of reasons for writing and a range of readers are provided. Older and younger children in the same or different schools, parents and adults in the local community can provide appropriate audiences, while purposes of writing can vary from giving information about the school to prospective pupils to writing up science experiments for younger children, and from a script based on a favourite story to a letter arguing for improved play areas.

The relationship between writing and learning. Writing is not only a means of demonstrating knowledge, it is also a tool for developing thinking. Pupils should be encouraged to use writing to formulate hypotheses, explore their thoughts, ask questions and put forward tentative ideas. Half-formed ideas once written can often, with help, develop in productive ways. Such use of writing assumes a reader who acts as a facilitator of ideas rather than as a critic or assessor.

The pleasures and responsibilities of writing. Within the range of writing activities provided, learners should recognise the value of writing for their personal development. They should be allowed to write, on occasions, simply for pleasure, unhampered by any assessment and without regard to conventions of accuracy. Alongside such expression, learners should consider their responsibilities when writing for publication, recognising the power that the written word can have.

These objectives for writing have clear implications for the teacher's role in the writing activities. The teacher needs to be aware of the nature of writing, to have examples of many different written forms and to be aware of the wide repertoire of writers' behaviour. Teachers need to adopt flexible roles acting at one point as the sounding board for ideas, at another as the critic for a first draft and at another as the editor and distributor of finished work. Assessment of a child's progress in writing should include monitoring the number of different written forms attempted as well as evaluation of the learner's facility with structures in writing for different purposes and different audiences. A writer's performance depends on the nature of the writing task and thus assessment must take the task demands into account.

To quote from: *English from 5 to 16: The Responses:*

> Lively, supportive and purposeful teaching should, along with a child's increasing experience, assist pupils to appreciate the place of writing to fix and create meaning for themselves and others.

To end with some examples from children, a school in Hampshire helped children explore writing and writers when they invited Gareth Owen to come and read his poems. Cath Farrow, one of the teachers, describes how, before the visit, the whole school looked at his poems, discussed poets and drew pictures predicting Gareth Owen's appearance, shared their likes and dislikes, drew on the themes of his poems to develop their own prose and poetry and discussed their performance as writers. There is space for two examples of their writing, the first inspired by 'Come On In, The Water's Lovely', the second by 'Mandy Likes the Mud'.

Come On Up

Come on up the view is lovely
Of course I won't push you down
There are men filling holes
Of course you won't fall
I am up here
There are cars and mini-buses
You really will come up
On the count of three
One
It is really quite nice
Two
I will help you
Three
Oh dear, Mum's calling because it's tea
Just as you started climbing.
                              Alexandra

Jonathan likes red
Zoe likes to go to bed
Vicki likes to stroke a cat
Grandad likes to wear a hat
Holly likes to eat
But Abby likes sweets.

Jo likes to play with toys
Jodie likes to play with boys
Alex likes to mess up hair
Hayley likes her teddy bear
Mummy likes to wipe her feet
But Abby likes sweets.
                                    Abby

These pieces of writing provide particularly powerful messages when it is realised that Alexandra is seven years old and Abby is eight.

ACKNOWLEDGEMENT

I would like to thank everybody – coordinators, teachers, team members and children – involved in the National Writing Project for their contributions to the development of my thinking. The views expressed in the article are, of course, the author's own.

REFERENCES

CLAY, M., *What did I write?*, Auckland, N.Z., Heinemann, 1975
Department of Education and Science, *English from 5 to 16*, London, HMSO, 1984
Department of Education and Science, *English from 5 to 16: The Responses to Curriculum Matters 1*, London, HMSO, 1986
FERREIRO, E. AND TEBEROSKY, A., *Literacy before Schooling*, London, Heinemann, 1979
GOODMAN, K., 'Growing into Literacy', *Prospect* vol. XV (1), pp. 57-65
GOODMAN Y., 'Writing Development in Young Children', *Gnosis*, 8, pp. 8-14
STREET, B., 'Literacy Practices and Literacy Myths', Paper for University of Boston Language Development Conference, October 1986

The outline of a context-centred set of objectives on pages 129-130 was developed through discussions with Michael Jones and Mike Austin.

VARIETY, MORE THAN THE SPICE OF LANGUAGE

GEORGE KEITH

George Keith is Director of the Cheshire Language Centre at North Cheshire College, having moved there after teaching in Yorkshire and in Bedfordshire. He is Chairman of Examiners for English Language at A-Level (JMB) and co-author of *Primary Language Learning with Micro-computers*, (Croom Helm, 1986)

When *Language in Use*[1] first appeared in 1971 it was rightly heralded as a major contribution to the study of English language in schools and colleges, and it has remained so. Yet it has not been easy to assimilate the concepts and methodology underpinning the book and despite the publication later of *Using Language in Use*,[2] the hearty welcome given at first by many teachers turned eventually to frustration and disappointment when they were unable to find ways of sustaining its use. The collecting of linguistic data, for example, or the stylistic analysis of non-literary texts, sounded just the right things to be doing but proved extremely difficult in practice. There seem to be two main reasons why this has been so. First, the teaching of English language has for so long been under-conceptualised that few if any English teachers have the expertise to sustain the *Language in Use* approach. This is not altogether a matter of insufficient knowledge or lack of specific training but rather one of difference in perspective or attitude toward language in general. The replacement of a prevailing static notion of language (inert structures held together by mechanical rules – sometimes called 'basic English') with a dynamic concept of language as social behaviour, was bound to take its own time. Secondly, the investigative approach to language study recommended by *Language in Use*, demands a particular kind of teaching style in which resource-based learning, small group activities, tape recording and a spirit of scientific enquiry all play an important part.

In short, *Language in Use* was an innovation ahead of its time.

With, however, the advent of English Language at A-Level and the success of the pilot schemes, we are now in a position to catch up, as it were, with *Language in Use* and begin to formulate a theoretical framework for language studies which will address itself not only to the needs of post-16 students but will also inform language studies lower down the age range. Post-16, this has already happened in some Further Education colleges where *Language in Use* has gone through modified versions in response to accumulated teaching and learning experiences. Also in the intervening years there have been discernible changes in the style of English teaching, and in classroom management, which betoken a readiness for more challenging kinds of learning of a resource- and data-based kind. Moreover there have been shifts of emphasis within academic linguistics and an increase in understanding on the part of linguists, of the needs of class teachers. Modern linguistics has more to offer than it did 15 years ago and its interdisciplinary relations with other fields of knowledge have generated a range of topics in different theoretical areas (e.g. language variety, language and society, language change, language acquisition), highly suited to the needs of students in schools. This paper is concerned with just one of the areas which should form an essential part of a projected schools syllabus, namely language diversity.

THE CURSE OF BABEL?

Following the Bullock Report [3] there has grown a considerable public enthusiasm for language among teachers and educationalists, a sort of golly-gosh amazement at the pervasiveness, the influence and the sheer power of language in human society. Whether for good or ill, language and education have come to be regarded almost as synonymous entities and the new perspective this has opened up on the politics of schooling has proved both disturbing and invigorating. For some teachers the new emphasis on language has revived the flagging optimism of the sixties, for others it has given a completely new lease of life to their teaching. However, despite the power of language to invest our experiences with meaning, to transform our lives even, it remains a major human problem both inside and outside educational contexts, the most familiar difficulty being that of linguistic diversity. Even the comfortably insulated British tourist can experience dismay and panic or a sense of isolation when confronted with a foreign language, Hungarian for instance. With no linguistic support on hand, except perhaps some dimly remembered German from school days, communication is rendered impossible except through non-verbal means, which can be notoriously unreliable despite the current enthusiasm for the importance of body language. Well intended gestures can appear threatening, eye contact becomes unnerving, and even the wordless features of voice, such as pitch and intonation patterns, are likely to be misinterpreted. We do well to reflect upon the intensity of physical experiences attendant upon situations of this kind, especially in view of the rather abstract notions of language that have predominated in educational contexts. Going to school and going to live in a foreign country are very similar experiences so far as language is

VARIETY, MORE THAN THE SPICE OF LANGUAGE 135

concerned. Compare for example some lines by a cosmopolitan Yorkshireman, Tony Harrison,[4] with lines by an immigrant Jamaican, now living in Manchester, Alfred O'Connor.[5] Harrison has drawn our attention to dialectal differences between home and school in a number of poems, for example, 'Them & Uz', 'The Queen's English', 'The Rhubarbarians'. There is an especial poignance in the following lines from 'Wordlists':

> I've studied, got the OED
> and other tongues I've slaved to speak or read
> ....
> ....
> but not the tongue that once I used to know
> but can't bone up on now, and that's mi mam's.

The same sense of estrangement from a first language is expressed in a poem written by O'Connor, the title of which refers to his father's pride in his own language, Jamaican Creole:

A Fi-mi Language Dis

> When mi a picni inna de country
> mi gran teach mi fi talk
> jus de way everybody roun mi talk.
> Mi come fram de country part
> where wi talk real country Patwa.
> Only at school, wi talk more proper.
>
> Now when mi come a Inglan, is den mi change.
> Mi modda and fadda tell mi seh,
> 'Now yu inna Inglan, yu have fi learn de Inglish.
> Yu av fi talk same like de people – dem ya talk.'
>
> But mi fadda neva change.
> Him talk him Patwa all de time.
> Like him waan fi seh, "A fi-mi language dis."

In 'The Queen's English', there is a parallel with O'Connor's last verse. The poet's father spots a book of Yorkshire dialect poems on the station bookstall and says:

> 'ere tek this un wi 'yer to New York
> to remind yer 'ow us gaffers used to talk.
> It's up your street in't it? ah'll buy yer that!

The experience of being cut off from our spoken language roots is a universal consequence of schooling. The ways in which children are 'taught' to read plays a significant part in this estrangement as do the methods whereby many children are taught to write. One teacher, Mina Shaughnessy,[6] even went so far as to describe the English writing system as a 'second language' for most of the students she taught. Worldwide it has been acknowledged and well documented that beginning readers learn more successfully from texts which incorporate the normal speech patterns of their first dialect or language.

One very impressive and thorough-going adoption of this point of view is the Western Readers Project in New South Wales, Australia.[7] The Project's initial aim was to produce local environmental reading resources for multilingual school populations in western country districts of the state. Inspired by Peter Dargin, an English teacher seconded to direct the Project, youngsters of all ages, together with their parents, teachers and other adults dictated or wrote a wide range of texts which were then edited and illustrated to a professional standard of publication. The series of books produced (different sizes, styles and presentation) is comparable in range and quantity with reading schemes used in Britain but draws almost entirely on the language resources of local communities in which descendants from different European countries are mixed with different aboriginal groups. The content of the books includes children's own adventure stories written in collaboration with their teachers, old folks' reminiscences, bilingual picture books, children's retelling of myths and legends, Bush ballads and folk tales, and a wide range of informative and instructional writing. Aboriginal dialects and lexical diversities within Australian English are acknowledged as a continuum in which language users should be able to move confidently according to their needs and purposes. Drawing on personal experience, expressed in the varied linguistic resources of a local community proved to be not only a successful strategy for teaching reading and fostering diversified language use among young people, it also united teachers and learners in the cultural sources of inspiration that have fed such Australian writers as Henry Lawson, Banjo Paterson, Judith Wright, Ruth Park and George Johnston. However, despite its achievements, the Project has provoked economic and political controversy over the effects created by the existence of an alternative resource to established reading schemes.

The story of the Western Readers illustrates very clearly the reluctance of formal education to commit itself to first languages of home and community. With few exceptions children in the United Kingdom and in the countries of her former Empire learn to read in a code based upon a dialect of the South East of England belonging to what is, economically and politically, a predominantly powerful national group. From the linguist's point of view all languages and dialects are equal in their systematicity and their expressiveness which in turn makes them equal in potential and integrity as systems of communication. These factors do not however ensure their equality of status nor their opportunity for development, both of which are determined by economic and political realities. Standard English is therefore conceived as the true English and all dialects are lesser or debased forms.

Given the predominance of literacy and literary traditions over oracy and oral traditions, the complex educational consequences of linguistic diversity in Britain will not be resolved by English teachers alone and they will not be resolved tomorrow. We can however draw encouragement from the Western Readers Project as we can from the Central Manchester Caribbean Project. It was, after all, the Manchester project which was responsible for getting Alfred O'Connor's poems into print along with the writings in Creole and standard English of many other Western Indian students. Einar Haugen[8] in 'The curse of Babel', refuses to concede the myth that linguistic diversity is an enduring punishment under which all of us have to learn to live, and chooses, rather, to celebrate the diversity of human language. English teachers should do the same and indeed many are now doing so. 'Our problem,' says Haugen, 'is how to teach tolerance of difference and acceptance of people for what they are, not for how they talk.' This is true whether they speak English dialects or the tongues of other mothers, but for English teachers to teach tolerance of difference effectively, they need a linguistic perspective on language diversity, rather than a literary, or a nationalist, or a basic English one. Gains will then come not only in the promotion of tolerance but in students' better understanding of their own language resources and in their improved expertise as communicators. There are two elements here:

1 knowing more about language (both teachers and students);
2 being able to use language better.

The argument for achieving these ends by celebrating and investigating dialectal and language diversity is slightly circuitous and has to begin with a consideration of 'basic English', one variety of English traditionally prescribed for teaching about language and for improving language performance.

THE TROUBLE WITH BASIC ENGLISH

So far as parents, employers and teachers are concerned, the efficacy of teaching one form or other of basic English is seriously over-estimated. Basic English for native speakers is invariably conceived in remedial terms, as a medicine for correcting something that has gone wrong, or for bringing on something that has failed to happen. There is also the implication that it is a necessary recourse because English teachers habitually neglect correctness in favour of other language goals less obviously useful in the world of work, for example, creative writing.

It is equally true, however, so far as schools are concerned, that the significance and the value of linguistic diversity have, in contrast, been consistently under-estimated. How can English teachers be expected to reach out towards the varieties of African or Asian languages when they have not yet come to terms with the variety of accents and dialects in their mother tongue? In 1975, Peter Trudgill[9] advocated 'that the teaching of standard English should be confined to certain sorts of written work; and the bidialectalism approach should be used to teach it. More importantly . . . we should do all we can to advance the progress of the "appreciation of dialect differences" view.' The right advice, but a tall order. Progress along these lines has been slow and sporadic largely because there is a lack of any kind of coherent theoretical framework from which to teach English language in schools. If such a framework can now be agreed upon it will enable closer and more confident attention to be paid to linguistic diversity which, in turn, will help break down some of the nationalistic confines of traditional English teaching. It will also help teachers deal knowledgeably with the recurring assaults from advocates of basic English.

At first sight the problems of basic English and those of teaching English in a multilingual society seem poles apart. One set of problems is home grown, about 100 years old if you take a historical view of literacy education (teaching the 'hands' to read and write) or about 40 years old if you take the view that the modern world makes significantly more complex linguistic demands upon young people than ever before. The language problems posed by multicultural communities on the other hand, seem to lie outside the recognisably traditional concerns of English teachers and consequently beyond their expertise and effective reach. Bilingual Welsh teachers and English teachers with experience of ESL, or who have taught abroad, are the ones thought to have the expertise, not conventional teachers of English. The two sets of problems are in fact very closely related and demand of teachers a capacity to respond to that continuum of dialectal and linguistic diversity so creatively exploited (in the best sense of the word) by the Western Readers and the Caribbean Heritage Projects.

Variety and change are part of the nature of language but these are the very features which formal education finds difficult to accommodate. The Bernstein-Labov debate, of what now seems another age, highlighted the fact that what may be perceived as differences in the outside world are perceived within school as deficiencies. No doubt it is easier to teach in terms of a deficit theory but the habit of doing so has led to more problems rather than fewer. Before outlining an approach to teaching which acknowledges and welcomes linguistic diversity as an appropriate topic for investigation, it will be worth considering just what kind of language variety basic English is.

The classic version was devised for ESL purposes by C.K. Ogden in the 1940s for a Committee of Ministers on Basic English under R.A. Butler. It consisted of 850 words (reflecting the new vogue for key-word type reading schemes) to which new compounds, foreign and technical words could be added. About 70 per cent of the basic vocabulary consisted of nouns (or 'things' as they were called) while 10 per cent consisted of prepositions, adverbs and conjunctions ('operators').

There were only 18 verbs. In America, I.A. Richards promoted a modified version which had an even smaller basic vocabulary to start with, followed by a progressive sequence of additions.

Eminently sensible intentions lie behind the schemes of the 1940s which, along with their successors, have a winning simplicity about them and a look of practicality and common sense that almost immediately recommends them for use both abroad and at home. One feels that they ought to work but it is plain that they do not. They are founded upon an assumption that language can be learned in an encapsulated, intellectual way, as though the need for cultural contact and social interaction can be short-circuited in the interest of faster efficiency. What happened in areas of East Africa, South East Asia and the Indian sub-continent is that pidgin varieties of English continued to flourish despite the introduction of Basic. Regarded in those days as debased forms which they are not, pidgins (whether English, French or Portuguese) proved easier to learn and more effective for communication. Some in fact developed into Creoles which have in turn produced new cultural and literary achievements. Basic English, of whatever form, applied to successive generations of school children, always intellectualises and reduces the mother tongue to a set of grammatical abstractions to be practised, memorised and applied to written English. As schemes, they are easy enough to devise but they always fail to do what is claimed for them. At best they describe only the surface features of written language while at worst they seriously misrepresent the nature and functions of language. They are, in short, never basic enough. The real 'basics' of language are the generative sources of language production where thought and feeling are formed into strings of words expressing meaning. Processes such as these are learned through experience and interaction, not from grammar books, which at best can only describe norms and deviations. At worst, they prescribe remote styles of performance and spurious rules of usage. We ought perhaps to think of language in ecological terms rather than mechanical ones since the rules which govern language use have a peculiar elasticity, taut enough to convey plain sense and to locate time, space and relationships but vibrant enough to allow a wide range of ambiguity, metaphor and implied meanings regardless of intention. It is the complexity and variety of even the most mundane language use which has made basic English approaches almost as unhelpful and as peculiarly alien as inventing a new international language. In effect basic

English and Esperanto are one and the same thing – they are reductions of living language which can only have meaning for people already familiar and confident with the real thing. Oddly enough it is English teachers today who need a basic grammar of English, not students.

Teachers need a coherent set of principles, not for teaching to students, but to underpin the ways in which language studies may be undertaken in the classroom and to inform descriptions and explanations of language use, where the role of the teacher is not so much one of language expert as experienced investigator. There is an encouraging parallel here with literature teaching. In recent years the view has developed that literature should be a shared experience between students and teachers in which different responses to texts receive equal consideration. Teachers have become learners, prepared to read texts that are new to them as well as to their students, and also prepared to learn from their students' responses. The authoritarian stance of the English teacher as 'superior reader' who holds the key to meaning is giving way to the role of 'experienced reader', alert to varieties of responses and different constructions of meaning. Also, incidentally, the range of texts has extended considerably in recent years. More and more Commonwealth writing is being included in reading lists and some teachers are actively seeking literature from other cultures with quite different language traditions, a development which parallels the demand for the publication of more multilingual texts in which English and Gujerati, or Urdu for example, are printed alongside each other.

English teachers must be seen as authoritative in matters of language, not merely prescriptivist and authoritarian about basic English and largely inexperienced in the needs of non-native English speakers.

To suggest that we should allow a positive response to linguistic diversity to shape the content and method of English teaching, rather than retreat into a basic English ideology, is not a particularly new notion nor is it just a timely adjustment to the increase in the number of multilingual voices in school populations. What is relatively new is the insistence that English teachers need at least as much linguistic expertise as literary expertise, an area in which they are almost exclusively qualified. Moreover the expertise should be drawn from modern approaches to interactive uses of language rather than from structuralist approaches which have proved so disappointingly ineffective as a ground work for practical judgements. Important developments have already occurred in mainstream English language teaching and these should be identified.

VARIETIES OF ENGLISH: SOME INNOVATIONS

12 years on most English teachers are grateful for the remarkable influence that the Bullock Report[10] has exerted upon educational

thinking, though many now wonder just what continuing effect it has had on everyday practice in schools, especially in the secondary sector. Beneath the new orthodoxy created by Bullock lie, as ever, old confusions and contradictory attitudes about the nature and functions of language. There can be no doubt about the welcome reinforcement Bullock gave to primary and secondary teachers already committed to reforming the reading curriculum or to changing the classroom environment for oracy and writing. Bullock also gave a new impetus to action research and in-service programmes devoted to language and learning. Several aspects of the English: 16 to 19 Project,[11] for example, derive from Bullock and both the National Writing Project[12] and the new National Oracy Project[13] owe something to the groundswell generated by *A Language for Life*.

One noticeable feature of the mid-1980s, perhaps directly due to the influence of Bullock or to concepts of language and literacy endorsed by the Report, is the tendency of English departments and examination boards to formulate their English language syllabuses in terms of four varieties of language mode: reading, writing, talking, listening.

Traditionally, English as the national school subject *par excellence*, has been divided into English Language and English Literature. A reverential notion of literature as 'the best English' has long held sway over the common uses of English language and rendered English open to the charge of being a 'snob' subject. If there is now a crisis in the teaching of English Literature it has as much to do with this separation from English Language as with philistinism in contemporary culture, or new ideologies. Modern literary theory, with its strong linguistic roots and declared interest in the variety of readers' responses to texts, might almost be seen as a revenge upon traditional literary critical pedagogy. Even when there is evidence of attempts to reintegrate language and literature the effects of the division lie very deep. Many department heads for example will say with pride that their English syllabus is 'literature based' but it is not so easy to find a teacher who can say just as confidently that her departmental syllabus is 'language based'.

The alternative construction of the English curriculum into language modes offers a much wider conception, drawing attention as it does to universal human behaviour rather than to a particular cultural heritage. In no way does it lessen the intimate ties of sentiment and loyalty to the mother tongue but it does open the way for a fuller consideration of linguistic diversity. The concept 'language' and the activities of reading, writing and speaking are more embracing than either 'English' or 'Literature'. The four language modes, besides being an eminently practical way of looking at teaching and learning in English lessons, are themselves a demonstration of language variety.

Virtually all the innovative movements in mainstream English language teaching have drawn attention to diversity. *Language in Use*, with which this paper began, drew attention to varieties of form and function, devoting considerable space to dialectal differences and to contextual difference between speech and writing. *Web of Language* (BBC)[14] was especially successful in making primary school children aware of register differences and of the importance of contextual cues for language use. Again considerable attention was paid to differences between speech and writing. In Australia, Michael Halliday, continuing formative work already reflected in *Language In Use* initiated the Language Development Project which is centrally concerned with shifting teachers' and students' perceptions of linguistic differences. In Canada, James Benson and William Greaves, after 10 years of experimental teaching have produced *You and Your Language*[15] which is primarily concerned with dialectal and stylistic variations in language use. Another development in Britain which stresses diversity between languages and dialects, and the fundamental differences between speech and writing is the Language Awareness[16] movement. If the notion of extending 'English Language' into 'language studies' in one sense 'denationalises' English as a school subject, the Language Awareness movement invites much closer collaboration between English and Modern Languages departments:

> . . . it can be claimed that a first step, within the capacity of every school with ethnic minority children on roll, is to build into the curriculum a language element which brings together the diverse language experience of the pupils while offering to the different kinds of language teacher (English mother tongue, ESL, foreign language) a shared responsibility.[17]

Within that shared responsibility English language specialism would achieve a new significance:

> It is a modern-day paradox that while Britain is becoming, year by year, a more multi-lingual community, the English language itself spreads ever wider across the globe as the world vehicle language, especially in the fields of higher education and technology, and in specialist areas such as air traffic control, satellite communications and computer technology.[18]

All the movements cited here have in one respect or another placed the teaching of English language as a mother tongue in a wider linguistic perspective. The widest perspective of all is represented by the Linguistic Minorities Project.[19] In 1975 Bullock asserted:

> No child should be expected to cast off the language and culture of the home as he crosses the school threshold, nor to live and act as

though school and home represent totally separate and different cultures that have to be kept firmly apart.

10 years later any re-reading of Bullock must be done in the light of *The Other Languages of England*, the report of the Language Minorities Project which apart from providing us with a detailed picture of the extent and variety of multilingualism in Britain also suggests a framework in which English teachers can begin to share language variety in the classroom with a new linguistic awareness.

VARIETIES OF LANGUAGE: THE NEW JMB SYLLABUS[20]

With the arrival of English language at A-Level there is now an opportunity to engage older students in a serious study of varieties of language. Candidates are required to submit a project as part of their course work and in a moderation sample of about 400 candidates, over half of the projects are likely to be devoted to an investigation of some aspect of linguistic diversity. The topic may well be an aspect of dialectal variation, or of differences between speech and writing, or of social differentiation. Increasingly students are turning to bilingual topics as an expression both of their curiosity and of their contact with bilingual speakers. Four examples will illustrate the kinds of teaching and learning involved:

1 *An Analysis of Letters from a French Pen Friend*
The letters had been written over a period of six years and show different stages in the acquisition of a second language. In order to describe data the student needed to make explicit the grammatical categories which had underpinned intuitive advice she had been giving her pen friend over the six years. Matters of grammar needed to be distinguished from matters of style.

2 *An Investigation into the Spoken English of a Polish Grandfather*
Here the student tape recorded and transcribed stretches of her grandfather's speech observing in the process that some of his speech sounds were distinctly foreign while others were characteristic of Wigan speakers of English. The student hypothesised that the foreign sounds must be distinctive Polish phonemes which he could not eliminate from his speech while the recognisably Wigan accents were distinctive phonemes of a regional variety of English. Once again an essentially human study required the student to make careful and accurate description informed by some theoretical knowledge of phonology.

3 *Teaching English to a Turkish Neighbour*
What set out as a modest intention to describe the experience of helping a

Turkish speaker to become more proficient with English conversation led the student to observe some grammatical differences between the two languages and to concentrate on describing three of these: the use of definite and indefinite articles; the use of auxiliary verbs, as in the past historic tense for example; the formation of relative clauses.

4 *Code-switching and Code-mixing in a Multilingual Community*
In this project the student investigated the ways in which speakers of Urdu and Punjabi switched to English and back again during conversation. There was also a consideration of examples of words from one language becoming mixed into the vocabulary of another.

It is important to recognise that these examples are not the work of academic high flyers and were supervised by teachers prepared to put themselves at risk by learning along with their students. Support and advice were available from the consortium of centres offering the syllabus and each project title had to be submitted for approval by the chief moderator who, along with examining colleagues, was also prepared to give practical advice. Reports from teachers who have undertaken project supervision are very encouraging. The students themselves believe in the value of what they are doing and show a willingness to collect authentic data however inconvenient, frustrating and messy that process can be. Furthermore, the effect on their own use of written English is extremely beneficial largely because they are able to write with a new sense of subject expertise. In a learning context such as this, where there is regular consultation with a teacher and critical feedback from other students in seminars, students show a hitherto unsuspected ability to take care of their own basic English.

What kind of a conceptual framework then, for varieties of language, do these innovations require? The one offered below has been constructed out of the innovations described earlier and from experience at A-Level. It is intended as a comprehensive outline which can be applied across the age range in some form or other. Any part of it will serve as a starting point for explicit teaching about varieties of language; each part connects to any and every other part of the network of language studies. More and more audio, visual and textual resources in each area are becoming available while a pool of experience in teaching styles and methods is growing rapidly.

a) *Varieties of communication* – e.g. signal systems in different animal species; sign languages; gesture and vocalisation; body language; inventing a language.

b) *Different uses of language* – a range of models can be studied but students can also, from observation, construct their own which will in turn tell us quite a lot about how they perceive themselves as language users and how they might develop their own expertise.

c) *Difference between speech and writing* – a central area of theoretical and practical study in which the differences have consistently been misunderstood and underestimated. A study of the rules that govern how we talk to each other and of grammatical features in conversation is not only more accessible to secondary students but creates a new awareness of audience and registers for writing.

d) *Variations of dialect and style* – a topic that lies at the heart of home-school dislocation. Learning to produce bi-dialectal or bi-lingual versions of a text, for example, leads students to a very concentrated form of language awareness.

e) *Idiolectal variation* – a consideration of the infinite variations of idiolect and of the features that make individual voices personal and unique. The work on writing development by John Dixon and Leslie Stratta for example expressly encourages teachers to 'listen' to the individual voices of their students and help them grow in confidence as language users.

f) *The Indo-European connection* – the history of English words has always been a popular first and second year subject if reasonably well taught, but the wider topic of language families and language migrations enables us to teach a history of English and to investigate 'the other languages' of modern Britain.

g) *Language change* – normally this would rightly occur as a separate area in academic syllabuses but insofar as it is a form of language variation over time, it is also included here as a bridge to other areas of conceptual framework for language studies. There is however another, more important, issue underlying studies of language change and that is the question of attitudes and responses to change. For centuries languages have been studied in a historical (diachronic) way and this has had a very prescriptive effect on explanations of how language should be used today. Descriptive approaches of how language is actually being used and understood today are synchronic studies and vital for the promotion of tolerance and acceptance. David Sutcliffe's remarks in *British Black English*[21] convey not only a sense of excitement but also lend support to the need for investigative study:

> The birth of a new speech variety is the kind of linguistic event that used to go unnoticed or at least undocumented until years after it happened. Because of seventeenth- and early eighteenth-century prejudices against non-standard dialect and 'uncivilised' society, it is difficult to say now, at this distance, what the earliest Caribbean

Creoles were like when they first began to be spoken alongside the African languages, or even exactly what went into their formation. In the case of the transmission of distinctive Black Speech from the Caribbean to England, however, we have the opportunity to observe linguistic change and linguistic history at first hand. We can make tape recordings of the different age groups and ask questions of the people involved.

For young English students to encounter language in this way can be an extremely formative and humanising experience.

All these aspects of language variety are part of the undertow of language and as such are closer to the generative sources of an individual's speech and writing than an abstract, quasi-grammatical superstructure of basic English can ever be. Exploration of any of the areas given above leads to a more responsive contact with dialects and languages. What remains now is for teachers, if they can agree on a conceptual framework for varieties of language, to select and adopt content and resources from the increasing range becoming available for teaching in both mother tongue and multilingual contexts. Development of this kind constitutes a priority area for in-service programmes in the late 1980s.

TOMORROW'S LESSON

It must be admitted that the contribution of linguistics to the social and economic problem in which English teachers are enmeshed will be limited by prevailing attitudes but it is better to proceed from a linguistic rationale that is based upon sound principle rather than accumulated grammatical superstition and folk linguistics. This paper has suggested that English teachers should focus, in the first instance, on the fact that diversity is an essential part of the nature of language and that by investigating and exploiting diversity students can learn more about their own and other people's uses of language. Underlying all forms of language variation, however, and our perceptions of them, is the contrast between oral traditions of language use and literary traditions. Statistics about how many people in the world are bilingual or multilingual or about the rising tide of multilingualism in Britain are interesting but remote, while the EEC Directive on the Education of Migrant Workers, that the mother tonge and the culture of their country of origin should be actively promoted, is a daunting challenge to schools and education administrators. But one statistic that comes much closer to the English classroom is the fact that of the 5000 or so languages in the world only about 50 are written. This emphasises even more the significance of differences between speech and writing and throws into relief the remark of Goody and Watt in their influential paper, 'The consequences of literacy':[22] 'the relationship between the written and the oral tradition must be regarded as a major problem in Western culture.'

Among the four language modes it is generally agreed that talk enjoys a lower status than writing for example, but it is listening which has long been the Cinderella of the four. Consistently neglected because we are not at all sure how to teach it let alone assess it, it is the mode that now deserves serious investigation by students and teachers. Learning how to listen to each other, learning how we construct worlds of difference through talk, and learning to share each other's worlds and words are urgent necessities not only in the teaching of English, Humanities or Modern Languages but across the curriculum. One contribution that English teachers can make is to promote studies, not unlike those of the A-Level projects described elsewhere, in which attentive listening plays a significant part. The study of language varieties, if it is to have any value at all in schools for the development of students' own expertise and the promotion of cross-cultural understanding, must not be biased toward literacy. Speech comes first in human experience, and learning how to listen is a very appropriate starting point for language studies.

REFERENCES

1. DOUGHTY, P., PEARCE, J. and THORNTON, G., *Language in Use*, Edward Arnold, 1971
2. DOUGHTY, ANN AND PETER *Using Language in Use*, Edward Arnold, 1974
3. DES *A Language for Life*, HMSO, 1975
4. HARRISON, TONY *Selected Poems*, Penguin, 1984
5. O'CONNOR, ALFRED, 'A Fi-mi language dis' in *Versions: Writing in Creole and standard English*, Manchester Education Committee, 1985
6. SHAUGHNESSY, MINA *Errors and Expectations*, New York, OUP, 1977
7. Western Region Country Area Program *Western Readers*, Dubbo, New South Wales, 1981 onwards
8. HAUGEN, EINAR, 'The Curse of Babel' in *Language as a Human Problem*, ed. by Einar Haugen and Morton Bloomfield, Lutterworth, 1975
9. TRUDGILL, PETER *Accent, Dialect and the School*, Edward Arnold, 1975
10. DES *op. cit.*
11. DIXON, JOHN *English 16-19: The Role of English and Communication*, Macmillan, 1979
12. School Curriculum Development Committee (SCDC) National Writing Project, 1985 to date
13. SCDC National Oracy Project, 1987
14. BBC *Web of Language*, 1977. Now published under the same title by OUP, 1981
15. BENSON, JAMES AND GREAVES, WILLIAM *You and Your Language*, Pergamon, 1984
16. HAWKINS, ERIC, *Awareness of language: an introduction*, CUP 1984
17. HAWKINS *op. cit.*
18. HAWKINS *op. cit.*
19. Linguistic Minorities Project *The Other Languages of England*, Routledge & Kegan Paul 1985
20. JMB, *English Language A level syllabus*, 1987
21. SUTCLIFFE, DAVID *British Black English*, Basic Blackwell, 1982
22. GOODY, J. AND WATT, I., 'The Consequences of Literacy' in *Language and Social Context*, ed. by P.P. Giglioli, Penguin, 1972

ON ADVANCED LEVEL ENGLISH LANGUAGE

JOHN SHUTTLEWORTH

John Shuttleworth has taught English in schools and colleges in Manchester and Leeds. He is currently Deputy Director (Arts and Humanities) at Bury Metropolitan College and Senior Examiner for the JMB A-Level in English Language. His publications include *Considering Prose* (Hodder and Stoughton, 1984) and *Considering Drama* (Hodder and Stoughton, 1986).

Until recently, students who wished to take A-Level English faced a limited and limiting choice: they were able to follow only courses that concentrated on the study of literature and set books or combined such study with the more traditional forms of language work, such as the précis, comprehension and essay. However, two examination boards, London and the Joint Metriculation Board (JMB), have recently introduced syllabuses in English Language, both of which are available to centres throughout the country. The London board originally offered a course in language study as an optional paper within their existing literature provision, but this has now developed into an independent A-Level syllabus; the JMB English Language (Advanced) syllabus developed out of the interest and enthusiasm of a group of teachers, who designed a course which centres have been teaching since 1983. It is clear, certainly from the experience of the JMB, that such a course responds to student needs and has proved very popular with both them and their teachers and that continued expansion can confidently be expected.

Students who begin A-Level English Language will naturally approach such a course with the justifiable expectation that it will build upon much of the work and activity which they have pursued on their GCSE courses. Such students will have considerable expertise in language and will be skilled producers both of the spoken and of the written word in a variety and range of forms and registers. A student who therefore opts for English Language will have been fired, to some extent, with 'the excitement of writing' and so it is important that this fire is not damped down; students do not wish to have learning *about* language separated from an opportunity to continue to practise their productive and interpretative skills. As the JMB syliabus puts it: the aim is 'to combine learning *about* the nature and function of language in human thought and communication with learning *how* to use English more effectively'.

To have some understanding of how language works, students must be involved in some descriptive and systematic study of both the written and spoken varieties. It is important for them to realise that language is a system to be discovered; consequently they respond well to being given the opportunity to execute some personal investigative study into an aspect of language. However, before such an investigation can take place, they need to have some basic understanding about how language works and to be given some perspectives on language.

It is important to remember that just as most A-Level Literature students do not necessarily require a watered-down university literature course, neither do these students require A-Level 'Linguistics', for they have chosen to follow A-Level English Language courses. However, some suitable introduction to theoretical knowledge is clearly required if they are to develop an understanding of how language works.

Firstly, they need an understanding of phonology; for instance: how speech sounds are produced; the uses of phoneme theory; they need to know how stress and intonation patterns produce meaning and communication in spoken English; they need to know about accents and how to transcribe speech. Secondly, students need a basic introduction to grammar, particularly with reference to the historical and contemporary concepts of grammar, so that they can free themselves from the shackles of the prescriptivism they inevitably bring with them and move into more descriptive freedom; morphological and syntactic structures need some systematic study if students are to be able to cope with broader perspectives on language.

These very basic introductory forays into phonology and grammar need not be arid; learning through discovery is not a process excluded from an A-Level language syllabus and students are often surprised when they find out that they have an amount of expertise and knowledge about language they never knew they possessed. After all, it is *their* language. Some inkling of the systematic nature of language can be seen when students, for example, right at the outset of their course, are asked to formulate three or four simple rules about English that could be taught to foreign students; or asked how they can recognise that a particularly fractured piece of English was not written by a native speaker.

Students do welcome the opportunity to develop the wider perspectives on language that the A-Level courses offer them and such perspectives will include the national, historical, sociological, psychological, philosophical, cultural and linguistic; it should prove possible, for instance, for students to consider such issues as whether a 'universal grammar' exists; or that language is in a constant state of change (change, for example, in words and meaning, in written English, in sound systems and in the social context of these aspects); to study regional and social variations in English grammar or the problems of living in a multi-lingual community; to observe and describe the stages of language development in young children; to consider how meanings are conveyed or to pursue a stylistic approach both to literary and non-literary texts. Clearly the range of possibility for study is very large indeed and these examples could easily be augmented, but they may give an indication of the theoretical areas that A-Level language students do find of interest and value. Students do find language study absorbing; they find the descriptive analysis of the language system illuminating, but it is important that for students of this age a systematic study is not divorced from looking at a particular text or utterance in relation to its context. One of the ways that it is possible to avoid this divorce can be found in the requirement that students 'report on a personal investigation into a specified aspect of language use in everyday life using the knowledge acquired . . . about the Nature and Function of Language' in the earlier part of the course. This active investigation into language use can be of great benefit to students, encouraging, as it does, the formulation of a definite hypothesis for the linguistic study, awareness of the necessity of obtaining good clear data, with the concomitant awareness of possible weaknesses in methods of data collection, an analysis which addresses itself squarely to the data and a sensitive appraisal of what has been discovered. As a recent Examiner's report pointed out, 'it is clear that many of the candidates . . . have benefited from the experience [of the project] and that [it] offers them a unique opportunity to explore their own ideas and interests'. Some idea of the range of interests that may be stimulated by A-Level language study can be obtained by considering five of the topics students have submitted: a study of the accent of the student's grandfather, a Pole who has lived in industrial Lancashire for over forty years; a comparison between the language used in the 'Rover's Return' in Coronation Street and a discussion in a real Salford pub; a project to test the hypothesis that girls' vocabulary contains more colour words than boys'; an exploration of a number of metaphors for love and a discourse analysis of Prime Minister's Question Time. Personal investigations such as these, when based upon a secure application of theoretical knowledge, certainly demonstrate that language study for A-Level pupils can result in some valuable insights being gained.

To give students a thorough intellectual understanding of theoretical knowledge about language and its uses without offering them the opportunity of improving their own skills as both producers and interpreters would be selling them short. Whilst experience has shown that students are attracted to A-Level language by the prospect of being able to study such matters as why Geordies speak differently from Scousers, or doctors from dockers, or how their baby brothers and sisters acquire language skills, most of them are also attracted by the fact that they can continue to produce original work for a variety of specified purposes and audiences, as they have been used to doing in English lessons in their primary and secondary schools. One impetus to the production of these syllabuses was the fact that A-Level studies had given no real opportunity for children to continue with a subject that many of them so clearly enjoyed at school. If they remained unattracted by the prospect of studying seven or eight set books for two years, then effectively English as a subject of study was finished for them at age 16. There may, indeed, be a place for a course that concentrates solely on linguistics (many students who take these present language courses do continue with linguistic studies in higher education), but these are A-Level *language* courses and, as such, should additionally give students the opportunity to write in a variety of modes as well as concentrating on linguistic theory.

To make the teaching of language and writing skills to young people of this age as effective as possible means not only ensuring that they write with a specified purpose and for a specified audience, but also that they develop a critical awareness of themselves as writers. To this end, students can learn the complexities of re-drafting their original material and commenting on it, both during the various stages of composition and after the completion of the work. For instance, if a student has been sufficiently stimulated by his work on language acquisition, he may well find it attractive to write a story for an audience of young children. He must then decide on the age range of the potential audience, research and plan the writing and then produce an initial draft. For many students, used to the demands of the O-Level essay, this would have sufficed. The teacher would have read, marked and commented upon it and the student would then have embarked on the next writing task. (The opportunitites for re-drafting of coursework in GCSE may, of course, change this approach.) An A-Level student would, of course, be expected to develop and display more sophisticated writing skills, especially as he would have a real audience in mind for his story. Consequently, some audience response should be sought and whether this is from younger siblings, children of friends or by a visit to the local primary or junior school is immaterial. The student quite clearly may need to modify his draft in some way in the light of these responses, developing and maturing his skill as a writer in the process. It is not unknown for students to draft and re-draft their work four or five times before a final version is achieved. Students enjoy developing such skills in all the other categories of writing that Advanced Level courses demand of them – in addition to writing to entertain a reader, writing to persuade, writing to inform and writing to instruct. So, for instance, a report on the leisure provision for teenagers in a particular area must be capable of being submitted (and has been) to the relevant local councillors; an alternative student prospectus for a college should be issued to potential enrollers. Clearly, coursework is the only feasible method of assessing such writing skills and is therefore an essential component of any examination.

Students who are encouraged to approach writing in this way obviously develop a clear sense of purpose in their work and an awareness of how to achieve this purpose. They quickly become aware of many of the processes involved in writing and are able to comment objectively on their developing skills. The production of such a commentary in which they concern themselves with the process of writing in all its aspects is a very valuable part of an A-Level language course. Here they may be expected to give as much information as possible about the origins and sources of a piece of work, the adaptations and procedures followed; they may comment on any deletions, additions and revisions before the completion of the final version; they may give accounts of audience responses; they may reflect on style and register and other linguistic features; they may be encouraged to keep a writing log in which they trace and reflect on the progress of work-in-hand – but whatever approach to commentary is adopted by students, the discipline involved encourages them to become more deliberate and aware as writers, both in linguistic and in functional terms.

In addition to demonstrating both an understanding of theoretical models of language in describing and analysing data and an ability to be very aware producers of language, students at A-Level can be introduced to more sophisticated interpretative uses. As noted in the syllabus support material, there are some very practical skills in which they may be trained. 'Students (should be given) the experience of interpreting, adapting, editing and re-presenting source material to audiences other than those originally intended.' An interlocking picture of language studies begins to emerge. For, if students are to re-present material for other than its intended audience, they must be familiar with different modes of presentation and of register (such as, for instance, minutes, memoranda and agenda reports, technical reports or biographical writing) and must be able to write well and purposefully – all of which is dependent on their theoretical and practical knowledge developed in other parts of these courses. A high level of reading skill is demanded, for example, when students are asked to write a radio script for a schools' programme on the Libyan Embassy Siege of 1984, having had to read a number of contemporary and somewhat conflicting newspaper accounts in addition to a huge amount of information about the current political and social climate of Gaddafi's Libya; or when they have to produce a concert programme for 'The Black Knight', a rarely performed work by Edward Elgar, having read extracts from biographies, contemporary accounts of his life and times and various reviews of the early performances of the work.

Students have to learn to read critically and with a purpose, to be responsive to the various pressures that inform a particular piece of writing. They need to be sensitive not only to the content of the course material (with its potential both for repetition and for contradiction) but also to the variety of forms in which it is expressed and the variety of audiences for which it may originally have been intended. Difficulties which students may have with tasks of this nature are most likely to stem from inadequate reading skills which will permit only the most superficial familiarity with the material.

To conclude: the response of students to these new language study courses at A-Level is very positive. The opportunity to explore language more fully and more systematically; to collect, describe and analyse data; to develop and to mature their reading and writing abilities; to pursue research interests of their own – these are all approaches to language study and use that are encouraging and point to the future. If some way could be found, as in GCSE, of incorporating oral skills more fully than they are at present (a taped oral presentation in lieu of one written piece is acceptable as part of the JMB coursework), then such language study at 18+ is likely to be a strong growth area.

LANGUAGE ON THE ENGLISH CURRICULUM

JOHN KEEN

John Keen has taught English in further education and now teaches at Knutsford County High School. He is a chief examiner for A-Level English Language (JMB) and author of *Teaching English: A Linguistic Approach*, (Methuen, 1978).

What do we need to know about how language works? Judging by the collective wisdom of ordinary vocabulary, very little. Eskimos have their dozen words for snow, Arabic has its score of terms for camel, but everyday English makes few distinctions concerning its own structure. 'Word' itself is so exasperatingly problematic that linguists prefer to talk of 'morphemes' and 'lexical items'. A 'phrase' in ordinary English means an idiom or figure of speech, as in 'catch phrase' or 'to coin a phrase', not, as in language study, the unit of syntactic description intermediate between morpheme and clause. Terms such as 'subject', 'aspect', 'mood', appropriated for technical usage by grammarians, are far and confusingly removed in meaning from their colloquial homonyms. Linguistic units are classified on an unsystematic variety of pragmatic grounds; a word may be 'slang', 'long', 'descriptive', 'four-letter', as well as doubling as a unit of discourse when it is 'quiet' or 'of praise'.

If ordinary language tolerates conflations of level and dimension of description, commonsense knowledge about language accepts heterogeneous and even contradictory components of meaning within its understanding of colloquial metalinguistic terms. 'Slang', like St Augustine's concept of time, seems easy enough to grasp until you try to give it a sharp definition. Its main purpose is to provide a convenient general category of words and phrases proscribed for use in certain social situations, and as such is important for the etiquette of language behaviour. But our understanding of the criteria for using the term is governed by an ad hoc mixture of linguistic, personal, social and quasi-moral judgements, as this range of statements from a group of 13-year-olds shows:

1 Slang is a lazy way of speaking.
2 Slang is mainly used by young people.

3   Slang is like an alternative language.
4   Slang is used because people have different meanings.
5   Slang is a new or up-to-date way of speaking.
6   Slang is used when you do not want to be posh.
7   Some people use slang in their jobs.
8   Slang is used by some people to make them seem tough.
9   Slang comes from people missing parts of words out.
10 Slang comes from people who don't know how to speak properly.

By contrast, what distinctions of judgement, social and political role, mode, point of view, degree of confidence of assertion, level of formality, seriousness of intent, implied relation between addresser and addressee are contained in such ordinary terms for language interaction as 'say', 'mention', 'declare', 'come clean', 'prattle', 'harangue', 'allege', 'remark', 'confer'. And the judgement of English itself is surely right in this; that speakers need to understand language as it shines in use. We have to plan our days, tell people things, get on with our friends and colleagues, so we need to know the difference between suggestions and demands, hints and lectures, chats and conferences at a level of potential explicitness that is neither appropriate nor necessary for syntax and morphology.

As native speakers, our knowledge of discourse and our knowledge of language structure work at quite different levels and on different principles; we have an implicit grasp of the grammar of our language which cuts so deep and fine that there is a real sense in which we cannot make a mistake in it. But our knowledge of discourse is less perfect, and is more like a skill in the sense that it can be acquired by following explicit principles and lost through lack of practice. The most crashing egocentrics can improve their conversational skills by following simple rules like, 'Give other people a turn at talking'. Conversely, people who spend a lot of time alone may temporarily lose their interactional competence. But this does not happen with grammar. An English speaker emerging from solitary confinement does not forget the appropriate order of prenominal modifiers and say 'It was a dark prison small cell'.

Our knowledge of English grammar has to be implicit rather than explicit, if only to cope with its enormous complexity. If we think about it, we know that the underlying system of syntactic rules allows some structures rather than others – that, for example, 'I'll go if you'll' and 'I was angrier than frightened' violate principles within the system. But if even potential explicit knowledge of syntactic rules was a psychological condition of being able to use utterances constructed on their basis, we would have to spend so much time and neural energy processing them that we would hardly have a few minutes left for a civilised conversation.

There may be circumstances where explicit knowledge of form classes and their distribution is useful, notably in learning a second or additional language. Knowing that the adjective usually comes after the noun in French or that a verb comes after the subject and object in Japanese may give the learner a secure foothold in the early stages. Second language learners report the usefulness of various grammatical generalisations. Use of a structural metalanguage may enable teachers and students to mark out areas of a language system for convenience of focus and ease of reference. On the other hand, teachers may be making life more difficult than necessary for their students if they impose categories derived from a base language on to a target language where they are inappropriate, or artificially invent categories for a base language to facilitate transition into the target. More seriously, it may be that potentially able second language learners are alienated from new and exciting means of communication by the dogmatic requirement that they master an explicit grammatical description of their own language first.

While some limited study of grammar may have a place in learning, many other aspects of language deserve attention. The primitive morphology of English textbooks where students are required to rejig Greek and Latin prefixes fails because it is narrow, unsystematic and lacks the context of discourse. But if the word-structure of a text with a genuine purpose is foregrounded for communicative effect, then the potential for recombination that constitutes a basic principle of English word-formation can be explored meaningfully and in context. What possibilities for such study by older secondary students are there, for example, in this extract from a music review?[1]

> No sell out: Can we start by saying that Malcolm X has sold out? Or, to be more exact, that Keith Le Blanc's searing cut-up of X's chant-down on un-civil attitudes to Black Civil Rights is a sell-out in every West End record shop? I think we can.

The extract, which needs its whole context to be fully interpretable, refers to the fact that a Keith Le Blanc record made by editing recordings of speeches of Malcolm X, the US Civil Rights activist, is selling a great many copies. The house style of the journal from which it comes takes some time to assimilate, but the texts have clear purposes and well defined readerships, and raise issues about words in a way that cannot be simulated by ready-processed and contextless data presented as lists of roots and affixes. What other sources of new words are accessible to students? – science texts, computer manuals, fashion magazines?

Social aspects of language use are even more subject to what Geoffrey Thornton called preCopernican models of language. In some quarters the presuppositions are positively preCambrian:[2]

> People sneer at Standard English pronunciation as 'elitist', but the fact is that the development of such a clear and strictly regulated

method of speech has been an enormous aid to the primary purpose of language: communication . . . It is a mistake to see a correct accent purely in social terms. Good pronunciation is an unspectacular but essential part of the fabric of civilisation. Between the wars, and even as late as the 1950s, the BBC played a notable educative roll (sic) in improving the pronunciation of English by providing a dependable daily model of how it should be spoken.

More recently, in a spasm of inverted snobbery, it seems to have adopted a deliberate policy of pushing provincial accents. This is silly and deplorable. With so many barriers to understanding in the world, it is absurd to perpetuate the ancient confusions of speech.

In drawing up an agenda for language study in schools and colleges, we can distinguish three reasons why students might need or want to explore language at an explicit level:

1 It may be of practical help to them in their learning and language development.
2 It may help them to examine received ideas about language.
3 It may allow them to study topics which are interesting or important.

How far we go along this continuum depends on a variety of factors; what weight we give to language study compared to other aspects of English and foreign language learning; how seriously we take our responsibility as educators to challenge unproved assumptions and misconceptions in any area of thinking and living; what we consider to be interesting and important. We need to ask difficult questions about priorities, objectives, our students' perceptions. We need to be sure that our own knowledge and expertise is adequate, and that the educational context is conducive to fair and objective investigation of language. The social context certainly does not favour it. Pretheoretical generalisations about language tend to take on the characteristic features of prejudice: overselection of supporting examples, circular definition, dogmatism and lack of relation to the kind of systematic model without which observers tend to see in data those faults they know are there anyway. It is, for example, commonly assumed that spoken English is unstructured, deviates from a standard norm and contains many grammatical mistakes. These views are rarely challenged effectively by being confronted at the same level of generality, but principled observation of language use might offer enough opportunities for tentative comment and hypothesis to open productive discussion. So this anecdote from a 12-year-old, recorded in the fairly formal condition of a class discussion, reveals tensions between the narrative drive, the speaker's point of view and his awareness of the need for background explanation resolved into a syntagmatic vector.

When I was only a little boy I lived in Africa with my sister – and – Zimbabwe – we lived there for quite a while – about two years – till I was three and we came over to England – all – when I was about two – two and a half and my sister was three to three and a half – my mum and dad took us to – a party – and – it started rain – um – it was outside because it's so hot inside so – and it started raining – and – it's the African rain – rainfall you know where it's it's steaming – steaming hot rain sort of thing – so – um – we ran home quick and I was in the pram – and my dad and my mum went into the bedroom – just to see – see if everything was alright and – me and Samantha were in our cots – and – my dad looked – my dad could hear crack – crackling echoing round the room so – it was like creaking or something and they were looking around and my mum said John – like this – and there was a – big blue and yellow spider about that big – on the ceiling – and my dad panicked – he thought it might be poisonous so – it was like um – he got – he got my mum's high heel shoe and – ever so quickly – he walked up like this – and it moved and he jumped – he jumped back down – and it crawled all the way down the ceiling – mum – my mum was sort of like panicking and running out and um – he took a quick shot at it and got it in – the thing went straight through the spider.

The data can be used to confirm the view that speech is degenerate. Discontinuities abound: unfinished sentences – 'he thought it might be poisonous so – it was like um'; loops – 'I lived in Africa with my sister – and – Zimbabwe'; parenthetical explanations – 'it started rain – um – it was outside because it's so hot inside so – and it started raining'. There are self-corrections, pauses, fillers, generalisers – 'sort of thing', 'sort of like'. 'So' and 'and' are repeated continually. But if we accept that the means of utterance has a logic proper to its purposes and consider the speaker's position – wanting to tell a story to an audience which contains potential competitors for the floor about a highly personal incident which took place in a culture and climate unfamiliar to the listeners and whose main details the speaker has learned from hearsay – then the sense of pressure under which this boy's anecdote is delivered begins to emerge. Does he hesitate before he glosses 'Africa' as 'Zimbabwe' because he is unsure about the extent of his listeners' knowledge? Does he use 'and' and 'so' to signal his intent not to surrender the floor? How does he monitor his listeners' responses and level of shared assumptions in the explanation of African rainfall? Why, for instance, substitute 'rainfall' for 'rain', 'steaming hot' for 'steaming'?

These questions offer opportunities for students to rough out some of the relations between language and experience, and, if the process is sustained, to assist their language development and enable them to question assumptions and explore aspects of English significant to them.

We are only beginning to find out what aspects of language study are appropriate for learners' stages of cognitive and linguistic development, but we do know that highly general statements about language do not necessarily foster growth or understanding. Some activities, such as asking students to reshape a transcribed anecdote into a formal written account, work at a fairly low level of explicitness. Others, such as testing the validity of common assumptions about speech against a transcript, or exploring the motive behind a speaker's pauses, fillers, repetitions and false starts, require learners to externalise their intuitive knowledge to a greater degree.

Linguistics, operating at the higher levels of explicitness, draws a sharp line between what speakers know intuitively about language and what they do with that knowledge in concrete situations. Treating texts and utterances as realisations of an abstract system allows linguistics to construct itself as a coherent subject and to treat actual language performance as evidence of the nature of the underlying system. But language development moves continually between the poles of the competence-performance continuum in a dialectic made possible by the continuity between them. There is abundant evidence that in some sense children actively theorise about phonological, grammatical, semantic and pragmatic rules in acquiring language, and there is every reason to suppose that similar processes occur while 10- to 18-year-olds are learning a more sophisticated vocabulary, a wider range of functions for language or a greater variety of means for initiating and maintaining discourse. If we can understand how this works, we are in a position to give constructive support; if we cannot, then our interventions are likely to be pointless at best, stultifying at worst. A little of how this active hypothesising might work is seen in this story, written by Karen, a 12-year-old pupil in a London school:

Describe a Busy Market

It was cold, and was raining, Jack and Jane were walking, and talking about the film on TV last night. Jack said that it was a silly film, but Jane said it was romantic. Jane said the market would still be open and she really fancied a big bunch of grapes.

It was 5.30 and the market was like rush hour. There was a horrible smell of fish, people were shouting, pushing, and people were looking for bargains.

Jack noticed, well he could not help himself noticeing, five little puppies couped up in a little cage reddy to be sold to a big man very fat, and wareing a blue mack and a cap to match. Jack looked hard at the man's face.

'Come on Jack.'

They linked arms and went home.

Jane without her grapes, and Jack thinking about the puppies.

Karen

Karen's story is built on a series of images which carry a thematic contrast between the romantic and the realistic – Jane's and Jack's contrasting attitudes to the film; grapes and the smell of fish; the little puppies and the fat man. Jane's image of 'a big bunch of grapes' begins as a romantic whim. But seen as part of a distastefully acquisitive pattern of 'people . . . shouting, pushing . . . looking for bargains', and associated with the 'horrible smell of fish', the image loses its gloss, and is seen at its most unsavoury in the man buying the puppies, so that the transfer of meaning from a personal to a moral context reorganises the image and represents stages of Jane's, and perhaps therefore Karen's, disenchantment. The key to this discovery lies in the last line, an afterthought and grammatically part of 'They . . . went home', which subverts initial assumptions and transforms Karen's exploration of the meaning of 'romantic' into an exercise in practical semantics.

If we can keep sight of such early, intuitive attempts to map linguistic meanings onto experience, we can maintain a sense of the essentially human nature of language as its study becomes more objective, systematic and detached. What has long been a scandalous lacuna in the curriculum is now being filled as the possibilities for language study are realised in various ways. One significant framework for sixth form and FE courses, originally conceived by George Keith of North Cheshire College, is the syllabus for GCE Advanced Level English Language offered by the Joint Matriculation Board. This offers opportunities for students to write for a variety of purposes and audiences, to understand and rework texts for case studies, to undertake a project on language use and to explore such issues as the relation between language and society, how language varies and changes and how it is acquired. The course is assessed by a mixture of coursework and formal examination, and it operates on a consortium basis. The first candidates were examined, moderated and certificated in 1985; in 1986 the syllabus was scrutinised and approved, so any centre which can find or create a consortium can register with the JMB and set up a course.

Given that sixth form and FE students are neither miniature undergraduates nor apprentice theoretical linguists, one of the main problems for teachers of this syllabus is how to exploit their students' knowledge of language at its various levels of explicitness without mobilising folk-linguistics and prescriptivism, a task made more difficult by the lack of comprehensive and approachable published material with enough texts, examples and activities for classes to work out their own ideas. However, there is a general willingness to learn by sharing new approaches, and texts such as the following have proved to be useful starting-points.[3]

John-Crow[a]

(After 'L'Albatros' by Charles Baudelaire)

Some time, meck sport, young bwoy down a' Dungle[b]
Ketch john-crow, dem enarmous black bird
Dat fly all aroun', gliding all angle,
So beautiful an' happy-looking; out for dem food.

Once dey is tempted down wit' some little t'ing
Dese Bushas[c] of Sky come clumsy and shame!
Jus' hang down dem gargeous black wing
Drag in de dust like dem is lame.

Lawd! how dis bird so stupid and feeble,
So ugly! W'en up dere he was gran!
One a' de bwoy stone him wit' pebble;
Nex one mock how him stagger 'pon lan'.

Poet, man, is like dis Busha of Sky
Who ride hurricane, an' laugh after shot-gun;
Upon Earth dey scorn him, so easy fe' tie –
Him mighty wing' prevent him from run.

A.L. Hendricks

[a] A type of turkey-vulture, so known in Jamaica
[b] A slum area near the Kingston garbage-dump, portmanteau word 'Dung' and 'Jungle'
[c] Boss

Hendricks' poem raises issues which stimulate further discussion. Is it fair to adapt Baudelaire's poem in this way? Is the black john-crow an adequate symbolic equivalent of Baudelaire's white albatross? How do the other cultural 'translations' fare in the process of metamorphosis[4] – 'ces rois de l'azur' to 'Dese Bushas of Sky'; 'leurs grandes ailes blanches' to 'dem gargeous black wing'; 'la tempête' and 'l'archer' to 'hurricane' and 'shot-gun'? What is the social status of Creole in Jamaica and in the UK and why? What is the significance of Hendricks' choice of Jamaican Creole as the medium of translation when he could choose to write in Standard British English? How does Creole work in terms of phonology, lexis and grammar? How does the language of this poem compare with colloquial Patwa? What are the historical and linguistic relations between Creole and Standard British English? Would Hendricks' poem work without its reference to Baudelaire's?

Now that the study of English in the curriculum is no longer controlled by amateur grammarians, we have the opportunity to use texts like this, and many others previously considered unworthy of consideration, to open up significant areas. If we can develop in our students and ourselves the respect that comes from objectivity and well principled knowledge, acknowledging that the greater part of our understanding of language is, and always will be, intuitive, that linguistic snobbery is as contemptible as any other kind and that language is as complex and creative as the people who use it, we can learn to explore it and use its resources wisely.

REFERENCES

1 *New Musical Express*, 14 April 1984
2 Paul Johnson in the *Daily Telegraph*, 14 March 1984
3 *Poetry Review*, vol. 73, no.2, 1983
4 Baudelaire, Charles, *Les Fleurs du Mal*. Henri Lemaître (ed.), Garnier-Flammarion, 1964 edition.

TEACHERS LEARNING *THROUGH* LANGUAGE
Writing as well as talking

PAT D'ARCY

Pat D'Arcy worked in schools for 20 years, and now works as English Adviser for Wiltshire. She directed the Schools Council 'Reading for Meaning' project and now organises the Wiltshire 'Learning about Learning' project. She was Chairperson of NATE. Her publications include *Reading for Meaning* (Hutchinson, 1973); *Writing and Learning Across the Curriculum*, ed. Martin, Newton, D'Arcy, (Ward Lock 1976) and *What's Going On?* ed. Barr, D'Arcy, Healey (Heinemann Educational, 1982).

TEACHING *ABOUT* LANGUAGE

I can only speak for myself of course, but I have this vivid memory – of suddenly panicking in the summer holidays before I started work in my first school, about how on earth I would tackle teaching 'Language'. As an English Honours graduate I had no qualms (at that stage!) about how I would teach Literature, after all I had just spent three years prior to my PGCE training reading intensively and writing with enthusiasm about the novels, poems and plays of the authors I enjoyed.

I *had* also written one paper for my tutor in Old and Middle English, maintaining that grammatical rules were not inscribed on tablets of stone nor hurled to earth like thunderbolts; faced with my first teaching timetable I suddenly felt the need of such certainties to offer to my classes. I realised with horror that I had even forgotten the names for all seven (or was it eight?) parts of speech. I could remember, if I searched my memory, how to distinguish between phrases and clauses but I was no longer certain how many *kinds* of Adverbial Clauses there were.

What I did, quite practically, was to drop into Foyle's a week or so before school began and buy a couple of second hand grammars to refresh my memory. I soon became a dab hand at covering the blackboard in coloured chalk depicting Subject and Predicate, Verbs – Active and Passive, Finite and Infinite, Transitive and Intransitive. It was an elaborate game that I quite enjoyed, indeed my one Inspectorial visit in that first year, to decide whether or not I was fit to teach, happened to take in just such a board-covering lesson – I passed with flying colours!

The important question is, why had I forgotten all that knowledge *about* grammar and syntax which I thought I had learnt so thoroughly as a schoolgirl whose favourite subject was always English? The truth was that after I had taken my O-Levels, I no longer needed to consider such linguistic descriptions because they never consciously helped me to formulate thoughts or feelings. I never once, for instance, considered whether I should include a Noun Clause in Apposition – or an Adverbial Phrase of Manner. With my attention fixed on the meaning that I was seeking to express in response to a text (or more rarely in writing for myself), I was content to listen to the words as they rose, already structured, into my consciousness. On re-reading what thus appeared on the page, if it sounded confused or imprecise, then I would dip back again into a tacit search for alternative forms of expression.

I had only needed to know *about* the 'rules' of English grammar and syntax because I would be asked about them in an exam! Similarly my pupils at the Girls' Grammar School to which I was about to attach myself, would be expected in *their* O-Level English Language Paper to recognise a preposition from a pronoun and a compound from a complex sentence. I like to think that they also quite enjoyed gazing at my many diagrams rainbowed across the board but I doubt very much whether any of that 'knowledge' helped any of them to shape new meanings for themselves any more than in my school days it did for me.

I guess that my experience as a post-graduate student about to enter 'the profession' was not uncommon. Teachers usually feel more confident when they have something to teach *about*; as I look back now, however, across thirty years of English teaching, working with pupils for the first twenty and with teachers for the last ten, I realise more clearly than I did then, that teaching *about* does not necessarily lead to learning *about*, and that what is taught must have significance and value for the learner as well as for the teacher, if it is to be understood and remembered.

The ways in which primary and secondary teachers are encouraged (or required) to present knowledge about language may of course be clothed differently nowadays; after all, fashions change. The expectation may be that we teach about 'registers' or 'semiotics' or 'information technology' or the *model* of language that the Kingman Committee comes up with. Whatever the approach, if it is *about* language it seems likely that the stance will be an 'observational' one, requiring pupils to look *at* language from a standpoint which does not engage them simultaneously with grasping or searching for the meanings which lie behind and run through the words they hear or see. Meaning is quicksilver and elusive, often lurking below the net of words that seeks to capture it – studying the visible structure of the net may reveal interesting patterns but these are not the rich trawl that writer or reader is seeking to enmesh. Nor in my view will a knowledge of net patterns enable the fisher-for-meaning to make a good catch.

TEACHERS VERBALISING

An alternative to standing back and looking at – is plunging in. What is so valuable about our human ability to verbalise is that the act itself takes us beyond our present understandings towards new discoveries. Rather than halting the brain's flow of language for closer inspection, we should use its driving power to carry us – and our pupils – forward. The representation of experience is a creative act, never merely a repetition. As James Britton puts it:

> . . . what is organised is far more than words. Woven into its fabric are representations of many kinds: images directly presented by the senses, images that are interiorized experiences of sight, sound, movement, touch, smell and taste: pre-verbal patterns reflecting feeling responses and elementary value judgements: post-verbal patterns, our ideas and reasoned beliefs about the world . . .

This process of making new discoveries about the way we perceive ourselves and the world we inhabit, through talking and writing, listening or reading, is as necessary for teachers as it is for their pupils. As we know, however, teachers spend more time talking than listening – and reading than writing. Most English teachers I know have always been willing to talk enthusiastically about the latest book they've read; until recently I rarely came across one who talked with similar enthusiasm about her own writing. . . . Yet, as Frank Smith enjoys pointing out, children will not believe writing is a powerful and exciting process unless they come across other people in their lives who become powerfully excited when they write! Children, Smith says, are great club joiners – but only if there is a club around which looks sufficiently attractive to join.

Every year for seven years now, small groups of primary and secondary teachers in my county have given up a precious week of their summer holiday in order to become learners again together. Across age groups and across the curriculum, these teachers have taken part in many of the activities which happen in their own classrooms: sorting objects for common and diverse attributes, making Venn diagrams, making music, carrying out experiments in physics, investigating the lungs of a sheep, making batik, marbling, role playing, struggling with recalcitrant computers . . . Threading through every activity, has been the talking and the writing that helped the group arrive at new perceptions about the classroom experiences they were sharing with each other.

What our 'Learning about Learning' weeks have always revealed, is that teachers are far more confident as talkers than as writers. When it comes to exploring and shaping thoughts and feelings about which they are uncertain on paper (or on the screen), initially they freeze – seize up in much the same way that many of their pupils do. They suddenly become acutely aware that writing is visible, unlike talk which vanishes comfortably into thin air. . . . Like me, other teachers have dimly recollected memories of rules about written language which they fear may betray them into inconsistencies which talk doesn't reveal. They have forgotten – or perhaps never found out – that writing can help us to rediscover what we already 'know' and beyond that rediscovery, can take us into the exploration of new territory. They have forgotten that it is possible *through* writing to express uncertainty and confusion. Unless teachers become aware of this reconstructive power of writing for themselves, their approach to written work in their own classrooms will remain prescriptive – teaching about and commenting on, rather than encouraging pupils to plunge into talking and writing as a means of helping their individual efforts to 'make sense' of experience.

Here is what one teacher wrote after she had taken part in our first 'Learning about Learning' Summer Institute in July, 1980:

> I hadn't really written anything for years. I had scribbled notes, tried my hand at the odd poem but nothing that had to be shared with an audience, even of one! Now I was told that I had to write and what is more I had to share my writing . . .
>
> What does one usually do in such circumstances? Most people frantically search through their memory banks trying to recall a model previously established by past experience – in my case a pattern indelibly printed on my brain by a succession of English teachers and lecturers. It was all so simple according to them. In the introduction to any piece of writing the 'main idea' was outlined, in subsequent paragraphs this main idea was developed to hammer home the point (whatever that was) and finally, mercifully, came the conclusion, in which the whole thing was summed up, a sort of 'there, I told you so'.
>
> Now I was being asked to consider writing as a learning process. How did my prescribed model fit this new function? I started to write but as I wrote the model became increasingly irksome. The need for meticulous structure, for precise sentences, vetted mentally before they were allowed to arrive on the page, now proved positively repressive. As I struggled to make my meaning clear, syntactical structures, not ideas, defied me. The thoughts flowed too quickly.
>
> If I had stopped or slowed down to organise the syntax, some ideas escaped and were lost. So for the first time I abandoned 'the rules' and just sat and simply wrote. I learnt to sit and record my stream of thought and in doing so, I discovered a new freedom as a writer. Gone were the constraints I had accepted as part of the writing chore!

MEANING-MAKING: PATTERNS OF DEVELOPMENT

That teacher had rediscovered what it feels like to plunge into the current of language when it is flowing fast as thoughts take shape – and to allow herself, at that stage, to be carried along without trying to control every swirl and eddy. That is not to suggest however that talkers and writers should never be encouraged to reflect upon the words they utter aloud or on paper. The understandings for which we strive often require many attempts at re-wording as we seek to clarify our confusions or capture the complexities of thought and feeling. But in order to re-vise, we need to have something to look back over! What Sue was finding problematic was her attempt to generate new thoughts and *simultaneously* to edit them into a final form.

Looking back again to my own school days, I remember how I was encouraged to make the assumption that it was inappropriate to write anything down until I had 'got it clear' inside my head first. I was always a fast writer and a good speller, so the mechanics weren't a problem – but for many children, grappling with the technicalities of the language at the same time as seeking to clarify their understanding, is a task too Herculean to be borne. No wonder many pupils (not to mention many adults long past school age), regard themselves as hopeless writers! My fear is that now talk has come to the attention of the Examining Boards the same unattainable demands will unthinkingly be made, selfconsciously to edit at the point of utterance, thus rendering many more children similarly unconfident about their powers of speech. I am uncomfortably reminded of Herb Kohl's jibe – that if schools were to be made responsible for teaching children how to walk and talk we'd have more dumb cripples around . . .

In the Wiltshire 'Learning about Learning' Project, what our 'plunging in' has taught us as writers and as talkers, is that journeys towards new understanding take time and that often the exploratory stage takes the most time of all if the richness of past experience is to be recollected and new ideas are to be formed. American researchers such as Donald Murray, Donald Graves, James Moffett, Ken Macrorie and the teachers and students (aged 5-50+) with whom they have worked, all agree that where the writer's focal awareness is directed to the shaping of meaning, definable stages of development occur. These have been variously referred to as Rehearsal, First Draft, Revision; Fluency, Coherence, Correctness; Exploration, Drafting, Editing for Meaning, Editing for Mechanics, Re-presenting. Whatever the terms, there is the recognition that such journeys do have recognisable landmarks and that some activities (such as correcting spellings) are inappropriate, even damaging in the early stages. If on the other hand, the writer's (or the talker's) focal awareness is directed towards 'getting it right', on the grounds that correct handling of the medium takes precedence over the message, then we shall continue to foster an apprehension about language and how it should be used, for continuing generations of schoolchildren.

The diagram on the opposite page was recently constructed by Gillian Clarkson, one of our first 'Learning about Learning' teachers. Gill is currently seconded in a joint capacity to Wiltshire's Oracy and Writing Projects and she works with primary and secondary teachers across the curriculum. I find her diagram a useful reminder of the wide range of opportunities for both talking and writing that teachers need to offer to children if they are to become confident in their own search for fresh perceptions and further understanding. It illustrates clearly how necessary it is to provide different contexts for different stages in the pupil's learning. Neither talking nor writing can be divorced from the emerging meanings that each activity is calling forth – and taught separately as Talking and Writing, as though they were the moulds into which thought is subsequently poured.

The Bullock Report emphasised throughout that, whatever the language mode involved, pupils (and adults) become better talkers, listeners, writers and readers through engaging in those activities purposefully and meaningfully. I spend time in many classrooms in which children are constantly encouraged to break new ground through talking and writing about what they see and do and feel and think. In these classrooms there are no stacks of printed exercises for children to 'practise' on, neither do they produce one off, title first, pieces of writing in exercise books. Instead they and their teachers approach the business of moving to new understandings as a shared enterprise. Children are encouraged to respond to each other as well as to the teacher – through talk and through writing.

Often they keep their own or sometimes a joint 'think book' in which they are free to recollect, to reflect, to ask questions and express confusions. . . . Such entries provide a good basis for further talk and further writing but most of all for further thought. They are never 'marked' for mechanical correctness nor are they 'assessed' by the teacher for 'quality'. Whatever a child writes in a think book is welcomed for the seeds of further possibilities that it contains. Frequently the teacher keeps her own journal, to catch her ideas too, about what is happening in her classroom and is equally willing to share those thoughts with the individuals that comprise the 'class'. The teacher is signalling to her five- or 15-year-olds that writing, like talk, is first and foremost an activity which generates useful thoughts for the writer. One 10-year-old boy wrote in his journal: 'I like think-writing it kind of kick starts your brain.' Another child called it 'brainwaving'.

As we often realise to our cost, far more children have already achieved a competence as talkers, before they ever arrive in school, that many will never attain as writers in their entire lives. It is important that those of us

TEACHERS LEARNING *THROUGH* LANGUAGE

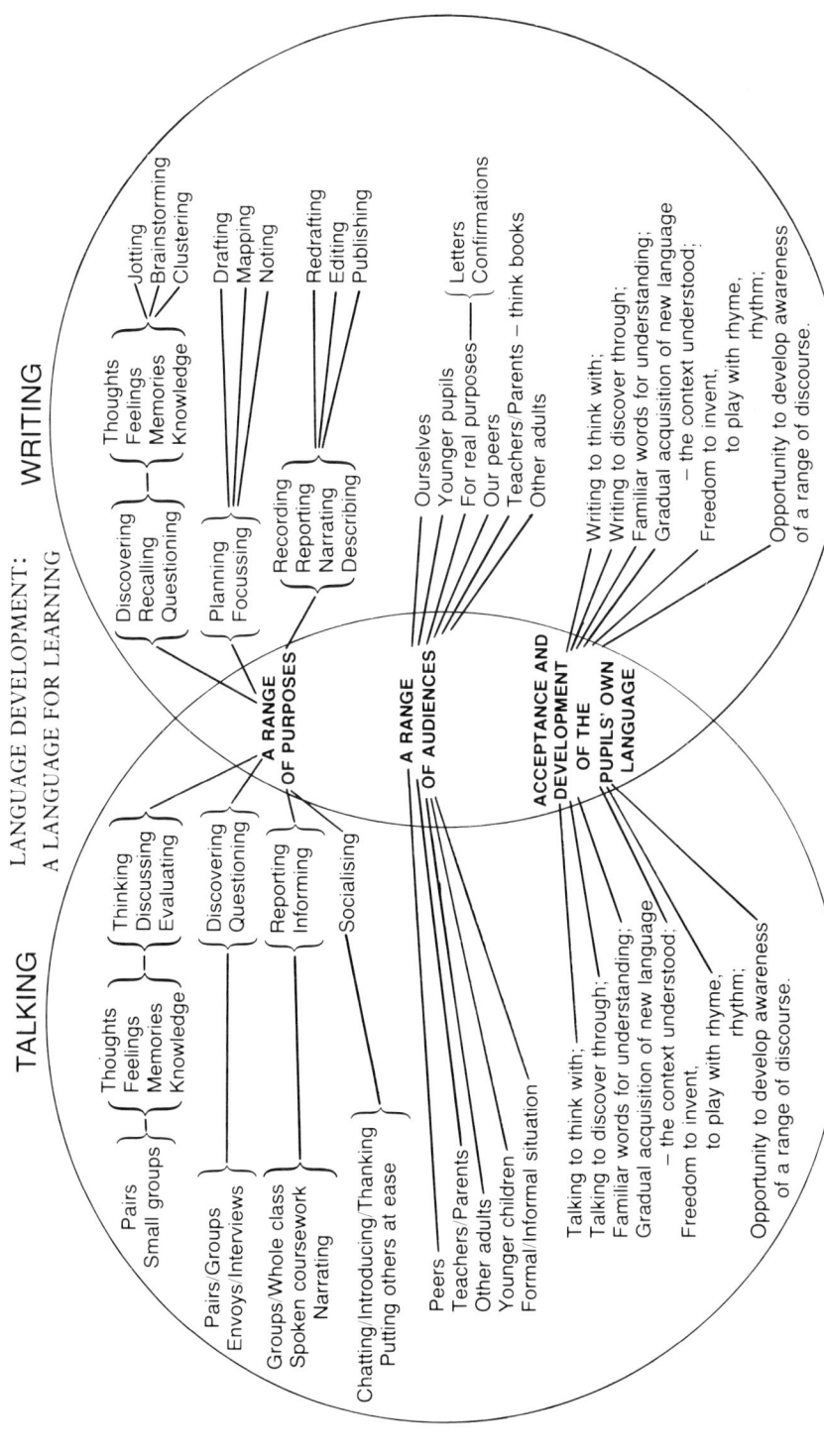

CREATING HELPFUL CONTEXTS FOR LANGUAGE USERS IN THE CLASSROOM

who care about education continue to ask ourselves why this should be so. What happens in our classrooms that so deprives children of confidence that they fear and mistrust writing not decreasingly but increasingly? Is it too little teaching or too much? In our conscientious concern to help children towards competence have we perhaps instead created an obstacle race by imposing editorial constraints from an early age and frequently adding a time limit too: 'I want all these essays finished by . . .'.

I remember the title for one of Donald Graves' early papers was something like 'Let Children Show us What They Know'. In classrooms where teachers are now willing to take part, to talk and to write *with* the children rather than *at* them, the collaborative nature of the whole enterprise encourages pupils not only to rediscover what they know already, but with persistence and excitement to pursue their discoveries further. In such classrooms children are not rendered powerless by the powerful, they are reminded constantly of their own powers: to recollect, to reconstruct and to re-present through language and through art, through non-verbal sounds and symbols as well as through words; all forms of expression are available to them for experiments in meaning-shaping. Their teachers are learning more about the possibilities that such activities hold out to pupils as they too become involved in the doing – not standing back but plunging in: 'And as I watched them, e'r I knew, I'd stripped and I was swimming too . . .'. I can only hope that the deliberation of the Kingman Committee will result in a view of language – and an approach to verbalising in the classroom – which recognises its dynamism. Fuelled by the individual's search for meaning, language flows. Cut off from such a search it becomes merely 'stuff' and often very unmanageable stuff at that.

ACKNOWLEDGEMENTS

I am indebted to the following writers for their willingness to shape and to share their insights into the nature of language, especially language 'on the move':

JAMES BRITTON, *Language and Learning*, Penguin, 1970
ANN BERTHOFF, *The Making of Meaning*, Boynton Cook, 1981
DONALD GRAVES, *Writing: teachers and children at work*, Heinemann, 1983
SUE JACKSON, *The Way Ahead*
GABRIEL JACOBS, *When Children Think*, Teachers' College of Columbia University, 1970
KEN MACRORIE, *A Vulnerable Teacher* and *Uptaught*, Boynton Cook, 1974, 1970
JAMES MOFFETT, *Coming on Center*, Boynton Cook, 1981
DONALD MURRAY, *Write to Learn*, Holt, Rinehart and Winston, 1987 and *Learning by Teaching*, Boynton Cook, 1982
FRANK SMITH, *Writing and the Writer*, Heinemann, 1982

Most of all I am indebted to the teachers in primary, middle and secondary classrooms with whom I work, who have shown me how we can all continue to learn more about the nature and the power of language, through their thoughtful engagement with those most active of all learners, the children.

MINISTERING TO THEIR NEEDS?

An analysis of Kenneth Baker and George Walden on language and literature

PETER TRAVES

> Peter Traves is English Adviser for Waltham Forest, having taught previously in ILEA. He has contributed to radio and television programmes on Caribbean Literature and written regularly for the *English Magazine*. Essays of his appear in *Eccentric Propositions*, ed. J. Miller and in *Multi-Cultural Education*, ed. M. Straker-Welds.

Any attempt to tease out the underlying assumptions about language and literature in the statements of Mr Baker and Mr Walden is fraught with difficulty. The central problem is that what we have available is not a clear and cool piece of analytical thinking but rather a series of polemical statements, anecdotes and veiled references to research. It is important that we bear in mind the fact that both ministers have involved themselves in polemical argument and not in academic discourse. What they have offered us is a succession of carefully timed speeches aimed at effecting the most favourable possible reception for overtly political initiatives. This is hardly surprising given the fact that both of them have made clear at other times their commitment to a government and a party which intends to extract the maximum possible political mileage out of education. The Tory Party clearly perceived a potential threat to its electoral chances in the widespread disquiet expressed over such issues as industrial strife in schools and the government's apparent lack of concern for public education. Under Kenneth Baker's leadership they have launched a concerted campaign to seize the moral and political initiative from their critics. It has been a ruthless and cynical campaign fought for very high stakes and it has to be said that, in its own terms, it has been very successful. Consequently, we would be naive to wring our hands in despair if we detect the heavy hand of distortion and selectivity in what they have to say. It is not part of their concern to present a balanced and considered assessment. They take that which suits their purpose and carefully delete that which might call into question the values and practices they wish to promote.

For example in his Alan Palmer lecture Mr Baker fulsomely praises:

a wonderful senior English teacher at a school in Suffolk which achieves notable results in creative and imaginative poetry. She stressed to me the importance of reading aloud to children; of reading stories and poems, of making children familiar with the beauty and intricacies of language, of encouraging children to read language aloud. And she comes up with the goods.

What Mr Baker does not mention is that the same teacher is wholeheartedly committed to mixed ability teaching, a methodology Mr Baker has ridiculed at other times, sneering at it as a system that produces only mediocrity.

I think therefore that we need to take full cognisance of the context within which the Kingman Committee has been set up and this means that any analysis of the Baker–Walden statements has to go beyond a purely literary or linguistic framework. Having accepted this it is still a difficult task as what they have said constitutes a curious mixture of crude utilitarianism and half-digested sub-Leavisite romanticism. On the one hand we have a near full-blooded 'language development for the needs of commerce' model, especially in the utterances of Mr Walden, and on the other, a muddled mish-mash of ideas about the relationship between language, nationality, and culture which forms the central part of Mr Baker's Palmer lecture.

In November 1986 Mr Walden gave a lecture at a conference of the National Association of Teachers in Further and Higher Education. The DES preamble to the text of that lecture was significantly entitled '"Language means business" says George Walden'. The main concern of the speech is the learning of foreign languages and the role that they could and should play in commercial life. The word 'relevance' is used only to refer to the commercial advantages accruing from the acquisition of a second language. Mr Walden makes a number of very significant references to the place of English in this enterprise. He says, 'I am sure that it is easier to learn a foreign language, especially a highly inflected one, if one is more closely acquainted with the structure of one's own. That is why we as a Government have set great store by improving standards of English in our schools. As you know, only last week, Kenneth Baker announced the establishment of an inquiry into the teaching of English in our schools.'

The first assumption Mr Walden makes is that a knowledge of the structure of one's own language will help in the learning of a foreign language. It is an assumption that he feels does not need support: he can simply assert, 'I am sure'. This kind of appeal to an agreed common sense forms a considerable part of the foundations of the thinking of both Walden and Baker. Language is rule-governed, it has a structure, so therefore isn't it logical that a knowledge of the rules will facilitate a more effective acquisition of languages? This is a lot less certain than it sounds.

In fact we have tried something very like this before and it failed. For many years the main method in foreign language teaching stressed the need to master grammatical structures before attempting to facilitate fluency in speech. At the same time a large part of English work consisted of exercises along the lines of clause analysis. It was not a successful combination.

Mr Walden makes a very explicit causal link between the desire for a greater concentration on linguistic structure in English teaching, in order to facilitate the acquisition of foreign languages, and the fact that the Secretary of State has announced the setting up of the Kingman Committee: 'That is why we as a Government have set great store by improving standards of English in our schools. As you know, only last week, Kenneth Baker announced the establishment of an inquiry into the teaching of English.' In Mr Walden's mind the case is very simple. We need to be more commercially competitive. Our commerce will profit if our business people are more fluent in the languages of our trading partners. We learn foreign languages through close attention to their rules and structures. We will be able to do this better if we are trained to analyse the structure of our own language. Consequently we need to bring English teaching into line with this view of things. Therefore a committee of inquiry has been set up. Such a view of language and language acquisition is a profoundly flawed and impoverished one. It is a model of language that reduces it to the crudest of tools, a tool to be developed and manipulated in the most superficial fashion. It allows no room for the complex web of relationships that binds language to social and historical factors. The sad thing is that we have failed to make this insight sufficiently accessible and sufficiently widely known.

Mr Walden was addressing a conference which took as its central theme the relationship between language and commerce so it might seem unfair to put too much weight on the fact that commercial need forms the cornerstone of his argument. We need therefore to set these remarks in the context of the government's approach to education in general. The speeches of Mr Walden and Mr Baker, the setting up of the Kingman Committee, and the concern for a centralised curriculum are not isolated initiatives. They need to be seen against a background of things like YOPS, YTS, vocational and pre-vocational courses, and the proposed City Technology Colleges which will be funded in partnership with private enterprise. They need to be seen also in the light of the growing pressure for education to justify its existence largely in terms of its relevance to the needs of industry and commerce. Finally, they need to be set in the whole context of Mrs Thatcher's drive for a new 'broad based capitalism, a new entrepreneurial culture'.

It is vital that we take note of what Mr Walden has said for it reveals the mainspring of the government's education policy. Our main task it seems will be to equip students for the market-place; the rest of what we do is just frills. The frills might be pretty but they are just frills in the end. Such a view of education might well be described as 'common sense' in so far as it has entered popular consciousness at a very deep level. It is a virtually unquestioned assumption though it may express itself in many different forms. It is the common sense of a broad cross-section of our society and it cuts across barriers of class, race and gender. Educationalists have tended to respond by appealing to a liberal and humane rationale for schooling. Such a rationale has a poor cutting edge and we need to realign our attack. Parents and pupils who see contracting job opportunities for school leavers are not likely to be convinced by arguments about the need to fulfil the child's human potential. It is time we made 'access to power' the central thrust of our argument, and that would include economic power but would go beyond it to include political and cultural power as well.

It is of course unusual to find such a bald statement of aims as Mr Walden gives us. It is more common, as is the case with Mr Baker, for the utilitarian commercial motive to be mixed in with a more humane or humanistic approach. Let me make it clear that I do not see this as a shrewd conspiracy to deceive. The fact is that a series of apparently contradictory strands of thinking have become bound together. Mr Baker is clearly a man who has a deep and abiding love for literature. It would be churlish to deny that his references to books go far beyond the obligatory nod towards 'culture' of the kind we might expect from Mrs Thatcher. He even goes so far as to indulge his own tastes in the texts he refers to and his affection for particular writers, especially poets, is very noticeable. If George Walden represents a fairly brutal form of 'common sense', Kenneth Baker might be said to exemplify a 'cultured common sense'. Ironically this makes the contradictions in his thinking far more obvious, although it also makes him a more formidable opponent in other ways. He is formidable because he can appeal to the language we have grown accustomed to describe as our own; the language of humane and informed literary criticism. He has hi-jacked the languages of both post-Leavisite criticism and of progressive education. In so doing he has been forced to conceal the fundamental contradiction between the apparently humane and enlightened appeals to a literary heritage and education and the mechanistic vision of market forces that underlies his political thinking. He is able to mask this contradiction by using a language which has been purged of political commitment and which, though it has been traditionally associated with an appeal to the imagination and the individual, and has frequently ranged itself against the forces of mechanistic dehumanisation, was never firmly anchored to any sympathetic political thought or action and has now been appropriated by its erstwhile opponents. One of the difficulties in grappling with what Mr Baker is saying is that to a large extent we feel at ease with the language he uses. In fact we cannot repossess that language and use it against him without fighting at a severe disadvantage. We need to redefine the terms and use a language appropriate to them. Such a language must be firmly rooted in a more analytical and committed analysis of social, cultural and political issues.

Mr Baker's Alan Palmer Lecture at Pangbourne College, Berkshire, was delivered on the 7th November 1986. It was the occasion on which he announced his intention of setting up a committee to look into the teaching of English. It is a very revealing, if rather muddled, piece of work. Mr Baker's central concern is with the contribution of the English language to a sense of national identity, to what he calls 'the Englishness of England'. He makes an immediate appeal to the language as a point of fixity in a rapidly changing world. 'Its role in our national life is probably more important today than ever before, for the simple reason that it endures at a time which has seen so much that characterised our country change and disappear.'

Such an appeal is immensely powerful. It draws on several of our deepest emotional resources. In particular it refers to a vision of the past in which the way of life of the English had a sense of continuity that went back to time immemorial. Blake's 'green and pleasant land' as Mr Baker calls it. A largely rural England with rural values. A settled people with a settled way of life that is now disappearing beneath the clamorous changes of the modern era. Only our language, the English language of Shakespeare, Milton and Wordsworth remains to anchor us to our ancestral rural origins. It is a powerful appeal and must be recognised as such. In part of course it draws on a deeply personal myth which most of us carry, of a time in our own past, usually in our childhood, which we often reconstruct as a period of relative simplicity and security. The fact that it may bear little or no resemblance to what we actually experienced at the time does nothing to undermine the force of this myth. This construction of our own past makes us more susceptible to the appeal of a similar construction of our national history.

But what period of history in our past is Mr Baker implicitly referring to and what were those characteristics of 'our country' which have changed or disappeared? The rural England he refers to, but does not define, was not in fact a place of fixed and unchanging values or lifestyles. Our conception of the English countryside is a relatively recent one, dating largely from the eighteenth and nineteenth centuries. Timeless, rural England was never an achieved fact. What has characterised our history is change. One has only to read Bishop Latimer's sixteenth-century 'Sermon of the Plough' to see how far back the nostalgia for a secure past which kept faith with its forefathers goes. Later in Hardy's *Under the Greenwood Tree* we see the profound sense of loss at the apparent dissolution of a settled rural culture that has characterised the English response to the history of the countryside and its people throughout the centuries. Each age has placed its own bewildering complexity against a settled past; a past always just beyond immediate memory. Furthermore, such a view of the past has always been related very closely to our own sense of national identity.

What does Mr Baker mean by 'the English' and what are the threatened characteristics of their way of life? Historically how far back do we have to go to find the quintessentially English nation he sees as under threat? Who is included in this English nation? Perhaps more significantly, who is excluded? 'What is it that constitutes a nation?' asks Mr Baker. Significantly he begins to search for his answer in a series of contrasting literary descriptions of England and its people. The way he uses these passages is extremely revealing.

He begins with a quotation from George Orwell:

> When you come back to England from any foreign country you have immediately the sensation of breathing a different air. . . . The clatter of clogs in the Lancashire Mill towns, the to and fro of lorries on the Great North Road, the queues outside the Labour Exchanges, the rattle of the pin tables in the Soho pubs, the old maids biking to holy communion through the mists of the autumn mornings. All these are not only fragments but characteristic fragments of the English scene.

One question to ask is, what might Orwell have meant by this? What did he expect his readers to respond to when he referred to 'the clatter of clogs' or 'the queues outside the Labour Exchanges'? As a socialist it is unlikely that he would have regarded these features as part of the 'timeless patchwork' of English life. They were characteristics of England in 1946 and the dole queues were the product of a particular social, economic and political history, a history that human beings have made and can challenge.

A second question is, what might this mean to Kenneth Baker and his Pangbourne College audience? It is presented here as if these details were rather quaint manifestations of our national character. There is a total absence of the political, social or economic factors which determined and shaped their development. They are there because that is the way we are, and that is the way things are. Poverty and unemployment exist as part of the time-honoured fabric of our way of life, they are the product of an immutable law of economic reality, not because we live in a system that allows them to continue to exist in the midst of ever greater general wealth.

Mr Baker then moves back to Chesterton and 'the slow growth of great parks, the dark enrichment of red wine in cellars and inns, all the leisure of the life of England throughout many centuries'. What we have here is an historical nonsense rendered into elegant prose. The 'great parks' he refers to were often the result of violent disruptions in the lives of the villagers and small farmers who were moved off the land. Far from being representative of continuity and maturation, they were in fact the product of sharp change and dislocation. Chesterton's measured prose excludes the life experience of the vast majority of people who toiled in virtual leisurelessness throughout the 'many centuries' of English history. Like other writers, T.S. Eliot and D.H. Lawrence among them, who have affected to make sweeping generalisations about the past, Chesterton too often substitutes sonorous sentimentality for a rigorous historical analysis. Yet all our literary training makes it difficult for us to admit that what we have here is simply daft, or ignorant, or at times in the case of Eliot or Lawrence, downright unpleasant.

Mr Baker then goes back another hundred years or so to Cobbett 'writing of the forced sale of a farmhouse which must have been in my own Surrey constituency'.

> When the old farm houses are down (and down they must come in time) what a miserable thing the country will be. Those that are now erected are mere painted shells, with a Mistress within, who is stuck up in a place she calls a parlour, with, if she has children, the 'young ladies and gentlemen' about her . . . The children (which is the worst part of it) are all too clever to work: they are all to be gentlefolks. Go to plough! Good God! What, 'young gentlemen' go to the plough! They become clerks, or some skimmy-dish thing or other. They flee from the dirty work as cunning horses do from the bridle. What misery is all this.

What might we respond to in this text? Certainly we can take pleasure in the aggressive, assertive prose which launches into the 'Mistress within, who is stuck up in a place she calls a parlour'. Kenneth Baker clearly sees it as an elegant piece of writing, a description I find curiously at odds with the attacking colloquial style. But surely what we need to respond to is the anger, the commitment and the despair which finally explodes in 'What misery is all this.' Behind the single event, which is after all a *forced* sale, we glimpse once again the process of change that has characterised our rural history. Not only that but more specifically the dispossession of those who live on and work the land by those who see it simply as an asset to be invested in and exploited. Mr Baker does not respond to this. He makes no mention of the historical processes that led to a situation where the countryside became depopulated and where the prestige of the lowliest of clerical work was raised above that of the most purposeful manual labour. He seems blissfully unaware here of the Cobbett who despised the encroaching power of the City, 'the placemen and the jobbers'. The anger and the purpose of the writing have been defused or deflected by a concentration on the timeless quality of the human characteristics Mr Baker supposes them to describe: 'Unemployment and Cobbett's complaint about young people taking skimmy-dish jobs has a contemporary ring to it – it is referred to now less elegantly as deindustrialisation.' The collapse of our manufacturing industry is not the same as the processes Cobbett witnessed even if some of the results bear a superficial similarity. What we have from Mr Baker is a response to literature which is divorced from any sense of the history within which that literature was produced.

He concludes this section with a brief reference to that most abused of texts, 'Jerusalem'; 'Blake, at the beginning of the Industrial Revolution, spoke of England's green and pleasant land.' What follows is the assertion that while much has changed, many features remain the same;

> Wars have been fought and won, an Empire was built up and dismantled and, ever since Orwell's days, the clogs have now gone. But we have unemployment and Cobbett's complaint about young people taking skimmy-dish jobs has a contemporary ring to it – it is referred to now less elegantly as deindustrialisation – and the glory of Blake's landscape has just about survived the threat of the developers, scientific farming and Dutch Elm disease.'

The inclusion of Dutch Elm disease alongside developers and scientific farming has a subtle but nevertheless decisive effect on the meaning. All three can now be viewed as 'natural' events, disasters that strike the countryside and over which society has no control and for which it has no responsibility. Developers and scientific farmers, however, are not incidental to our national way of life. They do not represent either a natural disaster, in the way Dutch Elm disease does, or an historical aberration. In fact they are a logical development of an economic system that regards everything, human or non-human, living or inanimate, as a resource to be exploited. It is fascinating the way in which the same man can wax eloquent about the threats to our landscape and can sympathise with Cobbett or Blake in their opposition to its exploitation, and at the same time can also be an enthusiastic member of a government that can contemplate selling off even the water supplies we depend on. It is a sharp example of the way in which we have allowed our responses to literature to be divorced from our responses to the rest of life and of the way in which we have attempted to wrench our understanding of culture and national identity away from any analysis of history and historical process.

For Mr Baker what survives and unifies is the English language. It is 'the thing that has held them (the English people) over the centuries . . . so the people of England, wherever they came from in the first place (Scandinavia, Ireland, France, Eastern Europe, Asia or the Caribbean) have been bound together by the English language.' There is, of course, a great deal in this. Language is a major constituent of a sense of national identity. A shared language was a hugely important factor in the forging of nation states, particularly in Europe and, in some instances, notably those of Italy and Germany, for many centuries it was almost the only expression of unity those people had available to them. However, the expression 'bound together' is a more complex one than it appears at first sight. Kenneth Baker uses the phrase to express the achievement of a harmonious sense of national identity. A common language has enabled people to rise above less significant differences to share an agreed, if not explicit, sense of nationhood. Historically this is not a tenable view to take, though once again it exercises a powerful pull on our emotions, on our 'common sense'. Language has not in fact produced a single unified English people all speaking the same language. What we have is an uneasy hegemony in which the languages of many groups were suppressed or pushed to the margins. The Welsh, the Irish and the Scots were almost literally 'bound' to the English and one of the strands of their captivity was language. The people of the Caribbean who came from African descent were not drawn into the family of our language as welcome newcomers. Rather they were brutally cut off from their own linguistic background and, in the process of their survival and resistance, forged their own 'English' language. Nor do all the speakers of English participate on equal terms in the hegemony of a national culture. Language divides as well as unifies. It marks off boundaries of place and class and plays a major role in 'naturalising' the domination of men over women. Such an analysis plays no part in Mr Baker's speech where he talks of the language as 'a living thing, healthy and robust enough to thrive in taprooms, pulpits and senior commonrooms'.

What then of the role of education in all this? Mr Baker likens language to a garden which needs care and attention: 'It needs cultivation and I am not at all happy that this is happening.' It is clear from what follows that it is the role of teachers to nurture the language and they are not doing so effectively. In response to the discussion paper *English from 5 to 16* the teachers, according to Mr Baker, failed to present a unified concept of language education. There is probably a great deal of truth in that. However the first thing that strikes me is the dubious nature of the original analogy. Language is nothing like a garden and historically it has never been cultivated in the organised and methodical way in which a garden might be. Language itself is an immensely complex phenomenon and its development is always closely associated with other factors in human history. The English language did not develop under the guardianship of schools or scholars, it survived and flourished for over a thousand years before widespread education was available to its speakers. Nor was it the product of a few gifted literary geniuses. It was, and is, the product of all the men and women who have ever spoken or written it. This is not to deny that our language has been influenced by the advent of compulsory education and general literacy but rather to argue that its survival or its quality is not likely to be determined primarily in the classroom. The factors which shape the development and health of the language as a whole are far too complex and far too powerful to be directed by teachers. Teachers have a more tangible, if less exalted, responsibility. Teachers can make a major contribution to the insights children have into language. They can facilitate the development a child makes in talk, writing and reading. What they cannot do is act as 'gardeners' in the cultivation of the whole language of a people. Mr Baker is badly confused on this point.

Where the Secretary of State is on stronger ground, and where in fact I find I agree with him, is in the potential of schools to encourage a more enthusiastic approach to reading. Individual schools and even individual teachers can have a remarkable effect on the way children look upon reading and on the amount of reading for pleasure they actually do. Where he goes wrong is when he tries to explain the apparent reluctance of children to read and when he tries to draw wider implications out of this.

In attempting to explain the decline in enthusiasm for reading many children exhibit as they get older Mr Baker says:

> We should not be surprised by this because it does not require long and painstaking research; it does not require careful penetrating analysis; it does not require nationwide opinion polls covering all ages, sexes and social classes to discover that a person cannot look at television and at the same time read a book. And there is no doubt that children spend a lot of time looking at television. The study of 'Popular TV and School Children' published by my Department in 1983 indicated that young people between 5 and 14 years of age spend an average of 23 hours per week watching television – that's about a fifth of the waking hours in a week.

This is a popular analysis and one that teachers themselves often subscribe to. In fact there is no real evidence of a causal link between the two. The question to ask is not 'how much television do children watch?' but 'has it in fact replaced reading as the main leisure time pursuit of the great majority of teenagers?' Was there a golden age in the past when millions of 15-year-olds hurried home from school to read *David Copperfield* all evening and every evening? Probably not. Ironically I think that this is one occasion when Mr Baker could have put more blame on schools and less on the dreaded box, for it is school which shapes the child's conception of what kind of an exercise reading is. The truth is that for too much of the time and for far too many children reading is experienced as either a dull routine activity or as a forbidding task. Reading is usually done on the teacher's terms – he or she chooses the text, the purpose and the conditions under which it is done.

Difficulty with reading is regarded as a dreadful thing and is identified as early as possible in the child's school career. That identification is an experience many children never live down. It does not have to be like this in schools, as many notable exceptions have shown, and we do deserve to be challenged on this issue. Mr Baker unfortunately largely misses the point and goes off at an ever more eccentric and ill-informed tangent.

He enters enthusiastically into the literature versus television debate and champions the power of the written over the visual image:

> But literature, the reading of good books, is in many important ways a superior, richer and deeper experience than watching television. A particular feature of the written or spoken word in isolation from visual image is the unique demand it makes upon the imagination. Written or spoken poetry and prose stimulates and enriches the imagination of the listener or reader. He cannot make sense of what he sees or hears without the full play of imagination. A society whose imagination is retarded or stagnating is a society which is looking at a bleak future.

This is amateurism at its very worst. Mr Baker clearly knows nothing about the creative nature of the act of perception itself. All understanding rests on a play of the imagination. We interpret visual images as we do written ones. It is a nonsense to oppose television and literature in this way. The problem is not that one is an imaginatively passive and the other an imaginatively active medium, but rather that we have been accustomed for too long to think of ourselves as uncritical consumers of both television and literature rather than as active and critical makers of meaning. It would also be interesting to know what Mr Baker's explanation is for the fact that the very culture he sees as under threat was developed in a predominantly non-literate society and that more books are sold and read today than at any time in our history.

Again Mr Baker isolates literary and cultural judgements when he says, 'I know there are books and books and too many so-called bestsellers today cynically cash in on a crude formula of sex and violence.' As with scientific farmers or developers we are not dealing with an aberration from the norms of our social values. Sex and violence have become commodities just like human labour to be invested in, bought and sold, exploited. Kenneth Baker is a senior Cabinet member of a government which has laid great stress on the merits of free and unfettered market forces and on the contribution to all our welfares of the unrestricted profit motive. Literature cannot expect to be exempt from the grand and glorious design.

The low level of the argument is reinforced by a particularly indulgent section where Mr Baker complains about how much books lose when they are translated into television. It is an ill-informed and poorly thought out argument and attempts to generalise about the natures of both mediums from a very dubious set of examples and premises. The varied level at which Mr Baker engages in this debate is typical of his approach in general. He moves from one issue to another, picking out potentially attractive ideas, latching on to common misconceptions and under-pinning the whole thing with an ultimate contempt for more rigorous thinking, a contempt which expresses itself in such asides as: 'I suspect I shall be told by many educators that I'm old-fashioned. But being old-fashioned is not the same as being wrong.' True, but being ill-informed *is* much the same as being ignorant.

What positive initiatives or insights are we offered? One of them is the notorious, some would say rather ludicrous, 'bench mark' suggestion;

> I would like to see bench marks for progress in English which actually set out lists for the sort of books or authors which children should be able to read and understand at particular ages and levels of achievement. For example, in the case of children of average ability: *Animal Farm* by age 12 or *David Copperfield* by age 15. The details are obviously for discussion but I regard the principle as important. You won't be surprised to know that I am told this is too radical or too centralist or too dictatorial.

The problem is not that this is too radical, or too centralist, or too dictatorial, but that it is too silly. The silliness of the suggestion rests partly in the fact that you could simply reverse the order of the bench marks he has chosen without anyone really detecting any difference. More importantly it fails to take note of the real issues involved. Children of 'average ability' may well be able to read *Animal Farm* or *David Copperfield* at 12 or 15 but the question is to what purpose should they read them? It simply isn't good enough to pluck a few titles out of the air and slot them into age brackets. What we should be thinking about is the range of critical reading activities children should be engaged in as readers. Our job is to empower children as critical readers and viewers so that they will be able to make real choices about what and how they read or view. It is pointless putting them over a number of literary jumps in the hope that a few will stay the course and learn to love the hurdles on which they may well have barked their shins. Besides which the whole concept of 'bench marks' is unsuited for the task in hand. A bench mark provides a surveyor with a universally agreed measurement of height against which to measure other features. A bench mark is, say, three hundred feet above sea-level, it can be shown to be that height and is agreed to be such by everyone concerned. Reading *David Copperfield* at 15 is not like that. Reading is much too complex and unstable a business for that. No two 15-year-olds will experience the same thing in reading the text or be engaged to the same degree. By all means encourage teachers to introduce a wider range of literature. By all means encourage the development of a more demanding reading curriculum. But don't confuse age-related texts with a realistic measurement of the efficacy of literature teaching in schools.

The final section of Mr Baker's speech takes us to the heart of the contradiction he is attempting to ignore. At one point he says of children: 'They are from birth immersed in a living language through which they increasingly learn to describe, understand and control their environment.' I agree with that whole-heartedly, but it is at odds with most of what he says elsewhere and, more significantly, with most of what he does elsewhere. Mr Baker and Mr Walden are really into the business of making children fit into a society over which they can expect to have very little power indeed. The main thrust of their thinking on language is that it is a tool to be exploited, not that it is a potentially powerful means by which human beings can effect change. The final sentence illustrates the contradiction:

But above all they should emerge with the confidence that comes from knowing that the language belongs to them and is in their keeping for the time being, and that is both a reassuring and awesome prospect.

The first part of the sentence stresses ownership, the second part custodianship. Ownership implies the power to change the thing we own and to use it to our own purposes. Custodianship implies the protection of something belonging to others and is a much more passive activity. Mr Baker touches on power but he rapidly modifies his statement. His vision for pupils is one where they continue to be passive consumers, only now they will consume *Animal Farm* rather than *Donald Duck* or *David Copperfield* rather than *EastEnders*. They will continue to have no say in the selection of the canon of 'great literature'. In Mr Baker's speech that canon constitutes itself out of its own intrinsic greatness. There is no acknowledgement of the fact that people and institutions have made choices and that we have the right to challenge the legitimacy of their position as arbiters of literary immortality. Mr Baker genuinely wants children to read and enjoy literature and that is a very worthy ambition. However, their role as readers will be to stand in awed wonder at the genius of other users of their language, at the power of these writers to describe human experience. As readers they are to divorce the experiences described in the text from the historical contexts within which those experiences were written or are being read.

Mr Baker complains that there is no model available to describe the working and role of language. One of the main tasks he has set the Kingman Committee is the production of such a model that can then be applied to the training of teachers and to the education of children. I can only presume that what he means is that either he is not sufficiently informed to know, or that those models which are available and have influenced the thinking of many English teachers are not to his liking. What has emerged and is still in the process of coming into sharper definition is a model that places language, including literary language, not above everyday experience but at the very heart of it. Language exists only in a social context: it is a purely social phenomenon. Consequently it cannot be studied in isolation from the study of social organisation and behaviour. Human beings speak or write in order to affect other human beings or to change their physical environment. The nature of the effect language aims at is of course infinitely varied and includes amusement, shock, despair, resistance and persuasion. The effect may be at the level of 'please pass the salt' or 'a state of war now exists'. In all its uses the meaning of language exists only in a specific social context. To re-read or hear it in another context is to change that meaning. As readers and listeners we use our understanding of social context to create meaning out of aural or visual images. The decoding of any piece of language implies an act of social analysis, even if this analysis is often at a relatively low level. Any attempt to isolate the study of language from a broader study of culture and history fails to recognise the actual role language performs. But ultimately this is not an academic issue, it is a political one. If language and knowledge about language have a potential for power and change, then it is unlikely that those who hold power in our society will be willing to encourage the realisation of that potential in those who, at present, have very little power.

A READER'S GUIDE TO THE KINGMAN REPORT

ALASTAIR WEST

Alastair West is English Adviser in Redbridge. After teaching English for 14 years in comprehensive schools, he spent 4 years researching adolescent readers, gaining his D. Phil. in 1986. He has contributed to *The English Magazine*, written a teacher's guide to the Archway Novels series (OUP) and contributed to a forthcoming collection of studies on school self-evaluation (Falmer Press).

To read intelligently is to read responsively; it is to ask questions of the text and use one's own framework of experience in interpreting it. In working his way through a book the reader imports, projects, anticipates, speculates on alternative outcomes.[1]

How should we read the Kingman Report? How should the text be read? It is little more than a decade since those familiar words from Bullock, describing the reading process, were written. Do they adequately describe how we are likely to read the Kingman Report? The answer most certainly will be yes. Well, at least up to a point. To make our meanings from the text of the Kingman Report we will doubtless interrogate the text, anticipate and speculate upon alternative outcomes and do all the things that Bullock commends we should do as readers. But we are also likely to do more than that, for we are wiser now than we were about reading. And it is that more with which this article is concerned. The account given in Bullock of how we read is not so much inadequate because wrong as that it is incomplete and partial.

The story of reading proposed in Bullock is an essentially participatory one in which reading is seen as an activity shared between reader and writer. At the time, it represented a considerable and welcome advance in our thinking in that it gave due weight both to the simplicity and the complexity of the reading process. In consequence we have rediscovered and pondered old truths in such writers as Sterne:

> the truest respect which you can pay to the reader's understanding is to halve this matter amicably, and leave him something to imagine, in his turn, as well as yourself.[2]

and found confirmation of them echoed in more recent theorists such as Eco who said that 'texts are lazy machineries that ask someone to do part of their job'.[3] This emphasis upon the reader's active making of meaning in the reading process has produced undoubted classroom benefits in all sectors of education. The implications of this view of the shared nature of meaning-making have been teased out in countless changing classroom practices in recent years. The dreary round of comprehension exercises which reduce reading to a search for isolated gobbets of information and which ignore the wholeness of both text and reader; or of reading schemes which fragment the reading process into an assemblage of dubiously separable, but carefully structured and expensively marketed subskills are both mercifully less frequent than once they were. Bullock thus has argued and validated teaching approaches which are more holistic in their view of readers and texts and of the interaction between them, approaches, moreover, which lend themselves to more enjoyable, imaginative and ultimately purposeful classroom activities for both teachers and pupils. Amen to all these undeniable benefits. And there should be no question of surrendering any of these hard won gains for reversion to the discredited practices which they supplanted.

But ten years is a long time and we are at sufficient distance from those days to be more critical of some of the assumptions in Bullock. 'Bathe the child in language' is not an injunction that we would in any way care to deny. But it has less assured resonance than once it did. We know now that we need more than that phrase's heady optimism to help us to effective action. Such comments, we can see now, belong to a discourse of confident progressivism whose day has passed. Its conceptual framework omits too much that we have since come to acknowledge as important. The limitations of the Bullock discourse have been pressed upon us through direct experience and through theory in different ways. The revolution in literary theory has profoundly unsettled many of our assumptions; recent government policies have transformed beyond recognition the educational landscape in which we used to operate upon those assumptions; and the discourse in which many of those assumptions were expressed has been appropriated and differently inflected by the government responsible for those changes. These factors have all played their part in distancing us from the context of Bullock. And so, in many ways, there is good reason to welcome the Kingman Inquiry as an opportunity to restate and redefine what we are about in the altered circumstances in which we find ourselves. To progress beyond Bullock we need to reaffirm the great deal in it worth retaining, whilst at the same time developing approaches to secure our view of education as 'the means by which men and women deal critically and creatively with reality and discover how to participate in the transformation of their world'.[4]

To make that move we will need, amongst other things, to modify our view of reading and see what has been happening elsewhere in neighbouring parts of the educational universe. In the same year that Bullock was published, for example, the American critic Harold Bloom argued that 'nothing is to be gained by continuing to idealise reading as if it were not an art of defensive warfare'.[5] Clearly Bloom was reading in a very different part of the library. Nor was he working there alone. And the body of theoretical work that informs his comment does concern us as teachers, for it includes the nature of narrative, the reading process, the status and formation of texts and interpretations, and, not least, of course, the varying views of language which underpin them, together with the social and political theories to which they are inextricably related. What emerges from the debates in these areas is a view that

> reading and writing are important because we read and write our world as well as our texts and are read and written by them in turn. Texts are the places where power and weakness become visible and discussable, where learning and ignorance manifest themselves, where the structures that enable and constrain our thought and actions become palpable.[6]

It is a view of reading which builds upon and renders more complete the one we have inherited from Bullock. What is emphasised in many of these 'stories of reading'[7] is not, however, so very new, although the terms in which they are expressed have a somewhat alien ring to those of us schooled in the familiar discourse which derived from romanticism and culminated perhaps in Bullock. It is not new, for what is being argued marks the return of rhetoric, an acknowledgement not just that interpersonal context is crucial, but that all utterances are socially and historically situated, and that the meanings derived from them change according to the positions held by those who make them. It is a much less innocent view of reading, in which the social and the political are restored to a domain from which they have long been excluded. Tomkins summarises the shift well:

> The insistence that language is constitutive of reality rather than merely reflective of it, suggests that contemporary critical theory has come to occupy a position very similar to, if not the same as, that of the Greek rhetoricians for whom the mastery of language meant mastery of the state . . . The similarity lies not in the common focus upon literature's audience . . . but . . . rather in the common perception of language as a form of power.[8]

The contrast with Bullock is striking. It must be said at once that such a rhetorical view has not won universal acceptance. It has prompted restatements of the old humanist position by some theorists such as Iser, for example. But the debate is a real and an intense one, and a great deal is at stake. Given our current concerns with language and knowledge about it, we cannot afford to ignore this debate. The whole theoretical upheaval that has followed in the wake of structuralism has turned again and again upon language, endlessly language. Before proceeding to see how all this theoretical debate might affect our reading of the Kingman text, we could usefully sharpen up some of the differences between Bullock and post-Bullock approaches so far as reading is concerned.

Thus, to read in the manner proposed by Bullock is to engage in an interactive process, a shared activity that is seen in purely individualised terms: 'it magnanimously allows the reader the right to construct meanings for the texts as if there were no ideology of the ruling class and no social mode of reception determined by it'.[9] It is based upon an individualistic, interactionist model of communication which takes for granted that 'the individual constructs himself, the discourse he utters and the texts he reads under weak general constraints such as "appropriateness" '.[10] It ignores both the social and institutional contexts in which readers and readings exist, and the uses to which texts and particular readings of them are put. It overlooks the extent to which reading responses are socially determined and to which the reading codes that we employ are equally socially and culturally constructed. It proposes reading *with* the grain of the text rather than *against* it and although the reader's active role in this process is highlighted, the dominant partner in the relationship remains still the text. Texts in this version of reading tend to retain a univocal meaning and any limited plurality of meanings remains circumscribed within a set of assumptions and conventions that are generally determined by those social groups whose interests they best serve. Indeed, many of the activities devised upon this model seem designed to find ways of delivering the reader as willing victim to a particular selection of the rhetorical effects of the text. The reader's personality and interests are taken into account only in order to render them that much more susceptible to those effects.

So, in the light of our changing understanding of the reading process and the consequent demise of the innocent presuppositionless reader who presents him/herself before the text with open responsiveness, how then should we prepare to read the Kingman Report? Bullock urges us to question the text and use our framework of experiences in interpreting it. But what questions should we ask? And what experiences should we draw upon in interpreting the text? Bullock is not very helpful on that score. The more rhetorical view of reading advanced by recent theorists prompts questions that could be asked of any text, fictional or otherwise. In essence, it proposes an account of reading as a form of social practice in which all texts, and their writers and readers, are embedded in social and historical circumstances which shape the meanings produced, meanings moreover, which are produced for particular purposes and occasions.

It would be helpful at this point to introduce some good old fashioned empiricism. After all, the proof of the pudding is in the eating. But since, at the time of writing, the Kingman text is not published, we must content ourselves with some anticipatory preparation. We can read the context if not the text. And since we know that any text is 'a tissue of quotations drawn from innumerable centres of culture',[11] we can reasonably think about the intertextuality of the Kingman report. Our traditions and training may cause some momentary unease at such preparation before the very text has been written. But we should not be deterred from preparing for this exercise of 'defensive warfare'. We cannot, as Jameson reminds us, retrieve innocence as readers because it is an illusion.

> We never really confront a text immediately in all its freshness as a thing-in-itself. Rather texts come before us as the always-already-read, and we apprehend them through sedimented layers of previous interpretations or, if the text is brand new, through the sedimented reading habits and categories developed by those inherited interpretative traditions.[12]

All that we can hope to achieve in these days of lost readerly innocence is to keep our wits about us and to retain a sense of our own positionality as readers if we are to produce our meaning from the text rather than reproduce someone else's. We must strike a balance between being guided by the text and manipulated by it. We have to set our intentions and purposes against those of others who have produced the text and mediated it to us. Rather than deliver ourselves up to the intended textual effects, eagerly helping out the author(s) at every turn, as Bullock might have us do, we need to remember that 'an ideological bias can lead a critical reader to make a given text say more than it apparently says, that it is to find out what in that text is ideologically presupposed, untold'.[13] So what kind of questions might we reasonably have in mind whilst reading the Kingman Report? There are obvious limits to what can be done without the text, but a start can be made.

WHERE DOES THIS TEXT COME FROM?

Recent theory restores history to our texts and readings and ways of reading. All texts are socially and historically situated. They bear a complex relationship to other texts which precede them and co-exist with them. To acknowledge this as we read will entail more than just attention to the words on the page. The origins of the Kingman text lie, for example, as did such predecessor reports as Bullock and Newbolt, not in the disinterested sense of inquiry of any individual or group, but in the sense of crisis as seen by those in central government with authority over the national education system. This crisis relates to questions of control over the education system, to questions of educational standards and of the needs of society, all as perceived by those who govern it and who have called the text into being. The context for the report includes the many other educational initiatives whose effect has been to redefine the shape and structure of the educational system and of the conditions of those who work within it. It is thus but a small part of the prescribed treatment that follows on a particular diagnosis of this moment in our history.

This would appear to be par for the course. Both Newbolt and Bullock were summoned into existence by a similar sense of panic and crisis. And it must be said that there is a long tradition in this country whereby the declaration and definition of such crises in the state education system are made by those who have had least recourse to it for their own children. The system has long been designed and administered by one social group and used by another, in socio-economic terms, usually subordinate, one. A re-reading of the Newbolt Report, for example, is instructive. It reveals how various contemporary socio-political tensions and conflicts are entwined with an apparently disinterested advocacy of literature to develop children's personality. The committee's concern over 'the social question' and what they took to be the imminent collapse of the established social order into Bolshevik revolution was very real.[14] Their educational analysis and prescription was accordingly determined in large measure by this socio-political anxiety. The social distances between the committee and the population for whom provision is to be made is very apparent in their comments about working class language and culture. A comparable social distance is apparent between those who formulated its recommendations and the teachers who were exhorted to implement them. The text is clearly addressed from HQ about the provision to be made by other people for other people's children.

It is obviously more difficult to perceive the effects of such ideological implications in events that are closer to us. But some of those effects upon Bullock have clarified since 1975. The participatory view of reading, for example, is not unlike ideas then current which stressed a conflict-free participatory social democracy and political consensus. Similarly, whilst the report draws upon socio-linguistics, it detaches itself from connections with social theory. Moreover our understanding of Bullock, and equally of Kingman, cannot be disconnected from the prolonged industrial disputes in the education system which preceded them.

All this is partly, of course, a question of the inevitable implication in the ideologies of our time to which we all are subject. But although we cannot escape that process, a degree of scepticism and hard analysis affords a measure of protection. As does a realistic appraisal of one's own social, historical and cultural positionality. Many of the more recently developed reading strategies are specifically designed to confront the fact that 'the text says more than it knows and knows more than it says'.[15] To question the origins of a text is to do more than chart its pedigree. It is to probe the social forces which led to its existence and question whose interests it was designed to serve.

Whatever else it may become, the Kingman text cannot help but be a political document now. It will take its place and be used for a variety of purposes in a variety of public arenas. It is also a political initiative which, on even the narrowest construction, will cause some disturbance to the established power relations in the system as yet another means whereby curriculum control is drawn to the centre. As with many such centralising tendencies, the effectiveness of the control is not the point at issue. What is important is the assertion and exercise of the right to make that move. More widely, it can be seen as an authoritarian move which amounts to the redefinition of educational problems and the relocation of problems from elsewhere to the education sector. It will not be the first time that education has been held to account for deficiencies in the economic sphere. It is a familiar strategy which entails blaming the victims, holding them responsible for their disadvantages. Problems of material provision – teacher supply, teacher salaries and conditions, accommodation inadequacies and shortage of resources – are all thus condensed into a more economically manageable concern with curriculum content. Nor would it be the first time that education, and particularly the language curriculum, has been the site chosen upon which issues such as social unrest and civil disorder may be addressed. The hidden history of English shows that more than other subjects it has been prone to social and ideological pressures at all stages of its development. So we should not be surprised that part of the context for the Kingman text is a political rhetoric in which social disturbance and the failure to employ the standard dialect may be bracketed together under the label of loss of respect for authority. Historically, those in authority have often been tempted to forge a connection between respect for the standard dialect and respect for the established social order, between 'correct' rule-governed use of language and rule-governed behaviour on the streets.[16] There is nothing new in this, nor anything peculiar to this country.

All of which serves to say that the sense of crisis, so sharply perceived by the forces which have called for the inquiry, is not now, any more than it was on those earlier occasions, universally shared. Indeed many of those who work, learn or have children in the state education system would articulate, then as now, a rather different sense of crisis. For them any anxiety about what children should know about language, however interesting a topic, would have to take second place to other considerations. About the fabric, provision and staffing in our schools, for example. Or, beyond such material considerations, they are more likely to have wished for an inquiry more directly related to aspects of children's language learning. But to work in the system or to have one's children educated in it confers no power to influence the terms of reference of such an inquiry. For many readers, then, the Kingman Report can hardly be expected to address their major educational preoccupations. The framework of their experience will be different and their positionality is likely to lead them to question both the need and the motives for such an inquiry.

WHAT KIND OF TEXT IS THIS?

The Kingman Report will take its place in due course alongside myriad other texts which share certain generic features. The government report after all is a quite distinct genre, however unrecognised in the literary canon. All texts owe at least as much to other texts as they do to their authors. Such constraints do not inhibit creativity but act rather as a spur to it, allowing authors to produce that shock of pleasure for readers as their anticipations are rewarded or thwarted. It may well be that we are in for some formal surprises with the Kingman Report. We will have to wait and see. But in the meantime what are some of those generic features that we might reasonably anticipate? What are some of the rules of this particular textual game to which we might expect this text to conform?

Some, of course, are isolated trivial surface features. Writers in this genre share with Wittgenstein, for example, a penchant for numbered paragraphs. Some are less trivial. The usual omission of an adequate bibliography, for example (there was none at all in the Newbolt report and only footnotes in Bullock), so that the report's conceptual framework must be determined by more indirect routes. It would be useful to know what reading list was given to committee members for the Kingman, and indeed earlier, reports. In this respect the convention of including a list of the witnesses to the inquiry is helpful; they at least, one assumes, would have read, perhaps even written, some of the books thought relevant to the committee. The mention of witnesses also gives a clue as to the origins of the report genre, which are essentially juridical in nature. And it is juridical discursive practices which exert so determining an influence upon both form and content of such reports. Consider the conditions of the text's production.

Let us start with the composition of the committee where there seem to be some recognisable generic rules at work. The principle of amateurism is strong in the committee tradition, so that members, or some of them, are likely to be selected for what, in the currently fashionable jargon, might be called their 'transferable skills', rather than any directly related expertise. At the same time, the need for that expertise amongst committee members appears to be recognised in direct proportion to the socio-cultural clout exercised by the subject or discourse under inquiry. Thus, it is likely that any current inquiry into law or medicine would include rather more members acknowledged by those professions as 'experts' than appears to be the case in the Kingman Committee which is operating within the very much weaker discursive territory of education. The 'experts', by and large, feature as witnesses, making their cases to a largely lay body. This is not unlike the jury system except that there is no provision for jury challenging, the jury in this case being selected by the equivalent of the judge. It is the 'judge' also who sets the terms of reference. Thus, from the outset, very uneven power relations are established between the authors of the report and the majority of its readers, particularly those readers who will eventually be subject to its findings. The determinacy of the text is much disputed in current theory, which distinguishes between overdetermined texts such as James Bond novels which are predictable and underdetermined ones such as *Ulysses* which are less so. The conditions of its production tend to make the report genre one of overdetermined texts.

Another juridical aspect of the genre stems from the fact that an inquiry presupposes some disaster, crisis or crime which requires retribution or amelioration. The report format, therefore, is predisposed to some kind of narrative in which praise and reward, blame and calling to account are apportioned amongst the participants. There is a tendency for some kind of division of the participants into heroes, villains and innocent by-standers. Despite its resolutely non-fictional status, it is difficult for the report form to avoid some degree of fictional drift, a slide into narrative. Thus in Bullock and Newbolt there are both heroes and villains for whom there are different modes of representation. Both reports cite the heroic examples of teachers whose exceptional personal qualities enable them to achieve wonders with their charges in the bleakest and most disgracefully provisioned of circumstances. And there are also in both reports some off-stage villains lurking at the school gates and threatening the educational enterprise. These tend to be portrayed in more shadowy terms, as forces rather than individualised figures. In the past such villains have included 'the ephemeral novel', the trivialising or euphoria-inducing media or the 'perverted power' of non-standard English. Both heroes and villains tend to be evoked rather than analysed. The oppositions involved are not unrelated to contemporary ideologies and stereotypes. The use of such techniques is not extensive, but their effect is powerful in that they tend to end-stop analysis or defer it altogether.

There are other questions about the genre raised by consideration of the conditions of the text's production. These largely stem from uncertainty amongst the reading public about the exact roles and functions of those responsible for the text and about the working practices which they choose to adopt. No doubt there are some general guidelines. But committee members presumably bring differing degrees of expertise and commitment to their task and so the function of the secretary is a crucial one within the committee structure. This function is generally exercised by a full-time official with relevant expertise and access to those responsible for setting up the committee. It is thus a potentially very influential position which confers extensive gatekeeping and mediating powers. Through this figure both the witnesses and ministerial intentions are interpreted to the committee, as, presumably, is the committee to the outside world. Although the exact relationships between committee members and this figure are not divulged and do not declare themselves, they no doubt vary between committees to as great an extent as does the relationship between officers and elected members in different local government committees. No doubt in the past there have been at the extremes some committees which have simply been articulated by a skilful secretary and others where the committee has over-ridden all attempts by a secretary to influence the course of the proceedings.

The process of the writing is equally unclear. Does the secretary or chair produce drafts which are then negotiated by members? Do members produce drafts of different sections which are then subjected to a final editing process? What kind of collaborative writing process is involved? And what kind of editing occurs? How does it differ, if at all, from the Open University publications which bear the subscription, 'written by John Smith on behalf of the course team' beneath the title? No draft of the text will be produced, for example, or auctioned at some later date. The best that we can hope for in that respect is the insight afforded into the report process by committee members' utterances that appear elsewhere. The latest to hand, for example, being an article in the *Daily Telegraph*. Apart from such leaks (are such articles leaks? how does the Official Secrets Act affect the committee's work?) we must rely upon speculation or professional gossip and wait for the later publication of (auto)biographies, interviews and collections of letters as we did for those upon which our current understanding of the full process and socio-political context of the Newbolt Report is based. What is clear about this mode of literary production, as evidenced by recent examples, is that there is always provision in contentious areas for notes of extension and dissent by individual members (Bullock) and even, in the most extreme circumstances, for departure from the committee and dissociation from the report (Swann). Given the general secrecy surrounding the production of such public texts it is perhaps inevitable that their readers are likely to seek out any signs of fissure – what recent theory refers to as the gaps or indeterminacies of the text – in their collective authorship.

The question of the report's authorship raises another generic feature. It is more than likely that the present report will be known as the Kingman Report or more simply Kingman to the cognoscenti. Unlike most other texts, however, such as Gibbon or Dante, which are known by a personal name, such reports rarely appear to be written by the people whose name they bear. Recent literary theory has made heavy weather of the redundancy of the author in recent years ('the birth of the reader must be at the cost of the death of the author'[17]) but we have lived quite happily without the author in the report genre for some time. Although known by the name of an individual, the text carries a collective and therefore a more impersonal weight. Uncertainty about the authorship lends authority in the public domain. We are used to talking about the relationship between reader and writer as a kind of social contract when dealing with a fictional text. But the terms of contract offered by texts in this genre are very asymmetrical, both the anonymity and stylistic features ensuring a text-dominant relationship.

Another obvious generic feature of the report is that convention requires that recommendations are made. The numbered recommendations at the end of the report, however they are organised as regards their presentation, generally fall into various opposing categories: those which require action by the commissioning authority and those which require action by people subject to its authority; those which entail expenditure and those which do not. And of course there are later further divisions between those recommendations which are acted upon or funded and those which are not. The convention of recommendations is a sharp reminder that reports are commissioned texts, that may or may not please the Maecenas who pays for them. There is always a question mark over both the acceptance of the report and the implementation of its findings by the commissioning agent. Their acceptance or rejection would appear to be related to some degree to the amount of publicity to which the inquiry has been subject. Thus the delayed appearance or non-appearance of scientific reports upon the effects of radio-active pollution upon molluscs in the Irish Sea attracted little media attention. Widely publicised inquiries in education, however, are less prone to such delay.

They are also texts which are commissioned by those who may perhaps not be in a position to receive the finished product. Indeed such is the speed with which Secretaries of State for Education have moved to obscurity or to greater things in post-war years that it is highly unlikely that the signature of the Kingman Report's onlie begetter will ever grace the page of receipt. This explains, perhaps, one distinction between the report form and other commissioned works where it is customary, in the dedication or scattered textual asides, to praise the munificence, wisdom or patriotism of their patron.

WHAT MEANINGS AND CONTEXTS FOR MEANING ARE POSSIBLE FROM THIS TEXT?

Meanings change according to the positions occupied by those who make and hold them. They change across time and across cultures. The idea that texts have a single meaning, or a very restricted plurality of meanings, was an early casualty in the recent theoretical upheaval. And since meanings were found to be so unstable, interest centred both upon the social processes by which meanings were made and changed and the textual features and reading practices which enabled them to do so. In the case of the canon of literature, for example, we are familiar with the broad outlines of the process whereby the dominant meanings of classic texts are constructed. The selection of texts, the ways of reading them, the range of acceptable readings and the licensing of readers are all largely controlled by what Kermode calls that 'self-perpetuating, sempiternal corporation', the university.[18] Texts, readers and readings are all subject to its licensing authority. Dominant meanings emerge, and oppositional ones are ultimately either assimilated or annihilated. There are obvious qualifications to be made, but we are familiar with the overall position and the discursive powers involved.

But for other texts the process is more complex. Which group for example will determine the dominant contemporary meaning of the Kingman text? And what will be the range and fate of its oppositional meanings? Even within education the range of groups is such as to ensure the likely production of divergent meanings: the Secretary of State for Education; the DES; HMI; NATE; teaching unions and so on. Each group and individuals within them will construct a meaning and these meanings will not necessarily stitch themselves together neatly. Beyond the world of education there are others that will have a stake in the construction of a dominant meaning. Any doubt as to the complexity of this whole process is dispelled by consideration of the reception of the HMI report on educational provision in Brent or of the initial *English from 5 to 16* document. Texts do not wear their meanings on their faces, and for many texts, particularly in this genre, a great deal more is at stake in fixing the meaning of a text than the words on the page. It is not just that all texts inevitably are shot through with the ideologies of their time. The process of the text's reception by its audience entails the active reproduction and challenging of those ideologies. A dominant meaning will emerge and oppositional meanings will persist. The hegemony, assimilation or extinction of any one of them, however, will be determined by changes in the power relations of those groups which made them or opposed them.

However fierce this contest for meanings might be, the emergence of a dominant meaning is not the same as its imposition. When a particular meaning for a text attains dominance, particularly in a hierarchical organisation, specific powers and opportunities are conferred upon it. For example, it is the dominant meaning that will impose itself upon those who have not read the text. Thus there will be many for whom, in a sense, the reading work is already done. All that is required is for them to pick up the meaning lying around that has been established by others. Again the reception of *English from 5 to 16* should lead us to be wary of under-estimating the power of this process: there were many more who had a meaning for that text than there were readers for it. Moreover, upon those who are about to read the text, the dominant meaning exerts an equally powerful influence. It is towards that dominant meaning that prospective readers must work for confirmation, or against it that they must assert their own and strive to avoid being judged aberrant. The dominant meaning is also the springboard for action and policy. Here it is worth recalling that dominance is not necessarily determined by the number of people adhering to that interpretation. There was a meaning for Bullock, for example, that was very widely shared amongst the teaching profession, but that meaning differed significantly from the dominant one attributed to the text. The difference was that in the dominant interpretation language was largely a cost-free subject.

But although subordinate meanings might fail to secure a powerful institutional base, the struggles for meanings can and do persist at all points down a hierarchical system. Because meanings are always dialogic, they are endlessly mediated between groups and individuals as particular texts are re-negotiated, re-interpreted and turned to serve specific local purposes in specific places.

Such a process occurs because texts are inevitably organised in a way that enables such plurality of meaning and makes authorial attempts to limit it very difficult. Any text makes certain assumptions (age-related objectives?) explicit or implicit, which can be challenged or accepted by its readers who can then decide whether to read with or against the grain. Any text is organised around a number of structuring oppositions (*knowledge about* as opposed to *use of* language) and alertness to the patterns which they produce can lead the reader to the ideological presuppositions of the text. What are the exclusions from the text? the suppressions? What is the knowledge required to read it? What are the gaps and why are they where they are? What is the price for accepting what the text offers as taken for granted? These are the kinds of questions that will be prompted for a self-defensive reader in a struggle for meaning that has both an individual and a social dimension.

WHAT SOCIAL FUNCTION DOES THIS TEXT SERVE?

Texts remain embedded in specific social and historical circumstances for as long as they are read or remembered. Meanings accumulate around them in a complex way. But once formulated, those meanings, whether dominant or oppositional, are not static. They continue to be used and it is the uses to which they are put, the practices associated with them and the effects that they achieve over time that reveal their social function. The relatively stable selection of fiction texts thought appropriate for study by 14- to 16-year-olds in school, for example, and the meanings and practices that have accumulated around them, cannot be severed from the dominant ideologies of our culture. Recent theory has undermined our confidence in the durability of particular texts as proof of their timeless qualities and concern with universal truths. They last only as long as the social groups or cultures whose ideologies they serve. If some texts do survive widespread social change and upheaval, then their earlier meanings most certainly do not. New meanings are produced for changed circumstances. The history of the meanings attributed to the Newbolt Report indicate that this process is not confined to literary genres.

In the short term, the social function of the Kingman Report is largely explained in terms of its origins: its relation to other government initiatives in education, the economic crisis, the industrial dispute in schools and so on. But in the long term, its function is likely to be different. Once the dust of its origins has settled, its major social function will become apparent. This is likely to relate to what might be called system maintenance. For one prime social function of this kind of report seems to be to validate and preserve the sense of the unity of a national education system. Despite all evidence to the contrary of various kinds of fragmentation, the assumption upon which the report is likely to operate is of a unified system. Both the origins and the terms of reference tend to make that inevitable. Unity, despite the existence of a commercially funded sector, the widespread differentiated provision between and within LEAs, the scattered persistence of selection at 11+, and the introduction of yet further forms of selection and differentiated provision via the MSC, let alone via those schools which opt out of LEA control. So the structure of the system is likely to be taken for granted, but more important is the equally likely assumption that such diversified provision has no effects upon the subject under inquiry. Unity within diversity is likely to be the assumption as regards the system. And the focus upon language enables a similar stress upon unity. What more powerful, or cheaper, basis upon which to call for a sense of nationhood, of unity? The enormous social changes since Newbolt mean that there can be no repetition of that report's relatively straightforward drive to hegemony for the standard dialect and its imposition of 'language-through-literature'. But whatever view is taken of linguistic diversity in the Kingman Report, we should recall the strategy that has been used so often in the past whereby the language community is presented as at once naturally unified and naturally stratified.

WHAT KIND OF READER IS PROPOSED? AND WHAT KIND OF READING POSITION IS AFFORDED HIM/HER?

We cannot know in advance what arrangements will be made for us as readers. But we do know how all texts make elaborate advance provision for their readers. This generally entails the preparation of a reading position, a place in the text towards which the reader is manoeuvred. From this place the reader is likely to view the proceedings in the most favourable light and be most susceptible to the rhetorical effects deployed. Above all it is a place from which it is most difficult to ask the kind of questions least welcomed by the author. In recent years we have become quite adept with fictional texts at spotting many of these plans and are consequently more choosy as to where we sit. We are more likely now than we used to be to turn round and say, 'What kind of reader do you take me for?'

The invitation offered to the report reader is likely to be more ambiguous than this because of the diversity of audiences envisaged. Should we be there at all? Who is the intended audience? Is the intended audience primarily the commissioning Secretary of State, or teachers, or the wider public? The difficulties in resolving such uncertainties in this genre produce interesting textual features. The most obvious of these of course is the employment of a carefully coded language designed to exclude large numbers of readers and to allow for the production of a variety of meanings by various groups of readers. There is sharply differentiated access to the text, the level of reader access being largely determined not just by readers' familiarity with its stylistic features, but more importantly, by the report's intertextuality. Only the initiated, for example, are likely to be alert to shifts of emphasis that are signalled solely by their difference from earlier 'official' statements. For many readers therefore the reading experience is likely to be similar to that of eavesdropping. But they will be intended eavesdroppers. Indeed the tensions involved in catering for audiences that occupy such different power positions can produce interesting benefits to the reader. Readers of the initial *English from 5 to 16* document, for example, were given an unprecedented opportunity to participate as readers. They were offered not just a reading position for the initial document, but were also invited to a share in the composition of its replacement. This was not a commercial ploy as in the case of Mills and Boon romances, whose producers go to a great deal of trouble to ensure, through invited reader responses, that they are marketing the most profitable product. Nor was it a sign of the Readers' Liberation Movement being taken seriously at the DES. The initiative related more bluntly to the changed conditions of production and the difficulty of catering for the teaching profession and a Secretary of State whose positions as readers were known to be poles apart.

A similar situation exists with the Kingman Report. We learned from the *Daily Telegraph* that the committee is aware of the hostility of the teaching profession to the inquiry and is anxious not to alienate it. We know that the Secretary of State attaches considerable importance to the inquiry, and we know some of the things that he hopes to hear. The reading position that is being prepared in this report is therefore likely to be an interesting construction. We will need to inspect it carefully before we decide to occupy it. Whatever the position offered the reader, we know that there will be a reply to the text because 'the word is always a two-sided act'[19] and 'every utterance awaits its reply'.[20]

REFERENCES

1 Department of Education and Science, *A Language for Life* (The Bullock Report), HMSO, 1975
2 Sterne, L. *Tristram Shandy*, 1759–67.
3 Eco, U. *The role of the Reader*, Hutchinson, 1979
4 Freire, P. cited in Barnes, D. and Clarke, S. *Versions of English*, Heinemann, 1984
5 Bloom, H. *Kabbalah and Criticism*, New York: Seabury, 1975, cited in Culler, J. (see note 7)
6 Scholes, R. *Textual Power. Literary Theory and English Teaching*, Yale, 1985
7 Culler, J. *On Deconstruction. Theory and Criticism after Structuralism*, Routledge & Kegan Paul, 1983
8 Tomkins, J. *Reader-Response Criticism: from Formalism to Post-structuralism*, Johns Hopkins, 1980
9 Barck, K. cited in Holub, R. *Reception Theory. A Critical Introduction*, Methuen, 1984
10 Fowler, R. *Literature as Social Discourse*, Batsford, 1981
11 Barthes, R. *S/Z*, Cape, 1975
12 Jameson, F. *The Political Unconscious: narrative as socially symbolic act*, Methuen, 1981
13 Eco, U. *The Role of the Reader*, Hutchinson, 1979
14 See Baldick, C. *The Social Mission of English Criticism 1848–1932*, Clarendon Press, 1983; Widdowson, P. ed. *Re-reading English*, Methuen, 1983; Batsleer, J.; Davies, T.; O'Rourke, R; and Weedon, C. *Re-writing English: cultural politics of gender and class*, Methuen, 1986
15 Macherey, P. *Towards a Theory of Literary Production*, Methuen, 1978
16 See Hawkes, T. *That Shakespeherean Rag*, Methuen, 1986; Baldick, C. *op.cit.*,
17 Barthes, R. 'The death of the author' (1968) in Barthes, R. *The Rustle of Language*, Blackwell, 1986
18 Kermode, F. *Essays in Fiction*, Routledge & Kegan Paul, 1983
19 Volosinov, V.N. *Marxism and the Philosophy of Language*, Harvard 1986
20 Bakhtin, M. *The Dialogic Imagination*, University of Texas Press, 1981

A VIEW OF LANGUAGE

'Every language has the *capacity* to take the form that its users require.'[1]

DICK HANCOCK

Dick Hancock has been County Inspector for English and Drama in Bedfordshire since 1975. Before that he was Head of the English Department at Churchill Comprehensive School in Somerset. He has been an Associate Tutor at the Institute of Education in Bristol, and for six years was Chief Examiner in English with the South Western Examination Board. He is the co-author of an English source book Language in Life *(Chambers, 1969) and has contributed articles on aspects of English and Drama teaching to a variety of educational journals. He is at present Chairman of a working party established by the National Association of Advisers in English to look at what children need to know about language.*

SOME PRINCIPLES

The capacity to use our native language, or 'mother tongue', is such an unconsidered yet indispensable part of our lives that it is difficult to examine it in a disinterested way. We cannot remember when we existed without it, and indeed it is possible to say that in reality we have never existed in a state devoid of language; the very first burblings and the rhythms of a body amount to a language, a communicative act. Our very first identifiable words, phrases, and sequences of longer utterances, clearly represent the developing results of a process for expressing our needs, to get what we want, and generally, to let others know of our existence. Whilst this process is more extensively developed in some young children than in others, most are able to acquire enough language to achieve a measure of independence by the time they start school when the process of socialisation is accelerated. Teaching in the early years is very much concerned with the development of language in maintaining a relationship with others. It is in the use of language that we have one of our most effective means of establishing our own identity and of existing in a reasonable state of harmony with others, but this 'language making capacity' also provides a powerful resource for teachers who can skilfully and subtly intervene and extend it into the learning process. This thinking leads to the establishment of an important principle: *the capacity to use language is innate but it is engendered and promoted through experience and can be guided into learning.*

A young child's use of language is inextricably bound up with the development of personality. In this way the language we use expresses who we are. Consequently, it must be recognised that all young children express who they are, the way they see the world, and how they relate to others, through the language they use. They do not exist separately from their language and they are the language that they use. This is of considerable significance for schooling and leads to the establishment of a second important principle: *the language of the child is the expression of that child and needs to be treated with respect, sensitivity, and understanding by the teacher.*

Just as young children appear to acquire language at different rates and show variations in the confidence with which they are able to use it, so language itself is not a fixed entity but is in a state of flux and permanent change. An obvious illustration of this concerns vocabulary; it is not possible for dictionaries to catch the true state of 'the word hoard' because as soon as they are published they are giving credence to uses which may no longer obtain and omit words in current usage. Yet words, too, shift in contexts, and can only be responded to in their contexts. It is this connection which is made in a work like the Collins Cobuild English Language Dictionary[2] which is based on 'what words do' rather than what they 'mean'. Using modern technology the lexicographers handle over 20 million words and focus on 70,000 of the commonest in terms of frequency in the ordinary spoken and written language and the patterns that can normally be expected to embrace them. Besides reminding us that language is in a state of growth such works also underline that there are patterns of usage which are best looked at from the point of view of 'how things are' rather than 'how they ought to be'. It is not, of course, a matter solely of words, but of structures, idioms, and aspects of pronunciation. Because of this it is difficult to think in terms of 'a model of language'; it is more helpful to think in terms of qualities which characterise language and which can be expressed in a third principle: *language is a dynamic concept, existing in a process of growth and not a fixed entity impervious to change.*

As language is such a powerful means of expression we need to examine some of the important ways in which it makes itself felt in the world we know – there are the different 'modes' of language activity, such as talking and writing; there are also different forms of language such as Standard English, slang and dialect; there are also 'new' Englishes such as Creole. To a large extent these 'versions of English' are bound up with the value systems of the groups that use them and they can also take on the quality of being esteemed or devalued. Just as writing was once considered to be superior to talking as a language act there are still many current misconceptions about 'the value' of particular language forms. Yet all can be effective ways of making sense of experience and of the world around us and of conveying meaning. No one form is inherently superior to another but all can be valued as acceptable forms of communication depending on function and circumstance. This conclusion can be expressed in a fourth principle: *no one language form is superior to another but is comparable in that it possesses the capacity to convey meaning.*

Language is, however, more than a vehicle for communication. Because it has evolved in particular circumstances it is also a rich cultural expression illustrated through its words, structures and idioms, and its whole orientation. Associated with it, too, are other forms of expression, including the gestural and the graphic. The development of technology, and in particular, videotext, word-processing, and inter-active procedures, are likely to affect the development of language. It follows that any consideration of language needs to take into account the culture that has produced it and the history that has helped to shape it; this can be expressed in a fifth and final principle: *language is a cultural expression and its study needs to take into account the circumstances that have produced it and the factors affecting its future development.*

SOME CHARACTERISTICS OF PRACTICE

It is important that the practice of developing language is underpinned by the sort of thinking which characterises these key principles. Effective practice is likely to be distinguished by the following:

1 A learning 'environment' in which language is clearly alive. This is likely to be reflected in the learning circumstances and can be expressed in the verbal 'feel' of situations, for example the exchanges between pupils and teachers, and between pupils themselves, which need to be sustained and extended and to have the quality of dialogue and not that of 'a question and answer' session; the expression of different types of writing activity with purposes clear in the writer's mind and audiences identified; reading which ranges across powerful imaginative works but which also includes positive searching of texts for information of many kinds; and resources which include up to date encyclopaedias, dictionaries, and stimulating material of all types.
2 A realisation that context is of critical importance to language use. An obvious example relates to the atmosphere of the learning situation; for instance, a sympathetic and encouraging situation is likely to be the most effective one for promoting talk and extended discussion and can be the basis for work in more formal situations which, whilst being perfectly appropriate, may require a different style of language use; the one can prepare for the other. In this way it is necessary for teachers to be aware of the overall significance of context for promoting language activities. Pupils can be helped to

see the importance of context, too, in their use of language; this is likely to range from seeing patterns and correspondencies in words on the page to seeing how form and style can be appropriate in particular situations.

3 A readiness to accept that the language which children bring to school represents their identity and will be responded to sympathetically. Treated as a resource itself it can provide the points of development which will enable the teacher to extend the user's repertoire. This also implies that the teacher will know 'where each child is' in language, not in a precise sense, but in terms of overall grasp of the processes of communication. It is likely that this will be recorded informally so that teachers can build up a picture for their own professional use which will indicate significant points of development.

4 A vital interest in the way in which language manifests itself through the sound of words, and the delight to be taken in the use of particular words in a particular order – the use of style as well as a response to it when it is found in others.

5 An emphasis on 'appropriate' uses of language and the effectiveness of communication rather than on the idea of 'correctness'. As many uses of language are not matters of 'correctness', but rather matters of judgement, a more difficult concept to acquire, it is important for aspects such as style, tone and format to be given prominence in English teaching. The reports of the Assessment of Performance Unit[3] record that the major obstacles that pupils still have to overcome when writing do not lie with punctuation and spelling but rather with the need to look at the overall structure of the work in hand and the overall 'effect' it has. This is likely to lead to such questions as whether to use written language, or speech, the appropriate tone to adopt, the length to be aimed at, the importance of openings and conclusions and the overall organisation.

6 The encouragement of 'reflectiveness' on the part of the language user whether reading, writing, or talking, so that there is more emphasis on a considered approach to using language in order to help pupils become more conscious about the form and style to adopt for particular purposes.

7 The maintenance of records of progress, for, whilst it is not possible for pupils to reach particular 'points' at specific ages, the development of language is too important to learning and to future prospects to be left to chance. It is likely that these will vary in form and nature depending on the needs of the pupils as identified by the teacher. However, it is likely that the teacher will need to keep a record to include representative samples of pupils' writing and/or examples of particularly distinctive work, a reading inventory which instances books read, possibly with a periodic 'self-profile' when the

readers analyse reading tastes and habits, a commentary by the pupils on how comfortable discussion feels and whether there is a feeling that they can 'hold their own' together with any specific difficulties encountered. Clearly, this is pointing to the area of self-assessment and is implying that the pupils begin to accept responsibility for their own learning in language. Accompanying comments could be available from the teacher although it would be most helpful if an agreed 'negotiated' view could also be arrived at. An aspect of this could be the drawing up of 'a contract' which, accompanied by a clear account of a helpful way ahead, leads both pupils and teacher to see that specific attention is being paid to language needs. One of the recommendations of *A Language for Life*[4] was that records of children's work in language, including some expressions of achievement, should be able to accompany children when they change classes and change schools. Although this happens to some extent it is by no means the norm. The existence of such positive analysis would be very helpful to teachers who take on what is, after all, a role which continues to develop what has already been acquired.

8 A shared terminology for talking about aspects of language. Whilst it would not be helpful to have a 'universal' handbook of terms to talk about language as individual circumstances are likely to demand particular responses rather than the application of general terminology, it should still be evident that the teacher has an awareness of helpful terminology when talking to children about language. This, obviously, has specific implications for the education of teachers.

9 Evidence that language is not seen as existing in a vacuum but that it is enmeshed with all forms of human activity. This is likely to be expressed in the range of activities undertaken and will clearly relate to the world of the arts, to contentious issues, to scientific endeavour, and to other important aspects of human life.

10 A healthy curiosity about language and a fascination for it on the part of the teacher which, in turn, will help to produce in pupils the conscious realisation that language exists for them to create their own worlds and to construct meaning.

DEVELOPING A PARTNERSHIP

It will be readily recognised that the acquisition and development of 'the mother tongue' is a complex process and that its facilitation does not permit of easy or simple solutions. What will be agreed is that it is a human activity which is intimately bound up with ourselves and our interaction with others. It must also be remembered that a large part of the process must take place in contexts which are not school ones. However, the acceleration of language development and a sensitive intervention in the process are the proper concerns of all who have a specific role to play in the learning process. Teachers and parents have the most critical parts to play but others with perceptions of schools such as governors and employers also have important roles. Learning is never just a matter of schooling and this is particularly true of our confidence and capacity to use language which is very much a result of the background and the way in which language is viewed by people in positions of authority and influence. Consequently, the following points relate specifically to all who have a part to play in this endeavour.

All *teachers* whether working in primary or secondary education, and no matter what their 'specialism' or particular curriculum focus, need a language element in their initial training which illustrates the importance of language in learning. Furthermore, it is necessary to see that the element of language features in courses in in-service education programmes. Teachers need to be aware that their own use of language matters as they provide role models for their pupils. This is not a matter of 'elocution', or of having an 'approved' accent but it is very much a matter of pupils being able to see that their teachers have a grasp of language which enables them to encompass a wide range of learning situations. The teacher also needs to be able to communicate to parents some of the key ideas about language use.

As much of a child's language is developed in the home it is important for *parents* to see that they can be influential in helping to determine this, especially through the forms of conversation and the powerful medium of story. The degree to which children are able to form important concepts by means of this process are now well documented in such works as *Young Children Learning* by Barbara Tizard and Martin Hughes[5] and *Language, Learning and Education* by Gordon Wells.[6]

By taking an interest in the learning process and by becoming familiar with how children learn and develop their own language, *governors of schools* can also be of great value in supporting a broad curriculum which nurtures and sustains language. The HMI Primary Surveys[7] have clearly illustrated that language cannot flourish within the confines of a narrow curriculum.

Employers also need to be thoughtful when looking at the levels of competence in the young people they are recruiting. The power to communicate must be of great importance to both employers and employees. Undue emphasis on matters of neatness and accuracy in written presentation can prevent the development of an overview relating to language competence overall. In their turn employers also need to recognise that the contexts they create in the workplace, and the sort of relationships which develop, will have an important bearing on how people communicate. Certainly, employers will also always need a communications element in their training programmes for staff.

when the child is best served by close co-operation between these two parts of his/her life.

5.1 NCPTA notes that the work of the APU in assessing language performance finds evidence of rising standards. Summarising the APU's work, Geoffrey Thornton (DES 1986) concludes that teacher attitude is crucial in determining pupil performance. If pupils are encouraged to feel that they are good, or reasonably good, writers then they will be enabled to approach new writing tasks with confidence.

5.2 There is a grave danger that benchmarks at 7, 11 and 16 will emphasise failure and undermine the confidence which the APU found so essential to improved language performance. The 'backwash' effect of benchmarks on the curriculum is likely to be very considerable, and would, NCPTA considers, have a narrowing and constricting effect, similar to the narrow and repetitive coaching for the 11-plus.

5.3 The emphasis of the GCSE in both oral and written language takes account of 'different levels of ability' and 'a diverse range of skills'. NCPTA considers that this emphasis is incompatible with the fixedness implicit in the notion of benchmarks.

5.4 As well as the general stultifying effect of benchmarks on the curriculum experiences of children, NCPTA believes that they are particularly unsuitable for children aged seven, many of whom have great difficulty in settling into the routine of school life which may be immensely different from the particular variety of their experience.

5.5 Some LEAs will take 'rising fives' as young as four and a few weeks; some may not admit children until they are almost six years of age. How could results tested at benchmark aged seven therefore be fair?

5.6 NCPTA favours an emphasis upon the recast objectives for English as given by HMI in *English from 5 to 16: The Responses*, whereby 'experiences' within wide individual variations and 'expectations' of varied languaging activities are outlined. NCPTA agrees with HMI that high aspirations are appropriate for all pupils. Such expectations can be most fruitfully directed at problem-solving activities in language, and may be used in compiling profiles of pupils' achievements and formative assessment.

5.7 NCPTA believes that emphasis of this kind will be more likely to carry the confidence of parents and also the teaching profession which was largely critical of the section on Objectives in the original *English: 5 to 16* document.

The most appropriate use of any kind of sensitively applied testing would appear to us to be to determine the need for Special Needs provision. The emphasis should therefore be on diagnostic, rather than 'blanket', testing.

6. Oracy

NCPTA has welcomed the recognition of spoken English skills in the new GCSE examination and hope the Committee will stress the importance of oral competence. Such competence, however, extends beyond a checklist of 'skills', and methods of oral assessment should be broad and imaginative.

7. Literature

As we have already stated, NCPTA recognises communication and creativity as the primary functions of language. We see literature as a vehicle for developing both these areas and feel that literature is an essential part of the English curriculum.

7.1 Both traditional and contemporary texts should be used.

7.2 It is vital that children come to enjoy reading (for pleasure, information and research) and this goal could easily be destroyed by strong prescription.

7.3 NCPTA believes that teachers are best able to choose the texts that are appropriate for their own classes. We do believe that certain texts make themselves inappropriate or unacceptable, but we firmly believe that we should as a country employ a good, professional teaching force capable of making that decision. NCPTA would be most unhappy at the thought of central censorship.

8. To develop their language skills children need a richness of language experience. Books should be a natural, everyday part of their world. The opportunity to talk in small groups with adults, to be able to listen and to be listened to and valued as a contributor is essential.

It would be possible to draw up a list of language experiences that could be appropriate as a child's language entitlement over a school year, on the lines of HMI's recast objectives in *English from 5 to 16: The Responses* referred to above.

There will be resource implications if we really want to offer our children the richness of language experience that will help them develop as individuals and so further enrich our language.

9. From Knowledge to Understanding

Finally, NCPTA is anxious that the Kingman Committee is not so enamoured of its search for a 'model of language' that it falls into what Bullock called 'the confusion of everyday thought' of separating 'knowledge' into something which has an existence independent of someone who knows. Knowledge about language does not reside in reciting lists of rules, and bringing knowledge into being is 'a formulating process', highly personal, which 'must be brought to life afresh within each "knower" by his own efforts'. (4.9) That process of formulation is likely to be stultified by too ready obeisance to knowledge-as-benchmark.

EVIDENCE SUBMITTED TO THE KINGMAN COMMITTEE

by the National Association of Advisers in English

The setting-up of the Kingman Committee was preceded by a great deal of rhetoric. Much of what has appeared in the press has had more to do with polemics than with the educational interests of the children of this country. In this statement we have chosen to concentrate exclusively on those interests and to respond to the request expressed in a press statement issued on behalf of Sir John Kingman by the DES on 18th February, 1987. In it he requests comment on four specific matters; it is those four matters which this statement addresses.

1 'The Needs of Society in Present-day England as They Relate to Individuals' Ability to Communicate in Speech and in Writing'
The abilities of this kind needed by society in its individual members are well summarised in the National Criteria for English in the GCSE examination. They appear there as the Assessment Objectives. These criteria were established after consultation on a massive scale and can safely be assumed to represent the abilities regarded as important by those teaching and assessing English in examinations at 16+. It follows that these are the abilities which all English teaching in the country is required to cultivate.

The Assessment Objectives laid down in the National Criteria are as follows:

1. understand and convey information;
2. understand, order and present facts, ideas and opinions;
3. evaluate information in reading material and in other media, and select what is relevant to specific purposes;
4. articulate experience and express what is felt and what is imagined;
5. recognise implicit meaning and attitudes;
6. show a sense of audience and an awareness of style in both formal and informal situations;
7. exercise control of appropriate grammatical structures, conventions of paragraphing, sentence structure, punctuation and spelling in their writing;
8. communicate effectively and appropriately in spoken English.

The skills listed above are clearly interrelated and interdependent and, whilst all must be assessed, it is not envisaged that each skill need be separately tested.

We believe that, just as the skills listed need not be separately tested, they need not be separately taught. We also believe that English courses with the above as their stated objectives are well matched to the needs of society.

2 *'The Needs of Individuals as They Relate to Skills of Literacy and Communication Generally in a Rapidly Changing Society'*
Clearly it is in the interests of each individual as a member of society to have as fully developed as possible those abilities (defined at **1** above) which society needs. This will enhance the value of each individual to society and correspondingly increase each person's self-esteem. Thus, we believe that pupils in our schools need an English curriculum which is designed principally to develop their potential as *language users*.

Pupils need to know:

- that there are language varieties, usually referred to as registers, which differ according to the communicative context (purpose, situation, distance, roles, relationships);
- that all language-users have a repertoire of registers and/or dialects and that the greater the repertoire the greater the range of communicative contexts in which the user can function effectively;
- that registers and dialects do not form a hierarchy; all are equally valid in appropriate communicative contexts;
- that language has power, and control of it confers power: it can enchant, offend, hurt, manipulate, persuade, alienate; it is the stuff of thought and feeling; it can be used as a means of control;
- that books have a special place in their language development and that there are particular concepts and skills related to their use;
- that language use confers and confirms membership of a group or community and is therefore closely bound up with identity;
- that there are important differences between spoken and written language; writing is not simply speech written down, nor is speech merely an inferior version of writing;
- that language is constantly changing;
- that language is systematic;
- that appropriateness is a more useful concept than correctness.

It does not follow from the above that pupils inevitably need to be *taught* all the principles stated. Knowledge in many of these aspects of language is gained naturally through a combination of experience, use and observation. Knowledge gained in this way is just as valid as any other kind since it is reliable and re-usable, even though it is often not explicit.

3 *'The Training – Both Initial and In-service – Of This Country's Teachers in Relation to Those Needs'*

a) All teachers

All teachers, not just teachers of English, need to have the kind of awareness about language matters outlined in 2 above. In addition, they need to know:
- that their teaching must take account of the fact that not all pupils of the same age are at the same level of linguistic development;
- that performance levels in language are task-specific; the research of the APU provides firm evidence of this fact, which makes it unsound to attempt to describe language performance and abilities in general terms;
- that the role played by language in the learning process is a vital one which needs to be fully understood by teachers of all disciplines to all age-groups;
- that the *basic skills* of English are those which enable language-users to communicate effectively and appropriately in a wide range of situations;
- that in order to develop their own language structures pupils must have effective access to a wide range of narrative and non-narrative texts;
- that the central emphasis of English language teaching should be on communication and on the making, understanding and interpretation of meaning;
- that 'formal exercises in the analysis and classification of language contribute little or nothing to the ability to use it' (*English from 5 to 16*, 3.8);
- that 'language exercises from text-books or work cards are not effective means of *initiating* the learning of language skills' (*English from 5 to 16*, 3.10);
- how language is acquired and develops and the differences between first and second languages in this respect;
- the use and purposes of literacy and its impact on our society;
- that the language of teachers conveys powerful messages to pupils about their worth, their role in the educational process, in the school community and in society in general.

It would be useful if there were agreement about the most appropriate metalanguage for teachers and pupils to use in order to talk about language. It should also be agreed that such a language is to be used for the purpose of description, not prescription.

b) Teachers of English

In addition to those matters listed under (*a*), teachers of English should know:
- that the role of teacher intervention in children's language development is crucial; how to make sensitive interventions which will be likely to foster enthusiasm, growth and development;
- how to use pupils' errors as growth-points in their language development;
- the importance of reviewing and revising in the process of composing speech and writing and how to assist in that process while still preserving the autonomy of the pupil;
- how to create in their classrooms a community of language-users in which mutual support and encouragement are the norm;
- that, all other things being equal, teachers who write make the best teachers of writing;
- how to relate the study of literature and the study of language to each other and combine the two studies into a unified and stimulating course;
- that the study of one's language (and the languages of others) is both worthy and valuable in its own right; it is a fascinating area of study which does not need to be justified by claiming that it will improve language performance; indeed, it is difficult to substantiate such a claim since all the research of which we are aware shows no positive correlation between theoretical linguistic study and linguistic performance;
- the literary forms and the different varieties of written and spoken language which children experience in their daily lives;
- that the assessment of English should be consistent with the principles stated above.

There are two points which we would emphasise in relation to the initial and in-service training of teachers:

(i) there should be compulsory 'language and learning' courses as part of the initial training of *all* teachers;
(ii) that English should be firmly established as a National Priority Area under the Local Education Authority Training Grant Scheme and that this step should be taken as a matter of urgency.

4 'English Language Teaching in Primary, Middle Years and Secondary Phases of Schooling'
Our regular visits to classrooms have convinced us that great progress has been made in the last twenty years. We indicate below some of the

creditable features of English work which are commonly observed today but which would have been rare in the past:

- children of all ages capable of extensive and complex pieces of writing;
- a wide range of writing being tackled successfully throughout the primary and secondary phases, frequently published;
- the exciting use of a wider range of quality fiction and poetry than ever before;
- an increase in the use of real and demanding contexts for writing and speaking, with 'real' audiences often raising the level of competence expected; these audiences are often drawn from outside the school community;
- the common experience of taking a piece of writing through a number of drafts;
- an increased awareness and understanding of the media;
- comprehension work related to realistic situations and real material rather than to mere desk exercises;
- parental and community involvement in the development of children's reading ability;
- a greater ability to talk effectively and wider opportunities to use talk as a means of learning, especially collaborative learning.

The work of the APU has shown that pupils in our schools achieve creditable standards, contrary to the popular mythology which has much greater publicity. The APU tests have also shown that the pupils' greatest concern is with the *conventions* of language; they do not need to be convinced of the importance of accurate punctuation and spelling, since it is these two features, along with neatness, which they use as the criteria of good and bad writing. When asked to nominate what they thought were the most important qualities in writing, 'one third of the pupils (the largest single group) took prescriptive views about the importance of the correct management of surface features such as spelling, neatness and punctuation' (*The Assessment of Writing*, Janet White, APU, p. 16).

It is those much more fundamental aspects of language teaching and learning, to which we draw attention above, which need a higher profile.

EVIDENCE SUBMITTED TO THE KINGMAN COMMITTEE

by the National Association for the Teaching of English

ABSTRACT

The Introduction presents NATE's view of the context in which the Inquiry takes place.

Section 1 then opens with an examination of the different kinds of knowledge, ranging from implicit knowledge gained through direct experience, to explicit knowledge of a kind gained through more conscious and reflective means.

Section 2 deals with widespread and dangerous misconceptions about the relationship between the possession of explicit academic knowledge about language, and the ability to use language accurately and effectively.

Section 3 concerns what we know about language, and points out that the academic study of linguistics, though useful to teachers, covers only a proportion of the knowledge of language that informs the talking, listening, reading and writing of the competent language user.

Section 4 consists of an examination of children's pre-school language development, including a consideration of early encounters with the written word.

Section 5 is informed by recent advances in our understanding of the processes of language learning in older children, and examines the ways in which pre-school language learning can be developed and extended in the school years.

Section 6 concerns the kind of teaching that is needed to make this language learning most productive, and draws on a range of effective practices that have been developed in school classrooms.

Section 7 addresses the kinds of teacher education courses demanded by the approaches to classroom teaching that we have outlined.

Section 8 concerns the in-service training of teachers necessary in an area where recent years have seen significant advances in academic research and in classroom practice.

Section 9 deals with the issue of assessment and shows how universal "objective" testing of the kind recently proposed would be an extremely

complex and costly undertaking, far more likely to produce constricting and damaging effects upon learning than to yield information with any degree of reliability or validity on matters as complex as children's command of the English Language.
The Conclusion summarises our main arguments.

INTRODUCTION

NATE is an organisation which represents several thousand schools and secondary English Departments as well as a large number of individuals working at all levels of education from the nursery years to sixth forms and beyond. Through our activities at local branch and national levels, our newsletter and our journal, we ensure that the Executive Committee of our organisation is kept closely in touch with the views of our members. This document is the product of wide consultations of this sort and has been unanimously endorsed by The Council of NATE branches and by our Annual Policy meeting held in April of this year.

In English teaching we can no more return to the practices of the past than we can in medicine or agriculture. The context has changed and the pressures and expectations are very different from those which surrounded the schooling of our pupils' parents and grandparents. The language demands of daily living and the world of work are greater than they ever were and our pupils need to develop a greater understanding of language variety than any previous generation. Without an effective command of spoken and written language, our pupils will be ill-equipped to earn a living, retrain for new employment, play their part in a multi-cultural democracy, or lead a full personal life.

The Association is well aware both of the work to be done to fulfil these ambitions and of unevenness in provision and practice. The national surveys of primary education (*Primary Education in England*, DES, 1978) and secondary education (*Aspects of Secondary Education in England*, DES, 1979) found much that was boring, repetitious and trivial, and clearly identified teaching practices which lead to underachievement and alienation. Such practices were not informed by any coherent body of underlying theory, nor was the teaching that of interested and committed professionals. In fact, many primary and secondary classes were, and are, being taught by staff with no recognisable qualification in this area, and little interest in it. In too many secondary schools, colleagues are given a couple of English classes to fill up their timetables on the basis of 'we all speak it, so we can all teach it' – a fact which hides a very real shortage of English teachers.

The national surveys did however identify the kinds of teaching and classroom activities which led to effective language learning and development, consistent with what we commend in this document. The Association welcomes such initiatives as the School Curriculum Development Committee's National Writing Project and the proposed National Oracy Project, and hopes that your committee will give fresh impetus to the wider dissemination of good practice in language learning. There is much of which one can be justly proud in the advances in primary and secondary English teaching, and while much remains to be done, during the past two decades, NATE has helped to build a coherent and highly productive set of practices informed by work in linguistics, psychology, sociology and the study of literature and the media.

What is clear is that there are no simple, inexpensive solutions. If we require informed, committed and skilful teachers of English, sensitive to the language needs of individual pupils, able to motivate them to learn, to monitor their achievements and share that process with them, the nation must provide the climate, the time and the resources to attract them and ensure that they can carry out their work effectively. The climate should encourage these teachers in their further learning, and their continuing development as active and effective readers and writers. The time should be available for such matters as discussing progress and development with pupils on an individual basis. And the resources must be provided in terms of suitable and sufficient books and materials, equipment such as word-processors, properly furnished suites of rooms, and access to libraries and to writers and talkers of a variety of kinds, both in and out of the school setting.

We are keen to help draw on the very substantial body of knowledge and sound practice that has been developed in this country, and to play our part in the provision of in-service training and the dissemination of good practice. Although we have been saddened to see many excellent and well-qualified teachers of English leaving both primary and secondary schools in recent years, we are optimistic that your committee will make recommendations which could lead to major improvements in the effectiveness of language learning in our schools.

Henrietta Dombey
Chair
The National Association for the Teaching of English.

KNOWLEDGE ABOUT LANGUAGE

1 The Problem of Knowledge
Before we address the issue of knowledge about language, we need to consider what we might mean by knowledge. Of the many kinds of knowledge, we would want to list the following:

Type 1 Knowledge gained through experience, which though definite, reliable and reusable, is not generally explicit nor describable in analytic terms by the user. *Examples:* the process of learning to speak; having the sense that someone is lying; riding a bicycle.

Type 2   Knowledge gained largely through experience and observation, which can be signalled to others by shared symbols and part explanations and which is credited because it relates convincingly to experience or previous knowledge of some kind. *Examples:* those clouds will break up; what constitutes a story; what is understood by classical music; road sense; the process of learning to read.

Type 3   Knowledge gained through cataloguing, analysis, theorising and hypothesis. This is knowledge of a more abstract kind with little direct relation to first-hand experience, which includes what Vygotsky called non-spontaneous concepts. It may also require the use of artificial languages with their own rule-governed systems. *Examples:* mathematics; geology; linguistics; computer languages.

We need to add a few important points:

1 Knowledge gained through experience is often acquired earlier than other kinds of knowledge and is the standard against which most people measure the truth, validity or usefulness of other knowledge.
2 Knowledge which does not arise directly from experience ('non-spontaneous concepts') will need to connect with knowledge gained from experience, ('spontaneous concepts') in order to be intellectually accessible. The process of education is centrally concerned with establishing links between spontaneous and non-spontaneous concepts.
3 Knowledge of a more abstract kind depends upon acceptance of its premises, and thereafter on its own internal logic and coherence.
4 None of these kinds is inherently more valuable than any other kind.

2 Misconceptions
Popular misconceptions about how language is learned do not help learners, or their teachers. One of the most pervasive is the belief that you must learn 'the rules' and then apply them correctly. This is demonstrably not so with language.

First, the few and partial 'rules' cover very little of the spoken or written language. Many important features such as pitch, stress, pause and intonation are used without any consciously known rules. Some generalisations can be useful in drawing attention to patterns and social markers, but they are neither comprehensive enough, nor reliable enough, to function as rules to guide use. Languages have changed and developed over thousands of years without highly developed analytic descriptions of their processes, and all the evidence is that such descriptions follow changes which speakers and writers of a language have already made. Linguistics is concerned with describing what is, rather than with prescribing what ought to be.

Next, the presumption that teaching such abstract knowledge of language as a system will increase the effectiveness and competence of individual language users is mistaken. In fact, to quote the Bullock Report (DES 1975) 'there is no evidence that it helps them develop their writing and speaking skills'. Indeed, there is evidence that it can inhibit the growth of competence, making some so hesitant that they can scarcely perform as speakers and writers at all (Harris). By introducing unnecessary formality and by distancing the work from the writer at too early a stage, in a way that tends to obscure rather than clarify, it can create an obstacle between the meaning children are trying to formulate and their expression of it in writing. It can cause particularly damaging confusion for those who are inexperienced in the use of Standard British English and for those who do not have the same features in their own first languages.

Another misconception, that all learning follows a hierarchical development towards knowledge of the more abstract kind which parallels the chronological development of conceptualising skills, is now being rejected across subject disciplines and at the highest academic levels. It is not only artists, musicians and athletes who learn mainly through experience and observation. Mathematics, science, modern languages and design technology are increasingly requiring experiential, problem-solving, cumulative patterns of learning. The best language teaching recognises that speakers, readers and writers learn to be good executants and performers principally through experience and observation.

The real nature of the knowledge of and about language that learners and teachers work with in schools is clearly defined in the introduction to *Language in Use* (Doughty, Pearce, and Thornton):

> Pupils bring to the classroom a native speaker's knowledge of, and intuitions about, language and its place in human society. In this sense, the task of English teachers is not to impart a body of knowledge, but to work upon, develop, refine and clarify, the knowledge and intuitions that their pupils already possess. Consequently, they are interested in language as it affects the lives of individuals and the fabric of society. They are unlikely to find the central concern of the specialist in linguistics – the explicit, formal and analytical description of the patterns of a language, immediately relevant to their needs.

This removes a further misconception: that models of language which might be offered by linguistics could take over from the now generally discredited prescriptive teaching of 'grammar'. As Gannon and Czerniewska put it in *Using Linguistics – An Educational Focus:*

There is no complete and definitive analysis of language – indeed, there never will be – each approach has insights of value to offer.

3 Knowledge of and about Language

We gain our knowledge of language largely through using it in order to construct and construe linguistic meanings in a variety of social situations and contexts. The first aim of linguists by contrast, is to set down in explicit and academic form, as knowledge of type 3, an account of the regularities and systems which may underlie the construction and construing of language. But our intuitive knowledge of language is so vast, complex and subtle, that linguists have managed to formulate only a portion of it. All of us know much more of language than we can ever make academically explicit.

Linguistics has so far had comparatively little to say about some of the major concerns of English teachers. We have in mind, for example, the ways in which attitudes, feelings and emotion are conveyed, the logic and structure of longer stretches of discourse like discussion and argument, and a comprehensive and rich analysis of oral exchanges. The aspects of language which have been formally studied have tended to be those which have been easiest to describe comprehensively, and thus more limited in their complexity and scope. Linguists have been successful with many aspects of the form of language such as phonemics, morphology, syntax and some aspects of lexis, while the forms and structure of language on a larger scale have been studied in other disciplines.

Language, however, is not a structure operating in a vacuum, and the social contexts in which we use language to make and construe meaning have a determining influence on the choices available to us at all levels. This has meant that form and structure cannot be divorced from social contexts and purposes, nor from the meanings it is possible to create and to understand. Thus knowledge about language has also been gained from sociolinguistics and from other social and cultural studies, and there have also been studies of the ways in which meaning is made, ranging from semantics and cognitive psychology to philosophy and aesthetics.

Teachers need a rich conception of language, one that recognises that language is interwoven with nearly all the ways in which we think, feel and act in society and is not only shaped by social context, but has itself a shaping function that operates on our private feelings and our most public institutions. A relevant model of language and the way it works has to acknowledge the interrelatedness of:

function and social context;
meaning and significance;
form and structure.

Such a model would operate at a variety of different levels, from sound, letter and word, through to the larger scale utterances such as

conversation, speech and book. Since the total of our explicit knowledge about language is still, and is always likely to be, partial and incomplete, and since that knowledge is drawn from a wide variety of fields, we should concentrate attention on developing modes of inquiry about language which are concerned with questions like:
who is saying or writing what, to whom, and why?
as well as:
how, by what means, and in what context?

4 A Model of Spoken and Written Language Development
Those involved in the education of children and young people are bound also to be concerned with the acquisition and development of language, and with the processes of learning, including the workings of mind and memory.

Among linguists who have studied the development of spoken language (Brown, Slobin, Halliday, etc.) there is now a considerable measure of agreement about how children learn to talk, not just in English but in all the languages studied thus far. They emphasise the fact that spoken language is acquired rather than directly taught, and that direct instruction seems to have very little effect on the process. Children learn to talk in interaction with their parents, and other adults and children (Wells). The fact that they can draw on shared contexts and shared experiences is important in enabling them to construct shared meanings. Adults ascribe meaning to children's earliest utterances and work with them to establish and develop their meanings.

In addition to this kind of interaction, where children's efforts are strongly supported by more experienced language users, children engage in a considerable amount of spontaneous practice. They run through their language repertoires in pre-sleep monologues, and play with the sounds, tunes, syntax and meanings of language (Weir). This kind of verbal play is often generated by important experiences and strong feelings; it is inventive, creative, and can be highly patterned and poetic (Chukovsky).

As children become more fluent speakers they try out new language forms, and it becomes clear that they are engaged in a constant and tacit process of inducing the rules of the language they are operating in. Their errors show them hypothesising about language, drawing analogies from linguistic forms they already know, over-generalising, and self-correcting. But children do not simply take on adult grammar bit by bit. They work with a series of transitional grammars which are successively discarded in favour of the more complex adult system. They receive constant feedback and information from the adults they talk with, but though they obviously make use of this linguistic information, they may not do so directly or immediately.

This model of spoken language acquisition offers a powerful analogy for our understanding of how children learn to read and write. It now seems more exact to think of children acquiring written language, than to view reading and writing as being directly taught. It is clear that all language processes are interactional and cultural. The balance of evidence, both from theoretical studies and from schools and classrooms, seems to be that spoken language development and the development of reading and writing have more in common than they have in distinction, and that educational practices based on the assumption that reading and writing can be straightforwardly acquired seem to be more productive than approaches which assume that reading and writing are difficult skills which have to be formally analysed and taught sequentially.

5 Learners and Learning

The evidence that reading can be learned in similar ways to spoken language comes partly from studies of young readers who can read before they go to school (Clark, Torrey), partly from studies of the 'reading-like behaviour' of very young children, from under two years of age (Holdaway), and partly from many contemporary classrooms where children are successfully learning to read without a commercial reading scheme (Bennett, Waterland). What young learners appear to need in order to become readers is: the kind of familiarity with the language of books that comes from being read to often; access to a range of books, of a kind that will give insight into the rewards of reading; the opportunity to have chosen books over and over again, so that a store of known favourites is established; the opportunity to read and look at books independently and often; and regular opportunities to read with the support and help of adult readers who will supply them with information. Some conscious awareness of the phonemes of spoken language appears to contribute to success in early reading (Bradley and Bryant) but above all it seems, children need a sense that reading is an important, pleasurable activity (Meek).

As young children engage with written language and its workings they employ most of the strategies they have already used in acquiring the spoken language. They develop an awareness of rules and patterns, use all the available cues to meaning, over-generalise and make errors which reveal the hypotheses they are adopting. It has been Kenneth Goodman above all who has drawn attention to the intelligence of children's mistakes when they are tackling unfamiliar texts, and has made clear how important the confidence to take risks is in learning to read.

Learning to write cannot be separated from learning to read, and studies such as Margaret Clark's have shown that young fluent readers often begin to write at the same time as they learn to read, or even before. Less work has been done on this area, although the number of recent books on early writing suggests that it is becoming an important focus for research and for classroom investigation. It is clear, however, that children are able, from the nursery years, to demonstrate their awareness of written language and of print and the ways in which these are used in public contexts (Ferreiro and Teberosky). Their oral story-telling, if they are used to being read to, often shows that they are taking on the tunes and syntactical structures of written language, and the shapes of stories (Fox, Dombey). They can spend a great deal of time in practising aspects of writing, often through spontaneous copying. When they are writing independently, their early attempts at words show that they are using the same capacity to hypothesise, generalise and work out rules and patterns that was demonstrated in their spoken language acquisition. Their spelling development shows them making better and better attempts at the standard spelling of words over time, given adequate information and support (Bissex). Where they are reading a great deal, having frequent opportunities to write themselves, and being given plenty of support and feedback, their written language development can be as rapid and 'natural' as spoken language development is for most children.

It must be stressed that the influence of imaginative literature is vital for language development at all stages in school life. It is not always realised how significant a role imaginative literature, whether oral or written, plays in enabling inexperienced users of English to develop their language repertoires, and particularly that of Standard English, nor what support it gives such children to discuss and write about known and shared texts. It is in reading literature which engages their imagination that pupils encounter some of the most powerful and ambitious uses of language, through which some of their most exciting explorations of the relation between linguistic form and meaning take place.

6 Productive Language Teaching
The first and most important way in which language competence develops is through use. Whereas linguists are concerned to describe language as it is, teachers are inevitably involved in encouraging a continuing search for better uses of language. Their role is to help their pupils assess the demands of situation and purpose, and move towards the language which best fits these: language that is more rational and more cogent, more lucid and more expressive, more fair-minded and more committed, more eloquent, more direct, more precise and more rich in meanings. All our inquiries about the natural and human world, all the ways we organise action in it, set up demands of this kind on language. Teachers in all curriculum areas have a responsibility to develop relevant uses of language.

In all English Language teaching the basic task is to enrich and extend children's experience of language, both spoken and written, and to provide a constantly expanding variety of opportunities to use spoken and written language in real and in imagined situations. Children will draw on everyday language (including home dialects and mother tongues) for these purposes, as well as on the growing range of language registers and varieties of which they are becoming aware.

Through discussing their reading and their spoken and written language work with teachers and other children, and through bringing some work up to performable or publishable standard, children can begin to focus on the form as well as on the content of the language they use. They can be helped to acquire, particularly through the activities of revising, rethinking and editing their writing, enough linguistic vocabulary (paragraph, speech marks, past tense etc.) which relates to the form and orthographic system of their writing to be able to discuss it when necessary, but this vocabulary will not be a key factor in their writing development.

Second, children's awareness of language as a system can be sharpened through role play, games and discussion. The case for this kind of approach was put cogently in *Language in Use* (Doughty, Pearce and Thornton), some of the lessons of which are only just beginning to be understood. In the introduction, the authors point out that the vast majority of pupils possess extensive knowledge of the language and that,

> In addition, as a natural consequence of speaking a language, they possess strong intuitions about its nature and function, but these remain for the most part undeveloped.

The strategy adopted in *Language in Use* is to 'start from that ... intuition and work towards a much more developed awareness'.

In this kind of approach, children are invited to use their powers as experienced observers of language and human behaviour to 'play out' particular aspects of language, such as the relationship between what people say and what they mean, or the language of news bulletins, or to discuss examples of spoken and written language in use. For instance, a group can be asked whether a story 'sounded like a fairy story', or invited to discuss the way in which regional speech had been indicated in a written dialogue. These activities which draw on children's extensive tacit knowledge of language, and which are as accessible to primary as to secondary schools, lead children to focus directly on aspects of language which they would normally regard as 'transparent'. By enabling children to reflect on language, such activities help them achieve more conscious control over what they already know. They make use of the very faculty of mind which is of most help to children in their general language development and their inductive process of language learning: the perception of pattern.

Third, pupils can engage in a more systematic study of, or research into, particular aspects of language, perhaps as part of a topic on verbal and non-verbal communication, a study of persuasive language in advertising and propaganda, or a project on young children's language. This kind of language study should be undertaken because it is both intrinsically interesting, and socially useful, not as a means of improving pupils' use of language. The more children are aware of themselves as language users and the 'linguistic ways of the world', the more likely they are to be:

- able to differentiate between the genuine and the dishonest and spurious;
- tolerant and understanding of others' language use;
- prepared to participate in unfamiliar, or stressful contexts, rather than opt out.

Of these three kinds of approach, the first two would be likely to be most valuable, since they build directly on children's existing competences. In general, teaching which assumes knowledge and competence will be more effective than that which assumes ignorance and deficiency. The positive effects of recognition of students' competence in languages other than English has been widely documented (Houlton). In general, there is now a greater awareness of the advantages that speakers of more than one language or dialect can possess because of their wider linguistic experience, where this experience is acknowledged and used. Where this has occurred, where language awareness courses have been rooted in the languages and varieties of English used by the pupils, there have been benefits for all students.

Many of the teaching approaches already described draw on pupils' knowledge of language and social behaviour. School students come to school with intuitions about the power that language has in society. By the time they are coming to the end of their compulsory education they should have a fuller and more explicit understanding, if they are to participate actively in the world outside school. We would not wish to claim this territory in the curriculum as the domain solely of the English teacher, but there are some strong traditions within English teaching which make the English classroom an appropriate place for such study. Some of the elements we have in mind have their origins in the differing traditions of literary studies, others are linguistic like the programme outline for *Language in Use*, others have been made available through studies of the media. Evidence suggests that for school students, knowledge about the relationship of language and society has to start from activities in which meaning is central. We have in mind, for example, techniques of analysis which involve establishing a range of readings of a text rather than a single interpretation, which distinguish between denotative and connotative meanings, and which enable students to relate the detail of a text (word choice, syntax, metaphor, etc.) to wider sets of attitudes and values.

For example, some recent work in schools has been specifically concerned with the construction of gender. It has been multi-dimensional in that it has included such topics as making new readings of old texts, field-work collecting examples of language at the level of the word, phrase, and sentence to examine underlying assumptions, study of group interaction to analyse turn-taking, and productive activities such as writing from alternative points of view, and making alternative advertisements for television.

In general, students have a right to understand the creative potential of language to express ideas and feelings, and a right to understand the ways in which it can be used against them to control or mislead. They have a right too to experience, through poetry, novels, plays and stories, language at its most powerful and memorable, so that they may also become aware of its expressive force and potential for development in their hands.

It is clear that the model of language learning we have proposed requires a corresponding model of teaching: one which is active, responsive, informed and empirical. All teachers need to have an understanding of language and its development. The model of teacher education which this implies is discussed in the following section.

7 Teacher Training
Teachers' understanding of how language works must be broadly construed. Teachers need to recognise the linguistic competence that children bring to school and to provide the best circumstances and support for development to take place, both in what pupils know about language and what they can do with it. They need, therefore, a model of language which is sufficiently dynamic to interrelate meaning, function and form, and which can be fully integrated with theories of development and learning.

Teachers for whom children's language is a major responsibility need a particularly coherent and well-founded understanding of what language is and how it works, but all teachers need some knowledge about the role of language in the all-round development of children and young people. All need to understand the complex interplay between the purposes for which we use language, the meanings we construct and the underlying systems of rules and conventions on which we draw. For adults, as for children, this means relating what they already know as users of language to more academic knowledge.

But students preparing for a career in teaching demand a different approach to the study of language from those who have chosen to follow a course in linguistics. They need to see and feel its contribution to their effectiveness as classroom teachers. Their focus needs to be a professional one: they need to set their study of language in the context of a study of learning. Student teachers need also a fully developed confidence in their own skill as language users, as readers, writers, talkers, and listeners. They need, for example, to know what it feels like to produce an effective piece of writing, to tell a good story, to contribute to a productive discussion, or to construct a coherent and satisfying meaning from a literary text. They need the experience of using language with imagination, effectiveness and sensitivity to the demands of the situation, for a wide range of purposes and in a wide range of contexts. This is vital if they are to support their children's learning to best effect, and to have confidence in their imaginative ability to make language learning attractive, challenging and intrinsically rewarding.

During the 1970s the courses developed at initial training, diploma and M.A. levels, most notably by the London, Leeds and Birmingham Schools of Education, became internationally known for their work on the theory and practice of Language and Learning, Language and Communication, and Language in Society. The nature of these in-service courses we discuss in Section 8, but we would note here that work in centres such as these has had a seminal influence on teacher training throughout the country. The most significant aspect of this influence has been to complement consideration of what needs to be learnt with a thorough exploration of the processes of learning engaged in by both students and pupils.

For in planning courses of language study for intending teachers we need to do more than itemise the knowledge that teachers of English should possess. We also need to ensure:

1. that students are encouraged to draw on their existing knowledge of types 1 and 2, and to extend this;
2. that the development of students as language users is given space and importance;
3. that students are given the opportunity to use their own experiences of language learning (as pupils and as teachers, inside the classroom and out) as starting points for their explorations of language;
4. that, where possible, students study linguistic topics such as the differences between spoken and written language under professionally relevant headings, such as the teaching of reading and writing;
5. that knowledge about language should not be seen as an end in itself, but as a means of enabling teachers to promote effective learning in pupils.

On all courses of initial training for teachers who will play a part in the teaching of English certain topics need to be explored. Our list includes:

1 *Language in society*
   a) expectations
   b) choices
   c) the construction of meaning

2 *Language and social identity*
   a) its relationship with feeling
   b) its part in personal identity
   c) its part in group and cultural identity

3 *The power of language*
   a) to persuade, manipulate and control
   b) for humour, fantasy, imagination and creativity

4 *Language and variation*
   a) languages other than English
   b) creoles
   c) accents, dialects and varieties (region, class and occupation)
   d) forms of discourse, written and spoken

5 *Standard written language*
   a) differences between written and spoken forms
   b) orthographic system (spelling, punctuation etc.)
   c) lexical, semantic and syntactic patterns/conventions

6 *Language acquisition and development* – for learners of English both as a first and a second (or third) language
   a) spoken language
   b) reading and understanding
   c) writing

7 *Language and learning*
   a) its role in cognition, including bilingual issues
   b) its heuristic functions e.g. role play

8 *Language in school*
   a) the language demands of schools
   b) language in classroom interaction

Because courses are different from each other in terms of participants and their destinations, they are likely to vary in the weighting they will give to these topics. They will also vary in the balance they achieve between, for example, enabling students to get a sense of, and reflect upon, their own abilities as speakers, readers and writers, and their techniques for description and analysis; and between study of pre-school language learning and the language demands society places on young adults.

Within the construction of courses, some of these elements may well be subsumed within components allocated for specialist curriculum work. But work on the languages and dialects which school children bring to the classroom might be part of general education work consisting of studies of pupils and schools. Work on classroom interaction or the language demands of school may be best studied from cross-curricular perspectives. We note however, that even with such arrangements, the available time on some courses may not prove sufficient to provide adequate coverage.

In this connection, we would like to state that the CATE criteria for the accreditation of courses for initial teacher training has led to a dramatic reduction in the time available for the study of language. The figure of 100 hours, which appeared in the Bullock Report as the recommended minimum for class contact time for language study, has now been reinterpreted to cover the associated study time and even related school experience. The stipulation requiring the equivalent of two years full-time subject study now means that it is very hard, if not impossible, for institutions to provide much more than half the previous class contact time for language study for those not specialising in English. The consequences of this will be very serious for primary education.

The understandings which teachers need to develop are complex, and it may be helpful if we give an example which shows something of this complexity. Intending teachers are likely to be particularly concerned with the way in which children learn to widen their linguistic repertoires and with the pedagogy that promotes such learning most effectively. But there are wider perspectives which are necessary for a thorough understanding of the social significance of what is being learnt, and of how this relates to other forms and usages in other places and times, of the way in which the child's meaning potential is being extended, and of the linguistic forms in which this is realised.

The topic of the oral language learning that takes place in the school years, treated from these points of view, might include a consideration of the following:

1 the social contexts in which our pupils use oral language now and will use it in the future, both in and out of school, and the various languages, dialects and registers associated with these;
2 something of the range, complexity and subtlety of the meanings conveyed through the spoken word, both in terms of content and ideas and social relationships;
3 the structure of larger forms such as narrative and conversation, the use of markers of formality and informality, the salience of intonation

patterns, and the apparent syntactic 'imperfections' of much semantically rich informal talk;
4 the relation of function to form in the business of learning the spoken language, the role of oral narrative, drama and small group discussion in focusing pupils on the social and semantic purposes of talk.

Whether we are dealing at any given moment with helping children to learn to talk through a problem with others, to organise a scientific report, to punctuate speech or to write a more powerful story, our aim should be to develop in future teachers a more precise idea of what it is they wish their pupils to learn, a sense of its significance and the way this varies between different social groups, an awareness of the way in which it might enlarge the range of potential meanings available to the pupil, a sense of the relevant experiences and expectations that pupils might bring to the task, and an understanding of how this learning might best be achieved. Students' confidence in their own ability to handle such uses of language effectively is, of course, a necessary precondition.

With respect to the initial training of all teachers, we urge the committee to recommend that:

1 Any model of the English Language informing courses of teacher education should include consideration of the dynamics of development, of social context and of semantics, as well as of linguistic form.
2 Components of language study take full account of students' professional perspective as intending teachers.
3 The DES minimum figure of 100 hours for language study be taken to refer to class contact time only.
4 Those preparing to be primary teachers or to teach English or related areas of the curriculum in secondary schools, be expected and encouraged to develop their proficiency as language users through more varied means than seminars and essays.

8 In-service Training
Because of the pace at which exploration in this area has advanced in recent years, and because of the rate at which productive teaching strategies have been developed, experienced teachers could profit from courses covering much of the territory we have outlined for initial training. However, since they have a considerably greater experience of language issues in a classroom and school context, they will also need regular opportunities to share experience and good practice and to review their policies and teaching approaches.

It is unreasonable to expect that colleagues who completed their initial training twenty or thirty years previously will have been able to keep pace with developments over that period unless language has been a principal professional interest. Those who took a degree in English Literature 20 years ago, for example, would learn much from courses explicitly addressing language, and much also from more recent approaches to literature and its teaching, and these in turn would provide a good base for learning more about language issues. Other courses of initial training have only recently paid much attention to language as a crucial issue in education, especially those orientated towards teaching subject specialisms at secondary or F.E. level. And primary teachers who qualified 15 or more years ago may have done so with negligible attention to spoken and written language or their development in and out of school.

Were the committee to make recommendations about the in-service training of teachers, we would feel it important to stress, as we did in *Language Across the Curriculum* (Torbe), that every teacher is a teacher of language, whichever sector of education they are working in. Thus there would be a need for local education authorities to mount INSET courses and training, not only for language post holders in primary schools and for teachers of English as a first or second language in secondary schools, but for all teachers whatever their principal interest or specialism.

However, the needs of specialists are particularly great. Many LEAs have recognised the importance of extending the knowledge and understanding of language of their most promising practitioners through one year secondments to courses offered by Schools of Education and by other institutions which have developed expertise in this area. LEAs' willingness and ability to support these courses is now being substantially reduced by recent changes in funding for in-service training, just when the Committee might consider recommending the extension of such courses to a wider range of teachers. Since LEAs have difficulty in seeing language as a local concern, if such provision is to continue, in-service training in language areas may need to be declared a National Priority supported by central funding under the Grant Related In-service Training arrangements.

Time is the obstacle on which many previous attempts at curriculum reform and in-service training have foundered. Only those most dedicated and free from other obligations will be able to attend in-service training at the end of the school day, at weekends or in holiday periods. If there is to be a serious attempt to improve the language experience and learning of our pupils, it will be necessary for HMI and LEAs to co-operate, not only in the provision of INSET courses, but in enabling teachers to be released to attend them and in providing the necessary financial support for teachers to make best use of them.

A particular problem which has been identified by HMI is the large numbers of teachers in secondary schools who teach English, special needs classes or ESL without any specialist training to do so, or any detailed knowledge of how language competence increases and develops.

There needs to be a substantial programme of in-service training for these teachers.

There is a similar need for those colleagues who work in special schools, off-site and support units, whose own training may not have included a language development component, but whose work is largely concerned with promoting more effective uses of written and spoken language.

As with initial training, the kinds of courses which would be most useful are likely to be those in which teachers take an active part and which draw on the knowledge about language which they already possess. Courses which allow teachers to relate new knowledge and theoretical insights to their own practice will foster the creative and imaginative skills needed to develop more effective teaching strategies and to increase the language learning of their pupils.

Topics which give an indication of this might include:

1 *Classroom provision for early reading*, which would include such matters as the experience of literacy the children bring with them on school entry, the literacy demands of the school curriculum and the wider world, a re-examination of the roles of the learner, the teacher and the parent, and a consideration of the kinds of text which have most to teach the learner.
2 *Approaches to active comprehension*, which would include the strategies of sequencing, word deletion and prediction referred to as D.A.R.T.s in *The Effective Use of Reading* (Lunzer & Gardner). By working through some example texts teachers will see that pupils can gain experience in problem solving, lay the foundations for detailed argument, and can focus in on the syntax and choice or order of words, as well as learn the subject matter of the text in an interesting and approachable way.
3 *Teacher interventions*, which would involve recording examples of classroom talk and interaction, or the collection of samples of written work, so that teachers could examine the times and kinds of interventions they make and assess their effectiveness in helping pupils become more capable language users.
4 *Action research* of various kinds, such as the collection of examples of talk or writing, or lessons given in a variety of curriculum areas, to examine what they seem to be contributing to pupils' language development and competence.

We would like to see the committee make recommendations on in-service training, including the following:

1   Those lacking initial training of the kind we recommend should not be permitted to teach English in schools without relevant in-service training.

2 Language learning and language-related issues be included in the list of national priorities under the GRIST scheme.
3 National support be provided for one-year full-time courses leading to a recognised qualification in language.
4 Every LEA and educational institution dealing with the compulsory years of schooling be required to collect examples of its best practice in the area of language and learning.
5 Every LEA be required to organise in-service courses on language and related issues, with the help of its own staff and H.E. institutions, to meet the different needs of its teachers and to ensure that sufficient resources are devoted to this over a period of time.
6 Support and co-operation be given to voluntary bodies of teachers working in this area, such as NATE, NARE, UKRA, CILT, and NAME.
7 SCDC and other organisations be enabled to fund research and the development of teaching strategies and materials suitable for teaching the language and knowledge about it in successful and imaginative ways.
8 Those teachers principally involved with the teaching of English at primary or secondary level in our schools be allocated half a day per week, or its equivalent, to take part in in-service work, conduct action research and help to collect good practice and disseminate it.

9 Assessment

The present Secretary of State for Education has declared a wish for a test or evaluation of what children have learned in each curriculum area at the ages of 7, 11 and 14, there already being an evaluation at the end of compulsory schooling for those who wish to take it – the GCSE.

It must be said that we have very serious doubts about the feasibility of this proposal on a number of grounds, and grave anxieties about the likely constricting influence on the curriculum which all forms of testing and assessment inevitably produce. There is a long history of failed and flawed attempts at the mass application of 'objective' assessment, all of which have had an inimical effect on the learning of large numbers of children. Such tests deal with a narrow range of competences, which then come to dominate the language curriculum, often squeezing out more profitable areas of learning and experience. It is the superficial which is most easily testable.

Further, if North American experience is any indication, a great deal more time and energy is spent on testing and the preparation for it than is devoted to actual learning and teaching. Too frequently the reward is the illusion of successful language learning, and the effect of failure is not the motivation to try harder next time, but discouragement and the loss of that essential confidence without which nothing can be effectively learned. We would also point out some specific difficulties for which there is recent British evidence.

First, as the complexity of the issues raised in this paper makes clear, the assessment of the skills, knowledge and competences in this area is unreliable and of limited validity. There are no simple tests which would have universal support, even in a well researched area like reading. The Assessment of Performance Unit has spent many years devising and trialling instruments to measure what children can *do* with language and it still has some way to go to satisfy its objectives. A move into testing what children know about language would be most problematic.

Second, the APU would be the first to agree that its instruments require careful and time-consuming preparation and administration if they are to be relatively error free, and a deal of careful scrutiny is subsequently required before any useful deductions can be drawn. We would be surprised if the APU felt that these instruments could be put into general use by teachers as part of their normal work as the Secretary of State has recently suggested. APU tests have not been designed for the purposes of individual assessment.

Third, attempts have been made to assess children's competence as language users across the secondary age range by groups like those working on the Oxford Certificate of Educational Achievement and the London Record of Achievement, who have found the territory extremely difficult to treat in this way, and have generally settled for some form of profiling statement by the teacher, validated by the examination board. The best of them involve the pupils in a shared evaluation of their achievements and increasing responsibility for their own learning. Even so, these systems are great consumers of teacher time and in-service support, and there are doubts about the feasibility of widespread unprepared introduction.

Fourth, any reliable system of even minimum validity is likely to be extremely costly to run, both administratively and also in terms of teacher time. The experience of trying to run a relatively simple assessment system at GCSE is already making large demands on schools' and teachers' time and the examining groups' resources.

It would be wise to consult widely and to consider the full implications very carefully before launching any precipitate proposals for universal testing or assessment in this area. The progress of an apparently straightforward proposal like the establishment of grade-related criteria at GCSE should occasion pause for thought.

In our view, an attempt to specify levels of achievement at 7, 11 and 14 would be damaging and limiting of teacher and pupil expectations; would narrow and restrict the language curriculum; and would give a misleading impression of what children and young people can do.

In the early stages of schooling, parental support and involvement are vital. But parents need far more detailed and extensive information than can be provided by tests, or even termly reports and parents' evenings. Through the daily comments of parents and teachers, the reading records which very many primary age children carry between home and school provide fuller and more productive information than any test can produce.

As children progress through primary and secondary school and move towards independence, such close and constant communication may become less desirable. But communication involving the sharing of the child's problems and achievements needs to continue in some form.

As pupils near the end of their formal schooling, records of achievement such as those we have mentioned above could provide more information of a kind that is valuable to employers, than could any form of 'objective' testing, but by far the most accurate and useful record of achievement in language would be a small folio of the best work the student has produced. Many employers have indicated to us a preference for seeing for themselves in this way, and having something available which candidates can talk about at interview.

We would urge that any evaluation of achievement in language is one based on as much real evidence as possible, that it is conceived very broadly, and that sufficient consultation is undertaken to ensure that it has the full support of teachers, pupils, parents and employers. At earlier stages of education the primary function of any assessment system must be diagnostic, in that it can provide useful information to guide future teachers of the pupil and parents.

We therefore urge the committee very strongly to recommend that:

1 No attempt be made to specify what children should know about the English Language at particular ages.
2 National agreement be sought on the areas of experience which children should be entitled to as suggested in *The Responses to Curriculum Matters 1* (DES 1986).

CONCLUSION

As we have shown, the teaching of English is not a simple or straightforward matter. Teaching that fails to take into account the purposes, intentions, social context and past experiences of the learner, is likely to be unproductive and alienating. Teaching that is determined solely by an academic and abstract conception of what is to be learnt, is unlikely to engage the learner or to increase either confidence or sensitivity to the demands of the situation. So, in so far as we are concerned with enabling our pupils to become more proficient users of language, we need to be wary of conceptualising the subject matter of English as knowledge of type 3.

This is not to say that language development at all stages is always the product of tacit learning. As we have suggested, conscious awareness of the 'sounds' made by initial letters, may be necessary for young readers if they are to develop a working theory about the sound-symbol relationships in our orthographic system. Explicit attention to the structure and ordering of paragraphs may help the writer produce a more coherent and cogent argument.

But such explicit attention to linguistic forms should not determine the shape of the syllabus. Instead it should be modest and unobtrusive. Purposeful use matters more than academically acceptable terminology or apparently logical progression through a hierarchy of skills. To deny or neglect the power and complexity of tacit learning is to remove the pupil's central driving force and to turn language learning from an active purposeful enterprise into a collection of mechanical responses which can never produce the command of English our children will need if they are to operate productively in and out of school. A fully developed understanding of the relationship between the individual and society and of effective language use, will only come about if pupils are encouraged to examine, order and extend their knowledge of how language is used in the world at large.

To facilitate these kinds of learning, teachers themselves need a wide and complex knowledge of language, in part more abstract than that of their pupils, but also enriched by knowledge of types 1 and 2. Such types of knowledge may have lower status in the academic world, but they are essential if teachers are to give their pupils an enthusiasm for language, good models of language in use and the productive interplay on which effective teaching depends.

There is certainly room for improvement in our schools. But there is also an exciting variety of productive practice, supported by a substantial body of underlying theory. If the teaching of English is to become more consistently effective, what is needed now is a more thorough treatment of language in courses of initial training, and the provision of time and money for teachers to operate professionally in the classroom, and to update and extend their professional expertise. A closer relationship between initial and in-service training would help to ensure that good practice is not discouraged and dissipated. We also need continuing and expanding financial support for research projects such as the National Writing Project, which recognise the strength of existing good practice and which both take that practice forward and disseminate it more widely.

Parents have a right to know far more about their children's school learning than they are often permitted at present. But it is abundantly clear that the information which they seek and value, and which enables them to play a more supportive role in their children's learning, is not of the kind which tests can produce.

REFERENCES

BENNETT, J. *Learning to Read with Picture Books*, Thimble Press, 3rd ed. 1985
BISSEX, G.L. *Gnys at Wrk: a Child Learns to Read and Write*, Harvard Univ. Press, 1980
BRADLEY, L. and BRYANT, P.E. 'Categorising sounds and learning to read: a causal connection' *Nature*, vol. 301, pp. 419–421
BROWN, R. *A First Language: the Early Stages*, Penguin, 1976
CHUKOVSKY, K. *From Two to Five*, Univ. of California Press, 1968
CLARK, M. *Young Fluent Readers*, Heinemann, 1976
DES *A Language for Life* (The Bullock Report), HMSO, 1975
DES *Primary Education in England*, HMSO, 1978
DES *Aspects of Secondary Education in England*, HMSO, 1979
DES *English from 5 to 16: The Responses to Curriculum Matters 1* (An HMI Report), HMSO, 1986
DOMBEY, H. 'Learning the language of books' in *Opening Moves* ed. Meek, M., Bedford Way Paper No.17, Inst. of Education (London), 1983
DOUGHTY, P., PEARCE, J., THORNTON, G. *Language in Use* Schools Council Programme in Linguistics and English Teaching), Edward Arnold, 1971
FERREIRO, E and TEBEROSKY, A. *Literacy Before Schooling*, Heinemann, 1982
FOX, C. 'Talking like a book' in *Opening Moves* ed. Meek, M., Bedford Way Paper No.17, Inst. of Education (London), 1983
GANNON, P. and CZERNIEWSKA, P. *Using Linguistics: An Educational Focus*, Edward Arnold, 1980
HALLIDAY, M.A.K. *Learning How to Mean – Explorations in the Development of Language*, Edward Arnold, 1975
HARRIS, R.J. 'An experimental inquiry into the functions and value of formal grammar in the teaching of English with special reference to the teaching of correct written English to children aged 12–14', unpublished Ph.D. thesis, Univ. of London, 1962
HOLDAWAY, D. *The Foundations of Literacy*, Ashton Scholastic, 1979
HOULTON, D. *All Our Languages (A handbook for the multilingual classroom)*, Edward Arnold, 1985
LUNZER, E and GARDNER, K. (eds) *The Effective Use of Reading*, Heinemann, 1979
MEEK, M. *Learning to Read*, The Bodley Head, 1982
MEEK, M. *Achieving Literacy*, Routledge & Kegan Paul, 1983
SLOBIN, D.I. *Psycholinguistics*, Scott, Foresman, 1979
TORREY, J. 'Learning to Read Without a Teacher: A Case Study', in *Elementary English*, vol. 46, pp. 550–556, 1969
WATERLAND, L. *Read With Me: an apprenticeship approach to reading*, Thimble Press, 1985
WEIR, R. *Language in the Crib*, The Hague: Monton, 1970
WELLS, G. *Learning Through Interaction: the study of language development*, Cambridge Univ. Press, 1981

Index

A–Level and post–16 English
   Language 133, 143–6, 148–53, 160, 207
adult/child interaction 59–60, 66
   see also teachers, parents
age-related testing and assessment 6, 18, 29–30, 53–4, 123–6, 242–3
   and bilingual pupils 94
   expectations at age five 42
   Kenneth Baker on 182–3
   NCPTA on 'benchmarks' 214–16
   records 204–5
   and secondary schools 113
   and task-specific nature of performance 72–3, 110–11
Aspects of Secondary Education 17
assessment *see* age-related testing and assessment, Assessment of Peformance Unit
Assessment of Peformance Unit (APU) iv, 16, 215, 222, 242,
   writing surveys 68–71, 74, 75, 204
audience 32, 34–5, 69, 113
   outside classroom 26, 222
   teacher as 128
   in written work 73, 105, 114, 130
Australia: Western Readers Project 136

Baker, Kenneth iv, 1, 2, 171–2, 174–5, 200
   on enduring and unifying nature of English 175–9
   on reading and literature 172, 180–3
'basic English' 133, 137–40
behaviourist theories 61, 63, 66, 83, 84
'benchmarks' *see* age-related testing
Better Schools (DES 1986) 39
bilingual pupils 43, **77–95**
   assessment 92
   attitude and motivation 85–6, 91
   collaborative learning 90–1
   importance of first language 79–82, 84–5, 87–8
   and Kingman Committee 77, 78, 93
   place of ESL in mainstream classroom 87–90
   specialist teachers 87, 89, 94
   teacher attitudes and training 78–9, 87–90, 94
   see also first language, ethnic minorities, race
Bullock Report (*A Language for Life*, 1975)
   2, 8, 18, 58, 140–1, 193
   four modes 16–17, 212
   importance of home language and culture 143
   knowledge about language 214
   language across the curriculum 101, 103
   reading 185–6, 188
   records and assessment 68, 205

commercial interests, language and 172, 173–4
competence 83, 109–10
context 38, 69, 127–9, 156, 184, 203–4
   and 'rules' of language 65–6, 210, 228–9
   see also meaning
Creole languages 24, 137, 139, 146, 202
   examples 135, 161–2
curriculum, national 8

Derbyshire Language Scheme 63–4
dialect 24, 138, 202, 213, 219
   importance of first dialect or language 135–7
   in secondary school English syllabus 145
drafting and editing 26, 114, 131, 214, 222, 232
   A-Level 151
   teacher's role 131
drama 26, 114, 115

education system, national 39, 190–1, 198
employers and employment 15, 75, 173–4, 206, 213, 243
English as curriculum subject 103–7, 108–15, 154–62, 191
   A-Level 148–53
   see also grammar, literature, teacher-training
English from 5 to 16 (DES 1984) iv, 5, 88, 196, 197, 199, 220
   on ethnic minorities 77–8
   on objectives 125, 216
English from 5 to 16: The Responses (DES 1986) iv, 1, 5–6, 131, 179
   on objectives 128, 215, 216
English as national language 77, 82, 212
English as a second language (ESL) *see* bilingual pupils

ethnic minorities 78
  Linguistic Minorities Project 142–3
  see also bilingual pupils, race
evidence to Kingman Committee 7
  submissions: NAAE 218–22, NATE 223–45, NCPTA 212–17
examinations *see* A-Level, GSCE

first language 79–82, 84–5, 87–8
  Bullock on 143
  importance to learning 136
  see also dialect, Creole
foreign language learning 9, 142, 172–3
funding and resources 217, 221, 225, 239, 241, 242, 244
  sharing ideas 115

gender 24, **96–9**
General Certificate of Secondary Education (GCSE) 29, 218, 242
  and A-Level English Language 148
  criteria 73, 102, 104, 218
  oral work 103, 216
government, present 171, 181
  education policies 4–5, 172–3, 186, 191
government reports 14
  generic features of 192–5
  socio-political reasons for 190–2
governors, school 206
grammar 5, 70–1, 104, 139, 163–4
  in A-Level English Language 149
  acquired rather than taught 155–6, 229
  see also knowledge about language

in-service training 146, 206, 220, 221, 238–41
  Wiltshire 'Learning About Learning' 165–8

Kingman Committee
  origin and setting up 1, 4–5, 172–3, 190–2, 218; *see also* government
  membership 2–4, 7, 192–3
  terms of reference 6–9 (set out vi)
    and bilingual pupils 77, 78, 93
    see also age-related testing, knowledge about language, 'model', teacher training
  the Report **185–200**
    audience 192, 199–200
    expected characteristics 192–5
    meaning and interpretation 196–7
    social function 197–8
    socio-political origin 190–2

Kingman, Sir John v, 7–8, 218
knowledge about language 28–9, 33–4, 38–4, 43–5, 116–22, 154–62
  A-Level studies 149–50
  NATE views 226–8
  NCPTA views 213–14, 217
  primary schools 43–5

language
  across the curriculum 9, 17, 33, 101–3, 168–9
    primary schools 43–5
    secondary schools 112
    teacher's role and training 205, 214, 231, 239
  and gender 96–9
  and individuality 51–7
  innateness 229–30
  and learning 25–6
  and media 26–7
  and play 60, 65
  in primary schools **41–50**
  in secondary schools 100–7, **111–15**, 116–22
  as self-image 204, 213
  as social interaction 32, 34–5, 39–40
  and understanding **208–11**
  see also oral language, literature, special needs, writing
language awareness 8, 9, 34, 88, 142
  see also knowledge about language
Language Awareness (Donmall) 5, 8, 9
language diversity *see* varieties of language
Language for Life, A see Bullock Report
Language in Use 29, 40, 75, 133–4, 141, 233
  (quoted) 227, 232
Linguistic Minority Project 142–3
linguistics 9, 11, 12, 20, 29
  and children with learning difficulties 65
  sociolinguistics 34, 38
  see also knowledge about language
listening 45, 111, 113, 147
literature
  and language development 18, 106–7, 141, 216, 219, 221, 231
  range of texts 38, 75, 140, 216
  traditional examination questions 24
  see also reading

Manchester Caribbean Project 137
meaning 22–3, 29, 30, 33
  see also context

media 26–7
　television 180–2
minority languages *see* bilingual pupils,
　Creole, dialect, ethnic minorities
mixed-ability teaching 115, 172
'model' of the English language 9–13,
　21–8, 183–4, 202, 207, 213
　a philosophical perspective 208–11
modes of language, four 110, 111–13, 141,
　147, 212
　Bullock on 16
　see also listening, reading, oral
　　language, writing

National Association of Advisers in
　English (NAAE): evidence to
　Kingman Committee **218–22**
National Association for the Teaching of
　English (NATE): evidence to
　Kingman Committee **223–245**
　knowledge about language 226–8
　language acquisition and learning
　　229–34
　teacher training 234–8, (in-service)
　　238–41
　recommendations 238, 240–1, 243
National Confederation of Parent-Teacher
　Associations (NCPTA): evidence to
　Kingman Committee **212–17**
National Foundation for Educational
　Research (NFER) 16, 68
National Oracy Project 225
National Writing Project 122, 141, 225,
　244
Newbolt Report (*The Teaching of English
　in England*, 1921) 190, 193, 194, 198

oral language 18–19, 26, 157–8, 216,
　229–30
　A-Level skills 153
　across the curriculum 101, 102–3
　levels of choice 34–5
　primary schools 43, 44–5
　secondary schools 111, 113, 115
　and writing 73–4, 145, 146, 219
　see also dialect, first language, speech

parents
　and minority languages 79, 87
　need for information 242–3, 244
　role in language learning 58–9, 66, 206,
　　212–13
　see also National Confederation of
　　Parent-Teacher Associations

play 60, 65
power, language as form of 24–5, 82, 174,
　184, 187, 219
　and gender 96–9
pre-school language learning 108–9,
　126–7, 201–2
primary schools, language in **41–50**, 123–8
　examples of work 46–50, 55–7, 123–5,
　　127–8, 131–2
punctuation 33, 70–1, 104, 113, 130, 222

race and racism 24, 81–2, 93, 98
reading 45, 111, 113, 114–15, 230,
　A-Level skills 152–3
　Bullock on 185–6, 188
　and ESL pupils 91
　need for variety 19
　post-Bullock theories 186–9
　see also literature
Red Book series (HMI) 15
resources and funding 217, 221, 225, 239,
　241, 242, 244
　sharing of ideas 115
*Responses see English from 5 to 16: The
　Responses*

second language learners *see* bilingual
　pupils
secondary schools
　English as curriculum subject 103–7,
　　111–15
　examples of work 158, 159–60
　language across the curriculum 101–3
　a personal account 116–22
Secretary of State for Education *see* Baker,
　Kenneth
sex (gender) in language learning 24, 96–9
slang 154–5, 202
sociolinguistics 34, 38
special needs, children with **58–67**
　linguistics 65
　survey in one LEA 62–5
　teachers 239
speech, quality of 36, 156–7
　see also dialect, oral language
spelling 33, 45, 104–5, 113, 130
　pupils' awareness of importance
　　70–1, 222
spoken language *see* oral language
Swann Report (1985) 2, 81, 88, 89, 194

talk *see* oral language
teacher training 30–1, 205, 206, **234–8**
　and bilingual pupils 89–90, 94

in language across the curriculum 220
teachers of English 221, 235–7
see also in-service training
teachers
  attitudes to minority languages 78–9, 87–90
  bilingual and ESL 87, 89, 94, 239
  and children with special needs 239
  of English, shortage of 224
  intervention by 36–8, 44, 221
  and language in all subjects 101–3, 220, 231, 239
  role in language learning 43, 59–60
  their power 24
  see also teacher training, in-service training
television 180–2
testing *see* age-related testing and assessment
Thatcher, Margaret 16, 173, 174
Thornton, Geoffrey 75, 156, 215

varieties of language 133–47, 202–3, 233
  and A-Level English Language 143–6
  Australia's Western Readers Project 136
  'basic English' 137–40
  home/school differences 135–6
  Manchester Caribbean Project 137
  some innovations 141–3
  see also 'basic English', Creole, dialect
vocabulary 36, 37, 154–5
  and gender 96–9
  about language 154, 205, 220
  and race 98
  specialised, for different subjects 101
Walden, George 171, 172–3
Wiltshire 'Learning About Learning' Project 165–8
writing 26, 34–5, 230–1
  A-Level skills 151–2
  across the curriculum 45, 101–3
  and age-related objectives 123–6
  APU surveys 69–71, 74, 75
  and ESL pupils 91–2
  'ideas book' 169
  need for a variety of models 74–5
  primary schools
    (examples) 46–50, 55–7, 123–5, 127–8, 131–2
    (objectives) 125–8, 129–32
  secondary schools 113
    (examples) 120, 159–160
  and speech 73–4, 145, 146, 219
  teachers' need to learn 165–7
  see also drafting and editing